AF581092

# Who Owns Beauty?

# Who Owns Beauty?

BÉNÉDICTE SAVOY
In collaboration with Jeanne Pham Tran

Translated by Andrew Brown

polity

Originally published in French as *À qui appartient la beauté?* by Bénédicte Savoy © Éditions La Découverte, Paris, 2024.



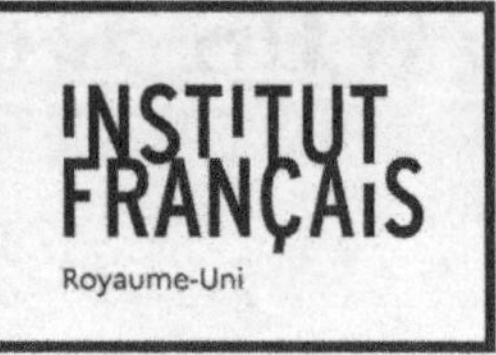


This book is supported by the Institut français (Royaume-Uni) as part of the Burgess programme.

Polity Press
65 Bridge Street
Cambridge CB2 1UR, UK

Polity Press
111 River Street
Hoboken, NJ 07030, USA



ISBN-13: 978-1-5095-6861-1 – hardback

A catalogue record for this book is available from the British Library.

Library of Congress Control Number: 2025933435

Typeset in 11 on 14pt Warnock Pro
by Fakenham Prepress Solutions, Fakenham, Norfolk NR21 8NL
Printed and bound in Great Britain by CPI Group (UK) Ltd, Croydon



For further information on Polity, visit our website:
politybooks.com

To Marie and Louise, who *do* own beauty

# Contents

# Acknowledgements

This book would not have seen the light of day without the infectious enthusiasm, professionalism, and patience of Jeanne Pham Tran. She came up with the idea of the delicate transposition of an oral course into a written text. She prepared the first manuscript, gave me the benefit of her valuable and judicious comments, and allowed me to clarify certain aspects and correct many flaws. She also assembled the elements necessary for the creation of the maps, and smoothed the final text. I would like to thank her most warmly. My gratitude also goes to the Atelier de création cartographique Afdec, as well as to Bruno Auerbach for his critical, precise, and friendly proofreading.

Without the support of Pierre Rosenberg, Marc Fumaroli, Carlo Ossola, and Antoine Compagnon, the Collège de France course that led to the present text would not have existed. Thanks go to Hartwig Fischer for the countless happy hours spent imagining the future of museums, to Felwine Sarr for opening my conscience to the heritage issues that arise on the African continent, and to the team of my research laboratory at the Technical University of Berlin for its abundant intellectual energy.

# Publisher's Note

This book is based on a course given at the Collège de France by Bénédicte Savoy in 2017: 'À qui appartient la beauté? Arts et cultures du monde dans nos musées.' She takes up in the introduction certain passages from her inaugural lecture published under the title *Objets du désir, désirs d'objets* (Paris: Fayard, 2017); extracts from a 2015 interview conducted by Cristelle Terroni for the website La Vie des idées (https://laviedesidées.fr/La-memoire-restituee-des-œuvres-volees); and, in conclusion, a few paragraphs from the postface, translated from German by Frédéric Gendre, that she wrote for the new edition of Arno Bertina's work, *Des lions comme des danseuses* (Paris: La Contre Allée, 2019 [2015]), under the title 'L'héritage des autres.'

# Introduction

At the end of the eighteenth century, in Paris and London, in Rome and in Weimar, the massive transfer of cultural goods and the real or symbolic violence that underlay them started to provoke reactions of unease in enlightened circles. In France, in 1796, Antoine Chrysostome Quatremère de Quincy attacked the policy of artistic conquests pursued by the French Directoire in Italy, and described in admirable and frequently quoted pages the sacred unity that, in his view, linked the object of art to its original context:

> Neither in the midst of the fogs and smokes of London, the rains and muds of Paris, or the ice and snows of Petersburg; neither in the midst of the tumult of the great cities of Europe, nor in the midst of the chaos of distractions of a needy people occupied with mercantile cares, can a profound sensitivity for beautiful things develop.[1]

In 1812, in England, Lord Byron protested against Lord Elgin's transfer of the Parthenon friezes from Athens to what he called England's 'northern climes abhorr'd'.[2] Half a century later, in 1861, Victor Hugo, revolted by the sack of the Summer Palace in Beijing by the French and British armies, denounced in what was to become a famous letter what he viewed as a crime perpetrated by European barbarism against Chinese civilization.[3]

These indictments have long been forgotten, and we have mainly just remembered the positive side of the accumulation of cultural capital between the eighteenth and twentieth centuries that forged the reputation of European museums. Admittedly, from the gathering and conservation of these objects, from the individual and collective emotions that they aroused, the very idea of a universal heritage was born. But what happened to the places where they were no longer to be found? How can we accept that the symbolic and real capital generated by these museums is not shared? And how can we not want – through museums, *thanks* to museums, because they have given us so much and we have taken so much – to seek to engage in a fairer policy towards the dispossessed?

Since the history of Europe has for centuries been the painful tale we are so familiar with – a history of enmities between our nations, of bloody wars and discriminations painfully overcome after the Second World War – we have within ourselves the sources and resources to understand the sadness, anger, and hatred of those who – in other tropics, further away, poorer, weaker – were subjected in the past to the 'intense absorbent power'[4] of our continent. Or, to put it simply: today, all we need is a tiny effort of introspection and a slight change in perspective to empathize with them.

Introspection is the effort that consists, collectively, in connecting the objects that our museums hold to the story of their arrival among us and to the people who still live in the places we once occupied. It means we need to show and to think; to consciously embrace the problematic part of our history as Europeans 'to whom everything came'.[5] It means we must pay extreme, constant, and critical attention to the voices of all those who, inside and outside Europe, see heritage as a political issue. In short, we have to try to do what Achille Mbembe encourages us to do:

> To move across [a multiplicity of places] as responsibly as possible, as the holders of rights that we all are, but in a total relationship of freedom and, where necessary, of detachment. In this process, one that involves translation, but also conflict and misunderstandings, certain questions will dissolve by themselves. Then, in relative clarity, we will see emerge the demand, if not for a possible universality, at

least for an idea of the earth as what is common to us, our common condition.[6]

Beyond the simple question of the 'belonging' of works of art, we must question their history and that of the populations on whose lives they had an impact; we must shed light on the past of these objects and the conditions in which they were exiled; we must expose in all transparency the historical, economic, and cultural contexts from which they were torn, and the way in which they were received in the enlightened and then industrialized Europe that appropriated and transformed them. To answer the question of restitution, we must first look at our history.

How can we justify that some people enjoy a heritage deemed to be universal while others are kept away from it, physically and economically? What are we to think of the fact that the latter are those who have been deprived of their possessions by the violence and asymmetries of history? What can we say to them? What are the consequences of the connection – real or felt, legally fixed or couched as a cultural demand – to these objects of dispute? What view(s) should we take of them? What do our emotions, individual and collective, refer to when faced with these icons of beauty?

Who owns beauty? The question is rhetorical: of course, nobody owns beauty. However, since the eighteenth century and the invention of museums as we know them today, certain objects have been chosen and exhibited precisely for their beauty. As 'objects of desire', they have been bought, stolen, hidden, plundered, offered, or donated; they have constantly given rise to germinations, aesthetic fertilizations, and unexpected crystallizations. However, any object 'transported' from one place to another also creates a 'lack' where it is no longer. This is why we will alternately adopt the gaze of the admirer, whose fascination can lead to the acquisition or confiscation of the work in question, and the point of view of the dispossessed, in whom the feeling of loss, injustice, and absence can lead to indignation and protest. Through objects, a transnational history of Europe and the world emerges, the writing of which engages in a dialogue between disciplines and historiographies.

The challenge of the present work is to think simultaneously about the 'movement' of objects, and the very varied conditions under which they were moved: pillage, archaeological excavations, scholarly expeditions, looting, acquisitions, donations, etc. Some of these terms already constitute a political reading of the events. This is particularly apparent when we try to translate them.

In French, *spoliation* ('looting') and *pillage* ('pillage') immediately evoke the period of the German Occupation. On the other hand, we avoid these terms when it comes to describing our own actions: when, under the Revolution and then the Napoleonic Empire, France seized works of art throughout Europe, we tended to speak of 'artistic conquests' or 'revolutionary confiscations' – gentle euphemisms to legitimize their capture. We therefore note that 'looting' tells the point of view of the victims, while 'artistic conquest' refers to that of the victors. The Italians still speak today of *spoliazioni* ('lootings') and *furti napoleonici* ('Napoleonic thefts') when referring to the French policy of appropriation in the 1800s. We find equivalent expressions in Spain, the Netherlands, and Luxembourg. Germany, which – like France – has been both victim and perpetrator, uses different terms for each situation: *Beutekunst* ('artistic spoils') to designate the confiscations of works of art carried out by the Red Army in 1945 that were suffered by Germany, and *Kunstraub* ('art theft') for the lootings perpetrated by the Nazi regime against Jewish families. Indeed, in the German-speaking context, almost untranslatable expressions have emerged in recent years to refer to the latter: *NS-verfolgungsbedingt entzogene oder kriegsbedingt verlagerte Kulturgüter* ('cultural property removed as a result of Nazi persecution, or displaced due to conflict'). In Russia, the term 'war trophies' is still used to refer to the collections of German libraries and museums that remained on the territory of the former USSR after the great wave of restitution to the German Democratic Republic (GDR) in the 1950s. In short, words always convey points of view.

This is why, after working for many years on these issues from a transnational perspective, I propose the more neutral term 'heritage translocations' – not to depoliticize the debate, but to include all types of appropriations of works of art and heritage that are carried out to the detriment of the party that is economically or militarily weakest. And I also wish to emphasize the multiplicity of points of view involved. For wars are only one subcategory among others. The dispersion of African art in the nineteenth and twentieth centuries was not only the result of war or colonization. After decolonization, it was also a result of the art market. Nazi lootings and archaeological transfers did not have the same goal or the same meaning: in one case, it was a massive and planned dispossession of works of art, linked to genocide; in the other, a displacement of fragments or entire works by archaeologists for scientific and scholarly reasons. It is not a question of mixing together what are distinct subjects, historical contexts, and dramas. The fact remains that all these objects that were taken, moved, or torn away by force, ultimately arrived in the same place, in the same receptacle – namely, the museums dedicated to the conservation of heritage.

Originally, 'translocation' is a term from gene chemistry designating an exchange between chromosomes caused by breakage and repair, an exchange involving mutations. Obviously, genetic heritage and cultural heritage are not comparable. And yet the analogy works: applied to lootings, it first has the advantage of putting a particular *place* at the centre of the discussion. This question of place (the place of origin and the place of conservation of a work of art; the place where it is and the place from which it is missing; the place deemed safe or risky for it; the environment that is deemed natural for it – such as a church, a collector's living room, or the sand of Egypt; and the environment that is felt to be unnatural, such as a museum, or a distant continent) is crucial for understanding, analysing, and identifying the emotions and discourses that have always been linked to the forced displacement of works of art, books, manuscripts, objects of natural history, musical instruments, archives, etc.

Taken in its primary sense, the notion of translocation also leads us to consider the 'breaks' and 'repairs' linked to displacements – the individual or collective traumas that they imply in the long term. Finally, it gives full place to the question of 'mutations', the multiple transformations that affect the displaced objects and the societies that receive them or lose them under the effect of displacement. The connection between these three elements – the place, the injury done, and the transformation – is decisive for understanding the logic of heritage annexations and their effects, and, in a certain way, the history of European museums.

Thus, the translocations of the works that we will be examining inform us both about the history of art and about global geopolitical relations, the rise of European museums and the history of the art market, the evolution of legal systems and the evolution of mentalities. They shed light on the very notion of 'heritage' which, in France at least, has been as important as that of 'secularism' or 'Republic' in the construction of the country since the nineteenth century (which is not the case in other European countries).

*

These questions have recently hit the headlines for several reasons: political and legislative initiatives by several governments; the advent of postcolonial and decolonial studies; and the growing demands for restitution from families, communities, or countries stripped of their goods.

A sign of this large-scale awareness is the enthusiasm that the cinema has shown for the subject: since the 1960s, and particularly in recent years, more and more fiction films have depicted the wanderings of emblematic works of art. The fact that American and Chinese blockbusters are investing millions of dollars or yuan to make films on this subject is evidence of the place that the question occupies in the collective imagination, particularly among younger generations. Halfway between history, the work of memory, emotion, and identity construction, these films advance at the same pace as historiography, but in a different, visual, and therefore more immediately striking, mode for contemporary audiences.

The most famous of such films has to be *The Monuments Men*, written and directed by George Clooney, and co-produced in 2014 by the United States and Germany. Adapted from the book by Robert M. Edsel, a huge bestseller in the United States, the film depicts the work of the Allies to recover the works looted by the Nazis during the Second World War. Released in 2015, *Woman in Gold*, the film directed by Simon Curtis, retraces the fight led by Maria Altmann to recover the portrait of her aunt, Adele Bloch-Bauer, painted by Klimt. Confiscated by the Nazis, it was then exhibited at the Belvedere Museum in Vienna. On the looting suffered during the Second World War, there is also the French film *L'Antiquaire* (*The Art Dealer*) directed by François Margolin, released in 2015, based on a true story: a young woman's investigation to recover the collection of paintings stolen from her Jewish family during the war. *Blood of War*, a film directed by Ukrainian Aleksandr Berezan, shot in 2011, depicts the evacuation ordered by Stalin of valuable items from the heritage preserved on the front line between the USSR and Nazi Germany, items that Hitler wanted to seize. In 2014, the Greek film *Promakhos* (*The First Line*) drew on the legal and political battle demanding the return of the Parthenon marbles to Greece. All these films are both mirrors of historical events and actors in current debates, since they express certain definite opinions.

But let us focus on a particular case, which, in its own way, sheds light on all the others. In December 2012, when Xi Jinping had just taken power, a blockbuster was released in China called *Chinese Zodiac*, a China / Hong Kong action film written and directed by Jackie Chan, set at the beginning of the twenty-first century. In a series of breathtaking kung fu scenes, the famous Chinese actor deploys all his agility, intelligence, and pugnacity to recover works of art looted from China in the nineteenth century and taken to France. Against a background of wonderful special effects, he too answers our question: who owns beauty?

Jackie Chan's film is relevant for at least four reasons. First, it refers to a real episode in the history of artistic heritage that links Asia and Europe. In February 2009, Christie's auctioned the collection of Pierre Bergé and Yves Saint Laurent in a spectacular setting at the Grand Palais. Two bronze heads of Chinese zodiac animals, looted from the Summer Palace in Beijing by the French and British armies in 1860, were up for sale. The announcement of their sale caused a profound stir in the media and in public opinion. The Chinese government tried to prevent the sale and obtain the restitution of these works. Finally, a Chinese buyer, supported by the Beijing authorities, refused at the last moment to pay, arguing that these objects were part of his country's national heritage.

Second, through the scenes of chases, stunts, and martial arts fights, *Chinese Zodiac* expresses a strong and explicit opinion. It is less heritage that serves as a pretext for kung fu than kung fu that serves as a pretext for a political message, in a Chinese context that was especially sensitive to the issue: between 2009 and 2012, in the time between the film's release and the Parisian event just described, nationalist rhetoric in China was experiencing a significant boom. When it was released in 2012, the film stayed at the top of the box-office charts in China, Thailand, Malaysia, and Russia for several weeks and grossed a total of $170 million, including $145 million at the Chinese box office alone. It was released in Hindi, Tamil, Turkish, Arabic, and many other languages. Not only was *Chinese Zodiac* seen all over the world, it was specifically seen by a young audience. Needless to say, it was not as successful when it was released in France and Europe. Who owns beauty? For Jackie Chan, the answer is clear.

Third, the film poses in a very schematic way the questions that structure an otherwise very complex debate. It addresses the idea of the ownership of a work of art. One of the characters, an old man in a wheelchair, the descendant of a British officer, speaks of the 'treasures brought back by his ancestors a hundred and fifty years ago, though they did not own them' and regrets that 'the bronzes are the property of only one or two people'. This reflection is deployed over two time periods: during the sacking of the Summer Palace in the Second Opium War in 1860, and during the controversy caused by the auction of the bronzes in Paris in 2009. The old man also makes us think about the accessibility of works of art: in his view, if these works remain the property of a single person, then they are not only lost to the original community, but also to the rest of humanity. The film highlights the question of the uniqueness of these works. No copy could ever replace them. So, in *Chinese Zodiac*, Jackie Chan absolutely *has* to get his hands on the originals.

Finally, the question arises of the 'right place' for these works of art. The film shows Paris as an 'unjust place': a group of students from various countries demonstrate in front of the Eiffel Tower to demand the restitution of the works to their place of origin. The banners of the attractive young activists, fired by zeal, read: 'No more sales of national treasures', 'Return these treasures to their country of origin'. The message is clear: objects of art belong to the territory from which they were taken. Geographical logic takes precedence over all others.

Naturally, the history of the translocation of works of art refers to different logics – military, political, scientific, cultural, etc. – but they are all associated with a relationship of domination, and very often with a 'feeling of belonging,' whether it is linked to a territory, a community, a cultural, ethnic, religious, artistic identity, etc., or whether it is a more complex form of recognition, identification, or even projection. Etymologically, the word *appartenir* in French, meaning 'to belong,' shares the same root as the word *parent*, which in French can refer either to a mother or to a father, and also to other relatives. Therefore, those who claim to be the owners or possessors of a work of art feel an attachment to it that implies feelings, emotions, and subjective perceptions that are difficult to verify or quantify, and often go beyond the domain of the law strictly speaking.

The question of the belonging (*appartenance*) of works of art, and of art in general, has long been the subject of in-depth research and publications among anthropologists, archaeologists, lawyers, and heritage specialists, at UNESCO, in museums, and in universities. Emblematic works include: *Who Owns Antiquity?* by James Cuno, *Art as a Plunder* by Margaret M. Miles, and *Whose Pharaohs?* by Donald Malcolm Reid.[7] For James Cuno, the president of the Getty Foundation in Los Angeles: '[A]ntiquities are the cultural property of all humankind – of *people, not peoples* – evidence of the world's ancient past and not that of a particular modern nation. They comprise antiquity, and antiquity knows no borders.'[8] And Cuno praises 'the concept of the museum dedicated to ideas, not ideologies, the museum of international, indeed universal aspirations, and not of nationalist limitations, curious and respectful of the world's artistic and cultural legacy as common to us all.'[9]

James Cuno does not here dwell on the question of the real accessibility of museums, which, because of border regulations (visas) or for economic reasons (mobility costs), are accessible only to a tiny minority of citizens from the countries of origin of the works, most of whom cannot ever hope to visit these so-called universal places.

This museological approach is coupled with international legal work on what English speakers call 'cultural property'; in French it is called – without any emphasis on the notion of property – 'heritage' (*patrimoine*) or 'cultural goods.' How does the idea of associating culture with property pose a problem?[10] 'Cultural property' has been the subject of two international definitions set within the framework of UNESCO conventions and frequently cited. The Hague Convention of 14 May 1954 for the 'Protection of Cultural Property in the Event of Armed Conflict' begins as follows:

> *Recognizing* that cultural property has suffered grave damage during recent armed conflicts and that, by reason of the developments in the technique of warfare, it is in increasing danger of destruction;
> *Being* convinced that damage to cultural property belonging to any people whatsoever means damage to the cultural heritage of all mankind, since each people makes its contribution to the culture of the world;
> *Considering* that the preservation of the cultural heritage is of great importance for all peoples of the world and that it is important that this heritage should receive international protection;
> *Guided* by the principles concerning the protection of cultural property during armed conflict, as established in the Conventions of The Hague of 1899 and of 1907 and in the Washington Pact of 15 April, 1935;
> *Being* of the opinion that such protection cannot be effective unless both national and international measures have been taken to organize it in time of peace;
> *Being* determined to take all possible steps to protect cultural property. ...[11]

From the outset, a certain tension is perceptible. It is stated that there is a 'cultural heritage of all mankind,' but it is immediately specified that cultural goods belong to different peoples.

The second text, signed on 14 November 1970 and ratified only in 1997 by France, is entitled 'Convention on the Means of Prohibiting and Preventing the Illicit Import, Export and Transfer of Ownership of Cultural Property':

> *Considering* that cultural property constitutes one of the basic elements of civilization and national culture, and that its true value can be appreciated only in relation to the fullest possible information regarding its origin, history and traditional setting,
> *Considering* that it is incumbent upon every State to protect the cultural property existing within its territory against the dangers of theft, clandestine excavation, and illicit export,

> *Considering* that, to avert these dangers, it is essential for every State to become increasingly alive to the moral obligations to respect its own cultural heritage and that of all nations ...[12]

In this document, UNESCO states that cultural property is one of the basic elements of each civilization. The recognition of a link between people, geography, and culture implies in return an ethical responsibility, with the mission falling to each state to ensure the integrity of its property as well as its maintenance on that country's territory: the text does not mention the idea of possibly demanding its return, even though this is a corollary.

While these texts have at least the merit of existing, they are full of contradictory energies and they certainly do not facilitate the conceptual work of heritage professionals. Moreover, their translation alone poses a problem since the concepts of 'museum' and 'heritage' are untranslatable in many languages spoken in regions that have been victims of dispossession.[13]

*

The first major texts that relate the question of beauty to that of property date from Antiquity. In the first century BC, Cicero formulated his set of speeches known as *Against Verres*. As a still young lawyer, Cicero had just obtained his first position in Sicily, at the age of thirty-six. The Sicilians had sought his help in a lawsuit against Gaius Lucinus Verres, the Roman governor of their colonized island. During the First Punic War (or Sicilian War) in the third century BC, the Carthaginians had plundered some of their treasures. During the Third Punic War, Rome recovered these precious works of art, objects, and carpets from Carthage (on the Mediterranean coast of present-day Tunisia) to return them to the Sicilians, thus demonstrating its loyalty to its colony. Less than a generation later, Verres seized these objects and had them transported to his home in Rome.

In this story, questions of ownership and restitution are already on the agenda. This is evidenced by Cicero's speeches, which he was unable to deliver in their entirety at the hearing, but which he published under the title *Verrines* (*Against Verres*) in 70 BC:

> There was among the Segestans a statue of Diana, of brass, not only invested with the most sacred character, but also wrought with the most exquisite skill and beauty. When transferred to Carthage, it only changed its situation and its worshippers; it retained its former sanctity. For on account of its eminent beauty it seemed, even to their enemies, worthy of being most religiously worshipped.... When that enemy of all sacred things, that violator of all religious scruples [i.e. Verres] saw it, he began to burn with covetousness and insanity, as if he himself had been struck with that torch. He commands the magistrates to take the statue down and give it to him; and declares to them that nothing can be more agreeable to him. But they said that it was impossible for them to do so; that they were prevented from doing so, not only by the most extreme religious reverence, but also by the greatest respect for their own laws and courts of justice.... Therefore, at last, the Segestans, subdued by much ill-treatment and by great fear, resolved to obey the command of the praetor. With great grief and lamentation on the part of the whole city, with many tears and wailings on the part of all the men and women, a contract is advertised for taking down the statue of Diana.[14]

Who owned the statue of Diana? The man who 'burned' for it and who had the administrative power to seize it? The city which had lost it and then found it again, which venerated it and which collectively felt the pain of its loss? This was Cicero's view. In addition to the matter of heritage, and the political, legal, and financial questions, there is also the issue of the emotions and the symbolic and real violence that this translocation provoked.

> Caius Heius is a Mamertine – all men will easily grant me this who have ever been to Messana; the most accomplished man in every point of view in all that city. His house is the very best in all Messana, – most thoroughly known, most constantly open, most especially hospitable to all our fellow-citizens. That house before the arrival of Verres was so splendidly adorned, as to be an ornament even to the city....
>
> There was in the house of Heius a private chapel of great sacredness, handed down to him from his ancestors, very ancient; in which he had four very beautiful statues, made with the greatest skill, and of very high character; calculated not only to delight Verres, that clever and

> accomplished man, but even any one of us whom he calls the mob ... They were open every day for people to go to see them. The house was not more an ornament to its master, than it was to the city....
>
> Shall Verres take away everything which is most beautiful everywhere? ... Was it for this reason that none of his predecessors ever touched these things, that he might be able to carry them off? ... But why am I borne on so impetuously? I shall in a moment be refuted by one word. 'I bought it,' says he. O ye immortal gods, what a splendid defence! ... For this defence seems to me to be got ready for everything; that he bought them ...
>
> [It is] you [who], under the presence of purchase which you put forward, in reality seized and took away these things by force, through fear, by your power and authority, from that man.[15]

Who owns these four statues, in the final analysis? The man who has the financial means to acquire them, says Verres. The person for whom they have no price, or else an emotional price, retorts Cicero. The lawyer continues by using the argument of the accessibility and visibility of works of art – a notion that the Republican and Napoleonic armies would not hesitate to take up again during the French Revolution and then under the Empire, when they decided to assemble in Paris all the collections of Europe.

For example, Vivant Denon, director general of the museums of France between 1802 and 1815, argued that the Louvre, renamed the Musée Napoléon, was much better equipped than others, financially and scientifically, to showcase works of art. Acting on his words, he explained to the director of the Brunswick Museum that the 900 pieces of porcelain from his establishment would be more advantageously exhibited in Paris because they 'would finally be useful to the public'! For Denon, beauty belonged to those who knew how to showcase and preserve it.[16]

The vanquished and dispossessed of the time were already starting to protest vociferously: beauty could not be the property of a people, even a liberated, egalitarian, and fraternal one, because it was not the concrete property of anyone. In 1798, following the arrival in Paris of works 'conquered' in Rome, protests were heard. August Wilhelm Schlegel, a German poet, philosopher, and critic, lent his voice to the statues seized in Italy. Speaking through them, he addressed the French in his poem entitled 'The Stolen Gods' (1798):

> Do you have a sanctuary for us?
> And can the charms of Greece be conquered by force of arms?
> Are the gods also the property of men?[17]

While the Galerie des Antiquités had just opened at the Louvre, the German poet and writer Friedrich Schiller expressed the same sentiments in this short poem dated 1802, 'Antiquities in Paris':

> That which Grecian art created,
> Let the Frank, with joy elated,
> Bear to Seine's triumphant strand,
> And in his museums glorious
> Show the trophies all-victorious
> To his wondering fatherland.
>
> They to him are silent ever,
> Into life's fresh circle never
> From their pedestals come down.
> He alone e'er holds the Muses
> Through whose breast their power diffuses, –
> To the Vandal they're but stone![18]

For Schiller, the person who owns beauty is the one who feels it in his or her heart, and not the one who appropriates it materially: the latter knows neither how to make it speak nor how to hear it. Beauty belongs to those who understand it. However, as is often the case, this argument is also hijacked, as much by the victors as by the vanquished. Many voices are raised in Western museums to demonstrate the 'benefits' (often the benefits of hindsight) derived from translocations and even lootings that, they claim, have allowed (and still allow) these museums to protect, even to 'save', many works of art which would otherwise have been destroyed, ransacked, dismantled by wars, or sold off in fragments by traffickers.

In 2014, after the lawyer (and wife of George Clooney) Amal Alamuddin came to England to negotiate the return of the Parthenon friezes exhibited in London since the beginning of the nineteenth century, the journalist Jeremy Paxman waxed indignant in the *Telegraph*: 'The Parthenon marbles belong in Britain, Mrs. Clooney. Had the ghastly Lord Elgin not plundered his works of art, they could have ended up in the footings of some Athens kebab stand.'[19] In other words, the 'others' from whom 'we' took works of art at a certain moment in history are not worthy, not capable – aesthetically, culturally, or morally – of preserving them. From there to expecting them to thank the kidnappers for their great magnanimity takes only a small step. What would Cicero have retorted if he had been there? He would doubtless have defended the Greeks against the British.

Then there is the film that made a great impression in 1964: *The Train*, by John Frankenheimer, with Burt Lancaster and Jeanne Moreau. It is the story of the derailment of the Aulnay train in August 1944. Resistance railway workers are trying to prevent the convoy, requisitioned by the Nazis and loaded with works of art, from arriving in Germany. A Nazi officer insults the railway worker played by Burt Lancaster: 'You are nothing, Labiche. A lump of flesh. The paintings are mine. They always will be. Beauty belongs to the man who can appreciate it. They will always belong to me or to a man like me. Now, this minute, you couldn't tell me why you did what you did!'[20]

Here, the argument that a work of art belongs to those who can understand it is turned against the simple man, the railway employee who has just derailed a train carrying works looted from France by the Nazis. But what does the spectator think? Does beauty belong to the Nazi soldier who claims to appreciate it at its just worth, thanks to his distinguished culture, or to poor Labiche who, admittedly, does not possess the codes of the dominant culture, but who acts for good and commits his life to the struggle against the Fascist power?

In the debates on translocation currently agitating cultural circles, we often hear voices claiming that 'we' have, in European museums, the technological and intellectual skills to conserve works of art, while the 'others' do not. Yet, in books, films, and newspapers, it is often the point of view of the ordinary person that is defended – of the one whose relationship to beauty is neither intellectual nor cultural, but ritual, intuitive, or emotional.

In the same period as *The Train*, in 1961, the German–Soviet war and propaganda film *Five Days, Five Nights* was released. This enormous production, the most expensive in the history of post-war cinema in the Eastern bloc, sold more than 2 million tickets in the GDR. The story takes place in Dresden in 1945. The Red Army enters the city completely destroyed by American–British bombings and extracts the masterpieces of the Dresden museum from the ruins to send them to Moscow. Some fifteen years later, these works are returned. The film was made to legitimize, a posteriori, their 'rescue' by the USSR. The way the museum is depicted in this film is meant to remind the audience in 1960s East Germany and the Soviet Union of what the news in the twenty-first century continues to emphasize: the translocation of works of art is a major cultural trauma in the history of European museums, whether they were victims or beneficiaries of past policies of heritage appropriation. By its very existence, the cinematography of translocation bears witness to the place of the subject in the contemporary collective consciousness and imagination.[21]

Observing the Red Army packing away the Dresden artworks, a young local painter, engaged during the war years in the resistance against the Nazi regime, is offended to see these paintings leave for the Soviet Union. Outraged, he denounces the theft. Suddenly, witnessing the emotion of the Russian sergeants in front of a Raphael Madonna, the painter understands his mistake. The veil that covered his eyes is torn: the victory of the Allies over the camp of hatred is reinforced by love of beauty. Thus, the film skilfully legitimizes the taking of the works from Germany in 1945 and their transfer to Moscow.

*

To the question 'Who owns the beauty exhibited in our museums?', two main answers therefore present themselves. The first claims that the works belong to a territory and have a link with those who live in the dispossessed regions. The other position affirms that beauty belongs to humanity and that museums provide access to it precisely through translocations. When working out one's own position, it is useful to focus on concrete objects and to question how they arrived where they are today – to ponder their provenance, their itinerary, their material and immaterial journey since their creation ... and the void they leave where they are no longer to be found.

In this book, I will follow the 'translocations' – which are also fascinating journeys across countries and ages – of singular works, representative of various diasporas from all over the world: archaeological and ecclesiastical objects, objects exhibited or buried in the sand, works of art which would never, in their original contexts, be described as such, so much are they 'subjects', agents, entities endowed with their own powers, and created in very varied political, historical, geographical, scientific, and technological contexts. I have decided to present the objects chronologically, according to their date of creation: from the bust of Nefertiti around 1340 BC to the *Portrait of Adele Bloch-Bauer* by Gustav Klimt in 1907. Only the last chapter, devoted to the treasures of the Abomey Palace made before 1892, does not follow this chronology.

I could also have classified these same objects according to the time of their first respective translocations by isolating distinct periods:

- the eighteenth century: a very prosperous period in northern Europe, when entire Italian collections were purchased and exhibited by the courts of kings and princes in Germany, England, and France;
- the French Revolution and the Napoleonic Empire: between 1794 and 1811, there were massive seizures of art and science objects carried out by France in Europe. The ambition and the discourse of the revolutionary and Napoleonic leaders consisted in legitimizing the appropriation by France of European heritage in the name of 'Liberty';
- the colonial period: between 1860 and the beginning of the twentieth century, this was the most important period in terms of heritage extraction from colonized or 'mandated' countries;
- the Second World War: a period of confiscation of works of art by the Nazis and systematic lootings from Jewish families in Europe.

I could also have chosen to classify the works according to their original type of belonging:

- some objects did not belong to anyone in particular (or belonged to this or that landowner) when they were found, having been buried in the earth for several centuries;
- some objects belonged to churches or palaces;
- some objects were seized in times of war, and it was claimed that they belonged to a particular locality or identity;
- some objects come from particular collections; and so on.

Finally, I could have chosen to classify the works according to the reasons and contexts that contributed to their being removed from their place of origin:

- a military asymmetry: wars, colonies, etc.;
- an economic asymmetry: one country richer than another, etc.;
- an asymmetry of knowledge: one country more scientifically 'advanced' than another, etc.;
- a political logic: annexation, occupation, colonization, gift and counter-gift, nationalization, etc.

In each situation, whether these objects were acquired legally or seized illegally, it is important to question now what we do with this heritage – both the objects themselves and the history attached to them. Of course, Western museums defend the idea of a 'shared and universal heritage.' In doing so, they obscure the mechanisms linked to the absence of objects in places where they no longer exist. And it is much more difficult for the historian to grasp and express the effects produced by loss and emptiness than to report the justificatory discourse of the victors or 'owners.' However, the discourses and practices linked to absence have, since Antiquity, reached us in the form of discourses spontaneous or organized, spectacular or discreet, political or poetic, verbal or visual. Moreover, the staging of what we could call the 'presence of the absence' of displaced works is a constant in the history of art and translocations.

The task of the historian is to grasp these affects in varied, sometimes unexpected, sources; to determine their origin (who expresses a reaction, when, and why?); to measure their authenticity and intensity, and their symbolic or political scope. Today, the history of emotions is still a young branch of historiography; its methodological and theoretical apparatus is still being developed. One of the challenges it faces is the connection between empirical work and theoretical models. For architectural heritage and monuments, Daniel Fabre recently proposed the concept of 'heritage-linked emotion.'[22] In the field of art history and museums, we can draw inspiration from this concept to think about the affective dimension of forced heritage translocations, and more generally the claims being formulated today by people, states, or communities wronged in the past.

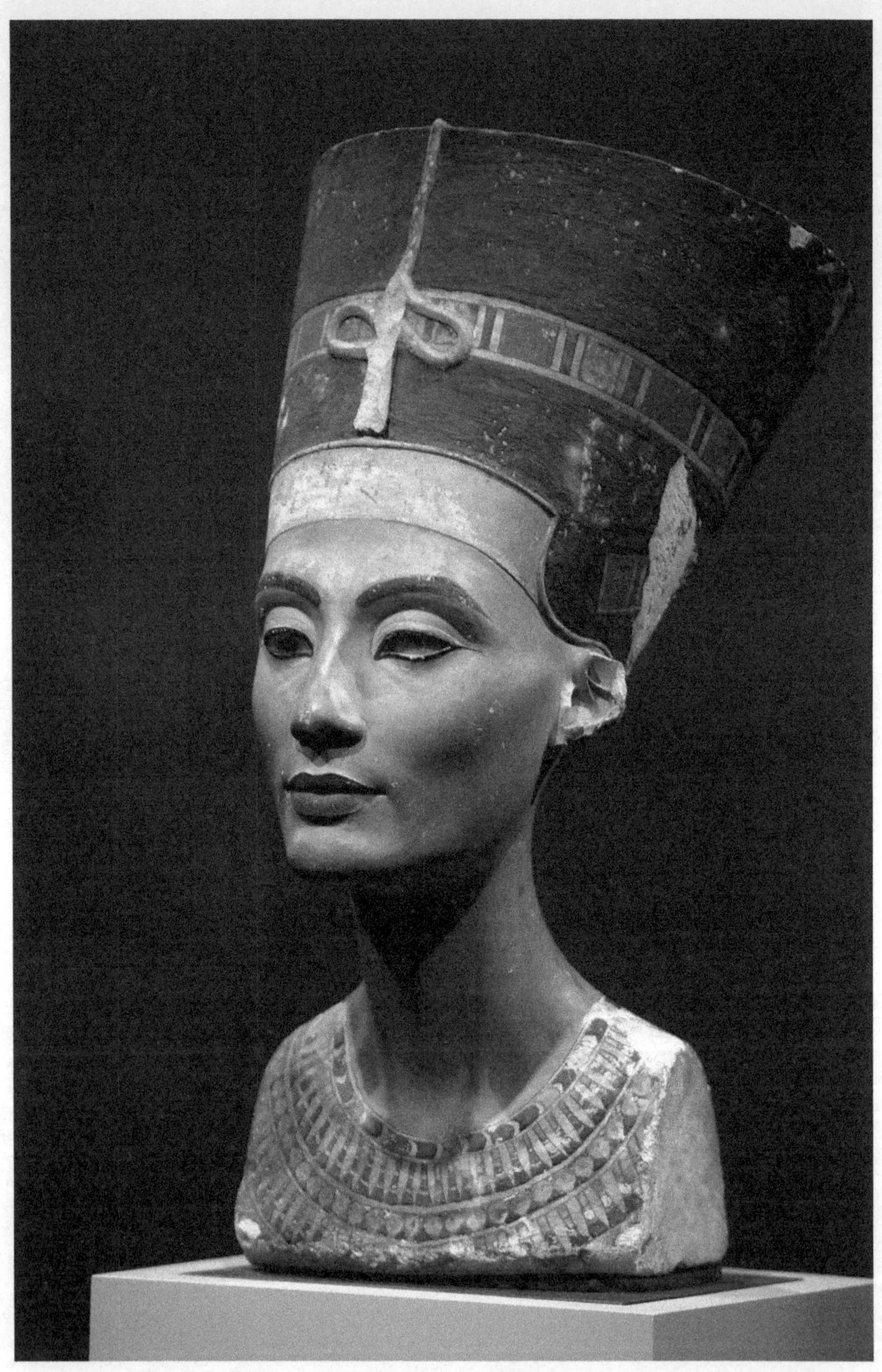

Workshop of Thutmose (Tell el-Amarna, Egypt), bust of Nefertiti, circa 1340 BC, limestone, plaster, quartz, wax, h. 50 cm. Berlin, Staatliche Museen zu Berlin – Preussischer Kulturbesitz. Photo © Imago / Bridgeman Images.

# 1

# THE BUST OF NEFERTITI

As an icon of beauty and powerful femininity, Nefertiti, the wife of the pharaoh Akhenaten, continues to exert her powers of seduction on the entire world thanks to an image that was made of her more than three millennia after her death. This image is composed of a small, 47-centimetre limestone bust covered in painted stucco: under an imposing blue headdress surrounded by a *uraeus* (a cobra that adorned royal crowns), we see a very slim face, with high cheekbones and a slender nose, and large almond-shaped eyes, one of which does not have an inlaid pupil, overarched by thick eyebrows. The figure has a slight smile and an elongated neck. Enigmatic and fascinating, she seems to be asking us the direct question, 'Who owns beauty?'

In what historical context was the bust of Nefertiti moved from the workshop of an Egyptian sculptor in the fourteenth century BC to the Neues Museum in Berlin at the beginning of the twentieth century? In 1912, the German archaeologist Ludwig Borchardt exhumed the famous bust from the ruins of Amarna. Shortly afterwards, he obtained permission from the Egyptian Antiquities Department, headed by a Frenchman, to export it to Berlin together with an entire collection that was exhibited in 1913 and immediately caused a sensation: Amarna art fascinated the Berlin avant-gardes. A veritable process of aesthetic fertilization took place. In the aftermath of the First World War, the French started to regret having let such an important aesthetic ensemble escape their grasp. In the 1920s, a now autonomous Egypt began to demand the return of the bust. In 1934, Hitler refused to return it. Who does it belong to?

## Cairo

The provenance of objects is part of their history, but it is also part of a legal framework, set out in past agreements. Independently of this framework, opinion is divided in the case of the bust of Nefertiti: should Berlin finally return this major work to Egypt? Does Nefertiti belong to those who helped excavate it and to their descendants, who could exhibit it in their beautiful museum in Cairo? Isn't it inextricably linked to the history of the German capital? Or does it belong, as we sometimes hear, to all of humanity?

What do we know in Europe about the positions adopted by Egyptian civil society on this subject? When it comes to translocations and restitutions, opinions are often clear-cut and even divisive. They rarely take into account the precise historical circumstances of the transfer of heritage, a knowledge of which is crucial for forming an opinion. It is rare for museums themselves to note these circumstances on the label of the works. The interested visitor often has to carry out his or her own investigations. In the case of Nefertiti, the web page of the Deutsche Orient-Gesellschaft (DOG, German Oriental Society) offers a first clue, in the shape of the list of actors involved in Nefertiti's arrival in Europe, either because they were commissioned by this learned society, dedicated to promoting archaeological research in the field of oriental antiquities and Assyriology, or because they signed the excavation or export authorizations. They included several famous French academics – Gaston Maspero and Pierre Lacau in particular, who were both professors at the Collège de France and directly involved in Nefertiti's move from Egypt to Germany.

The first surprise comes when the Nefertiti affair, assumed to be a German–Egyptian affair, takes the researcher to Paris. Why? Because just as many administrative archives are kept there as in Berlin or Cairo, and they inform us about the historical, political, and legal aspects that explain the presence of the bust of Nefertiti in Germany.

Many legends surround its transport. Some claim that the archaeologist had covered it with mud to smuggle it past customs, and that no one had seen anything; others state that relevant photographs had been falsified. As always, the less the proven facts are known, the more myths and rumours thrive.

Imagine the scene, at Tell el-Amarna, in December 1912. Thanks to the notes of the Berlin archaeologist Ludwig Borchardt, his correspondence, and his many sketches and excavation notebooks, and thanks also to the black-and-white photographs of Prince Johann Georg of Saxony, an art collector and amateur photographer who was travelling through Egypt at the time of the discovery, we are well informed about the conditions in which the bust of Nefertiti was extracted. It was found on the site of an ancient city in Middle Egypt, about 245 kilometres south of Cairo, not far from the current regional capital Al-Minya. It was here, at Tell el-Amarna, that the pharaoh Akhenaten had the capital of his kingdom built around 1348 BC; here, he decided to break with the religion of his ancestors to create a new cult, that of the sun, and to promote new aesthetic forms. Known today as 'Amarna art', they are distinguished by a complete break with the artistic canons then in place for several centuries; in particular, their realistic, almost naturalistic, representation of people and bodies was strikingly new.

The Prince of Saxony was travelling across Egypt in the company of his wife, Princess Maria Immaculata of Bourbon-Sicily, obsessively photographing the regions he passed through. Because they are not professional – sometimes they are poorly centred, and their subjects are partly out of frame – his photos are valuable documents for imagining the archaeological excavations in Egypt around 1900. In one of them, dating from the winter of 1912, we see men standing in front of a plot of land: Ludwig Borchardt and his team have just unearthed what is clearly the workshop of a sculptor, Thutmose, whose tools and works have remained almost intact under the sand. This was an unprecedented find: until then, the existence of Amarna had been known mainly from written documents. From now on, this singular period of Egyptian history acquired colours, shapes, a face – or faces: those of the living models whose imprint the artist had probably moulded in plaster, those of heads delicately sculpted in granite. And, among them, those of the royal couple: Akhenaten and Nefertiti. Their sudden emergence from the Egyptian sand, in the winter of 1912, astounded those present. Of the 'coloured queen', whom he did not yet identify as Nefertiti, the archaeologist Borchardt wrote in his excavation journal: 'There's no point in describing her, you have to see her.'[1]

Beyond the objects and their aura, the amateur photos of the Prince of Saxony allow us to view the discovery as an event inscribed in a social and political reality: one photo shows children and teenagers carrying baskets filled with sand removed from the hollows of the excavation site. An overseer in a white suit holds a whip in his hand. Several dozen Egyptian workers, identifiable by their traditional peasant clothing, are busy on the site, while a handful of Westerners in impeccable suits stand motionless above the cavities, bending slightly forward to scrutinize what is happening inside. Elegantly dressed ladies from the entourage of the Prince of Saxony are also present, in beige or white blouses, skirts and hats, sometimes sitting on chairs. The division between an upper level and a lower level, between Westerners and Arabs, between those who give orders and those who carry them out, between those who possess knowledge (or think they do, or will do so soon) and those who do not (or who possess other kinds of knowledge) is inscribed in the very space of the images.

While the Egyptian men and children employed on the site remain anonymous, the European actors involved in the discovery of Nefertiti are well known. The aforementioned archaeologist Ludwig Borchardt had been based in Cairo for several years, where he had created – and since 1907 directed – the German Imperial Archaeological Institute. An engineer by training, he was in close contact with the Deutsche Orient-Gesellschaft, which, from Berlin, financed numerous excavations in the Middle East – the one at Tell el-Amarna was carried out with the financial backing of a wealthy Berlin textile industrialist, of Jewish origin like Borchardt: James Simon, one of the wealthiest and most generous figures in the German capital. A benefactor of the DOG, he was also one of the main patrons of the Berlin museums, which he enriched with repeated donations, thus enabling the acquisition of extremely rare pieces. He was also involved in social work, financing hospitals and public baths in Berlin.

In Egypt, the main administrative contacts of German archaeologists were the French Egyptologists of the Antiquities Service, whose offices were in Cairo. Created by the Egyptologist François Auguste Ferdinand Mariette at the request of the Viceroy Said Pasha in 1858, this was one of the rare institutions whose management was still French when the country became a British protectorate in 1882. When the bust of Nefertiti was discovered at the beginning of the twentieth century, the challenge for the directors of the Antiquities Service was to ensure continuing French cultural and scientific influence while maintaining good diplomatic relations with the British and the international scientific community. Even after 1922, when the Kingdom of Egypt attained independence, the Antiquities Service continued to be headed by French Egyptologists, who were now civil servants of the Egyptian government. Only in 1952 did the management of the service finally pass into the hands of Egyptian scholars.

So, in 1912, when Nefertiti was discovered at Tell el-Amarna, Egypt was not an autonomous state: what was above ground, so to speak, belonged to Great Britain, and what was below belonged to France. Since Napoleon's expedition to Egypt at the very end of the eighteenth century, France had given itself a permanent archaeological mission in Egypt – part of what Éric Gady calls 'scientific imperialism'.[2] It took over the management of the Antiquities Service and established itself as the body that granted or refused excavation and export permits. But, around 1900, the English and the French were fighting over Egypt: on the one hand, the British authorities planned and built roads, irrigation systems, and infrastructure; on the other, the French antiquities administration was concerned about such major work, which in its view threatened the integrity of the subsoil and the treasures still buried. A sense of urgency took hold of the Antiquities Service, which granted international excavation permits and rewarded archaeologists and their financiers by being particularly generous in sharing the discoveries. The law provided for the formation of lots of equal value, divided between those who had excavated the objects and the Antiquities Service. In fact, for several decades, the French authorities, emphasizing the scientific interest of not separating coherent archaeological ensembles, allowed Egyptian heritage to leave the country – so much so that it can now be found scattered in public museums in

Boston, Paris, London, and Moscow. Gaston Maspero, director of the Antiquities Department from 1881 to 1886 and then from 1899 to 1914, explained this strategy in detail in his writings:

> The reform introduced twenty years ago in the irrigation system has returned to cultivation vast areas of land that had been arid for centuries: water was poured out in abundance, impregnating the objects contained there.... If, in the quarter century since c. 1900, the ancient sites attacked by modern industry have not been thoroughly explored, I have no hesitation in declaring that their entire contents of papyri, bronzes, stone and metal statues, terracotta, fabrics, utensils, weapons, tools, and amulets, will be lost to science. As they number in the hundreds, a mass uprising of scholars would be needed to get to grips with them in such a limited period of time: so we have asked to be allowed to carry out research, and I am happy to note that our intentions have been understood.[3]

Maspero estimated that researchers had twenty-five years to excavate and recover the essential works. These excavations were extremely costly and the time extremely short, so generous financial sponsors were clearly needed to attract scholars and archaeologists. In return, Maspero was magnanimous. The question of the ownership of the objects hardly arose: they were willingly given to scholars from the countries that took part in the excavations (Germany, the United States, etc.). They therefore belonged, by this logic, to those who paid for and organized the work and transport, to those who studied and showcased them.

Maspero noted: 'It was resolved in principle that no concession would be granted to non-Egyptologists and, in general, to anyone who did not come in the name of a University, an Academy or a foreign Government: the Egyptians were ipso facto excluded.'[4] At that time, there was no academy, university, or government in Egypt, no structured effort to train local Egyptologists, nor any effort by European countries to train them on their home turf. In fact, the institutional and epistemological asymmetry involved in the logic of excavations 'for science' excluded those working on site, who were kept in a form of ignorance or non-recognition of their knowledge. Thus, throughout Gaston Maspero's long mandate in Cairo, groups of important works of art were exported throughout the world without being shared out and without any major difficulty: the unity of the pieces or fragments coming from the same excavation prevailed over their place of ultimate conservation. This is how the famous statues of King Mykerinos and Queen Khamerernebty II were sent together to Boston in 1911, as was the intact tomb of the architect Kha, found in Thebes in 1906 and donated to the Turin museum, to name but a few examples.

But the situation changed in the months immediately preceding the discovery of Nefertiti. In 1912, tensions between the British and French authorities led to a tightening of controls, with the British now demanding that the regulations on sharing be strictly observed. The Antiquities Service and its director Maspero were reluctant to comply. They wanted to continue rewarding foreign archaeologists for their efforts. When the parties met at Tell el-Amarna in early 1913 to divide up the excavation, the German side was represented by Ludwig Borchardt and, despite the importance of the discoveries, Maspero was replaced by a very young collaborator who later became an eminent papyrologist, Gustave Lefebvre. An agreement was soon concluded, and the result of the division set out in these terms:

> For the Cairo Museum [the Antiquities Service represented by Gustave Lefebvre]: 1 painted stele representing Amenhotep IV and the queen playing with the princesses. Intact monument. Height 43 cm.
> For the D.O.G [the Deutsche Orient-Gesellschaft here representing James Simon]: 1 painted plaster bust of a princess of the royal family [this was Nefertiti].[5]

Despite the apparent allocation of equivalent lots to each of the parties, the painted stele being considered at least as important as the bust of the princess (Nefertiti), there was no real division. Indeed, Borchardt was very quick to request from the service the authorization to temporarily export all the objects found in Thutmose's workshop, not just the half that had fallen to Berlin. This was mainly for scientific reasons – in particular, because he considered the dividing up of an exceptionally coherent ensemble to be an act of violence against the interests of Egyptology. But there were also practical reasons: he wanted to have quality reproductions (photographs and plaster casts) of the sculptures made in Berlin, and he promised they would rapidly be returned to Egypt. Without having personally seen the pieces, Gaston Maspero unhesitatingly approved their complete transport to Germany. From an administrative point of view, the bust of Nefertiti had in fact legally left Tell el-Amarna for Berlin in January 1913, thanks to the agreement of Gustave Lefebvre, representing the Egyptian Antiquities Service. The direct transferral of this bust and the other sculptures from the sand of Egypt to the Berlin museum, from oblivion to light, was to have many consequences.

## Berlin

The European capital of tango, cabarets, transvestites, avant-gardes, rich patrons, hedonism and luxury, drugs and transgression, workers' and feminist movements, food fads and educational experiments, alternative sexualities and theologies – Berlin in the winter of 1913–14 was also the capital of the lumpenproletariat and urban misery, of the *Kaiserreich* and its colonies, of stark political, ideological, and social contrasts. In the artistic field, that winter witnessed what has since been considered a major event in the history of twentieth-century art: the first German Autumn Salon in the Galerie 'Der Sturm' directed by Herwarth Walden.[6] A brochure intended to extol the merits of the exhibition conveys with great immediacy the atmosphere of political and social confrontation that reigned in the city at the time: 'Hordes of howler monkeys splashing colours around / New uniforms for the insane / Hottentots in shirts'. By brandishing these insults published against them in the German press as so many trophies, the exhibition's organizers hoped to lure in an audience in search of sensations. They insisted on the international, modern nature of the movements presented – Expressionism, Cubism, and Futurism – and claimed that 'the First Autumn Salon is the most powerful art exhibition in Germany'.[7] In fact, if we re-read the German press notices from the winter of 1913–14, another exhibition seems to have shaken the public even more: that of the excavations of Amarna, which opened at the beginning of November 1913 on Berlin's Museum Island. The aesthetic encounter between ancient Egypt and the most radical artistic avant-garde movements was a stunning event.

What was then known, in Europe, about Amarna and its history? For about thirty years, specialists on the subject had realized that Akhenaten had rejected traditional Egyptian cults at the beginning of his reign, established an exclusive cult of the sun in their place, founded a new city for this reason, and maintained intense diplomatic relations across the world, notably with Babylon. It was also known that, after his premature death, Amarna had been abandoned; that the name of Akhenaten had been erased from the collective memory; and that it would be 3,000 years before the fascinating personality of this pharaoh resurfaced. Around 1900, the figure of Akhenaten moved outside specialist circles. Identified by some with Moses and viewed as the father of the first monotheistic religion in history, he became an object of fascination for many intellectuals.

On one central point, however, almost nothing was known: what did he look like? And the art of Amarna? Looking at some of the ornaments, wall paintings, and bas-reliefs found during the very first excavations, Egyptologists had a feeling that this art was different from the Egyptian style, but they prematurely concluded that it was merely a minor art, exaggerated and grotesque – a caricature. When the exhibition of the Amarna excavations opened in Berlin, the European view of Egyptian art suddenly changed. The objects discovered, entirely unfamiliar in style, had a radical otherness that opened up a scientific and aesthetic *terra incognita*. They were UFOs in the history of Egypt, and the academic experts had not had time to get to grips with them before the general public pounced.

Their heads resembled 'us', claimed the press reports: we could look at them and see ourselves as in a mirror; one felt as if they were part of the family. The many reviews of the exhibition highlighted the 'ease' of entering this singular Egyptian universe, which, according to the observers, required no prior knowledge, no particular education. These 34-century-old faces looked unmistakably like those of men and women one could pass in the street. Historical distance seemed to collapse. The men and women of Amarna, so to speak, were us. This was felt not only by anonymous visitors to the exhibition in Berlin during the winter of 1913–14, but also by eminent intellectuals who reported on it in their correspondence and works.

For the Berlin daily the *Vossische Zeitung*, 'the exhibition at the Egyptian Museum, where the new finds from Tell el-Amarna are currently being shown, is the great success of the season. Ancient Egyptian sculpture is being talked about almost as much as the tango, and Akhenaten is soaring to new heights of popularity.'[8] In a thought-provoking article published in the *Sozialistische Monatshefte* (*Socialist Monthly Notebooks*), Lisbeth Stern, an activist art critic and sister of the famous sculptor Käthe Kollwitz, produced a Marxist reading of Amarna art:

> The plaster casts could just as well be from today … and as far as expression is concerned, the features seem quite inconspicuous, like any face encountered in the street nowadays. On the other hand, the sculpted portraits are of an incredible purity of style and rigour. Almost as if they were the result of an ultimate aristocratic filtering of the human world. That being said, it is quite possible that the plaster casts were made from the faces of proletarians.[9]

Another political sensitivity, but the same intensely personal response, can be seen in the poet Rainer Maria Rilke who, after visiting the exhibition, urged his friend Lou Andreas-Salomé to go there too. She replied in February 1914: 'I went along with my husband and Ellen, all three of us were completely fascinated, and it gave us food for thought for a long time.... You must have noticed yourself how many Akhenatons resemble you?'[10]

For Rilke and his contemporaries, the faces of Amarna were not only fascinating: they were like them, they *were* them – a striking mirror effect that the novelist Thomas Mann would extend years later to an entire social group, relying, for the description of the protagonists of his tetralogy *Joseph and His Brothers*, on photographs of the Amarna sculptures in the Berlin museum. Hence his celebrated portrait of Akhenaton (alias Nefer-Kheperu-Râ-Amenhotep) as a jaded dandy, a perfect representative of the *fin de siècle*:

> In describing his face – beneath the round blue wig with its royal serpent that he wore today over a linen cap – we should not be discouraged by intervening millennia from making the apt comparison

> that he looked like a young, aristocratic Englishman of rather faded stock: tall, arrogant, and weary, with a large drooping chin that one could not call receding but that was nevertheless weak; a nose whose narrow, somewhat indented bridge made his broad, sensitive nostrils all the more striking; and deep-set, dreamily veiled eyes from which he was never able to raise the lids entirely and whose dull luster stood in bewildering contrast to the unhealthy, flushed red of very full lips, a hue that came not from rouge but from nature. The face was thus a mixture of sensuality and painfully convoluted spirituality – but still at a boyish stage and presumably even with something of a boy's playful recklessness. It was anything but handsome and beautiful, and yet it held a disquieting attraction.[11]

The time that separated Akhenaton from the Europeans of the 1900s seemed infinitesimal. In the same way, the sculptor of the Amarna heads seemed more modern than the avant-garde artists. Adolf Behne, one of the most influential Berlin art critics of the time and a defender of new movements, devoted an entire article to this sculptor in the *Dresdner Neueste Nachrichten* (*Dresden Latest News*): 'Today I will not introduce you to a living contemporary artist, but to the greatest artist who has ever existed. He is more contemporary than all of us, stronger than the Futurists and the Expressionists. His name is Thutmose and he lived fourteen centuries ago.'[12]

In the winter of 1913–14, the public came to the Neues Museum in Berlin to experience another Egypt, another Antiquity, different from the Greco-Roman canons taught for decades in the high schools of Imperial Germany and Europe. This different culture was quite *comme il faut*, as it came from Antiquity, yet it marked a 'break' in the radical and unprecedented realism of its forms. Thanks to the Amarna heads, a collective anchoring both in the distant and monotheistic past, and in a recent past different from anything known until then, could be (re)affirmed. New perspectives for the future were opened up. It was in this spirit that the weekly *Der Roland von Berlin* (*The Roland of Berlin*) reported its visit in November 1913:

> In the courtyard of the Egyptian Museum in Berlin, usually so motionless in its solemnity, and so little frequented, a dense throng of curious

> people gathers. It particularly includes ladies and young girls, who are enthusiastic about archaeology. Even columns of high school boys in colourful caps make their way through the crowd, kept at bay by pedagogues with stern eyes. The rustling of the wings of sensation can be felt between the papyrus-shaped capitals of the coloured portico. For once, the scholars who excavated this land have most definitely not exaggerated; they have unearthed real works of art and curiosities of an incomparable charm.[13]

In 1913–14, however – and this gives an idea of how much more intensely the 'wing of sensation' would be felt a decade later – the bust of Nefertiti was not part of the Amarna exhibition in Berlin. While almost all the pieces found at Tell el-Amarna were exhibited there, the 'coloured queen' remained invisible to the public and to the European scientific community. It was only ten years later, in 1924, that she would actually be placed in one of the museum's rooms. The first photographs of her, apparently, did not circulate until 1922.

Why this delay? First and foremost because, after obtaining permission from the Egyptian Antiquities Service to transfer all the pieces found to Berlin – a permission granted the day after the dividing up of the Tell el-Amarna excavations, and flying in the face of the restrictions sought by the British – Borchardt (who continued to live and work in Cairo) feared reprisals on the ground. He anticipated the huge outcry that the presentation of the royal bust of Nefertiti would cause, and recommended not exhibiting it. Indeed, if it had been up to him, even the other pieces would not have been exhibited. It was therefore against the advice of the archaeologist at the time that the DOG and the Berlin Museum had decided to present the whole – though Borchardt had at least ensured that the spectacular bust of the coloured queen would be kept in the private apartments of the patron James Simon. In the spring of 1914, after several months of presentation, the Amarna exhibition in Berlin had closed its doors and the treasures had been stored away, inaccessible to the public during the four years of war, then offered again to the eyes of admirers in November 1918, but in a graceless setting, and still without Nefertiti. It was not until 1924, finally, that the royal bust was publicly exhibited at the Berlin Museum along with Akhenaten and the other heads found at Tel el-Amarna. This belated exhibition, shortly preceded by the publication and wide circulation of a few photographs of the bust of Nefertiti, marked the beginning of Cairo's campaign to reclaim that celebrated piece.

## Restoring an international icon?

Back to Cairo in 1914. Just as the exhibition of the Amarna treasures was electrifying the crowds in Berlin, the Egyptian Antiquities Service and, more generally, the international group of Egyptologists based in Cairo were about to suffer the full consequences of the entry into war of the European powers. German archaeologists were banned from excavations and expelled from the country, which was still under English control. Their property and institutions were sequestered. A few months earlier, the head of the Egyptian Antiquities Service, Gaston Maspero, had given up his place to a close collaborator, the Egyptologist Pierre Lacau, who was on summer vacation in France when he received the order for general mobilization. He was posted to the East and did not return to Cairo. During the war years, the military and political antagonism of the powers at war was also expressed as a fierce scholarly antagonism.

Pierre Lacau was approaching forty; he was positioned on the second line near Verdun, with the units responsible for collecting the wounded and the corpses. His correspondence, now carefully preserved in the library of the Institut de France in Paris, gives a sense of the intellectual ravages that accompanied the horrors of war. In 1915, he received this message from his young colleague Gustave Lefebvre: 'My dear Friend, I learned that you were going to leave France to join your post in Egypt. That is also a combat post, and it is French work that you will be defending there, after having done more than your fair share of time in the trenches.'[14] Several months after the end of the war, in April 1919, Lacau himself confessed: 'It is absolutely impossible for me to think of any collaboration with any German. It is our duty to remember. A painful but necessary duty.... There is something that goes far beyond all scholarship, and that is morality. The scholarship of a murderer does not excuse his crime, it only makes it more hateful.'[15] It was in this context of Franco-German hatred and national self-assertion that the first requests for the restitution of the bust of Nefertiti were addressed to Berlin. They came several years after the war, when German archaeologists, having endured a long period of boycott by their European counterparts and a ban on excavations, were once again authorized to request concessions from the Antiquities Service in Cairo. Even though Egypt had in the meantime (1922) gained its independence, it was still the Frenchman Pierre Lacau who was in charge of the institution.

In 1925, Ludwig Borchardt, who had moved back to Cairo, tried his luck: 'Most honoured Director General, I hereby request you, in the event that the excavation permit granted to the Egypt Exploration Society for Tell el-Amarna is not renewed, to grant this excavation permit with the extension it originally had, to the German Institute for Egyptian Archaeology. Yours most truly, your humble servant, Borchardt.'[16] This letter was the first in a long series of requests, all refused by Lacau, demanding the return of the head of Nefertiti before he would consider them. The notes and documents preserved in his administrative archives show that he was aware of the perfectly legal nature of the export of the bust of Nefertiti to Berlin in 1913: 'M. Lefebvre did not recognise the real importance of this unique piece. This only proves that a man of indisputable merit and with an absolutely clear conscience can unfortunately still be mistaken.'[17] He acknowledges the scholarly errors made by his department, which he compares with the 'moral' error of the Germans of the time, who should not have agreed to take away a work of such importance:

> So the error is ours. M. Lefebvre represented us, and his signature fully commits us. I believe that we have no legal case. But morally we do, and it is a very serious case. Indeed, will we admit that the holder of the concession had the moral right to take advantage of our error and use it against us? Certainly not.[18]

A battle lasting several years ensued, with Lacau demanding the return of Nefertiti as a prerequisite for any authorization of excavation – a way of continuing by scientific and cultural means the war against the 'Boches', to use a recurrent expression in the Egyptologist's correspondence. For five years, until Ludwig Borchardt retired in 1929, requests and refusals followed one another. Then, through negotiations, the possibility of an exchange arose: Berlin would return Nefertiti to Cairo and Cairo would give them in exchange the statue of Ranofir, a high Egyptian priest. Proposed by Lacau, the idea was gradually accepted by the Berlin museums, encouraged in particular by the famous orientalist and specialist in Islam, the academic Carl Heinrich Becker, then Minister of Culture. In his eyes, the future of Europe and Germany depended on the good quality of their relations with the Islamic world. As such, he supported the project of returning the bust of Nefertiti to Cairo which, according to him, would mark the first stage in the building up of a new German–Arab friendship. King Fuad was associated with the project.

In Berlin, however – now the capital of the Weimar Republic and rent by intense political tensions between the extremist parties – public opinion was divided. The press took up the subject, with the possibility of restitution being the subject of numerous illustrated articles and repeated caricatures. One of them depicted a giant donkey with glasses, a three-piece suit and a red tie 'stupidly' handing the bust of Nefertiti over to a very small man with Arab features, wearing a red tarboosh, looking like a carpet merchant and apparently laughing up his sleeve as he presents in exchange a hideous statue of the priest Ranofir. There are also more offensive or plaintive versions. For example, in an article dated 1930 entitled 'What they are going to give us in exchange for Nefertiti!', a poorly framed, harshly contrasted, and overly dark photograph of Ranofir is placed next to a Nefertiti in all her splendour. Some people accused the German authorities of allowing themselves to be duped by accepting the departure of the woman who, since her exhibition at the Berlin museum, had become an international icon. Under pressure from public opinion, the project was finally postponed in 1930, but it resurfaced in 1933, just a few months after Hitler came to power. A date was even found to stage the restitution and thus revive German–Egyptian friendship: 9 October 1933, the anniversary of King Fuad's accession to the throne. In the end, the event did not take place: Hitler – who, according to press reports, had 'fallen in love' with Nefertiti – opposed it. The French-language daily *La Bourse égyptienne* ran the headline: 'Among the Nazis, Queen Neferet-Iti will remain a prisoner. This is what Chancellor Hitler has decided:

**Winter 1913–1914**: 'Amarna' exhibition at the Neues Museum (Museum Island, **Berlin**).
The bust of Nefertiti is exhibited in the private apartment of the patron James Simon in Berlin.

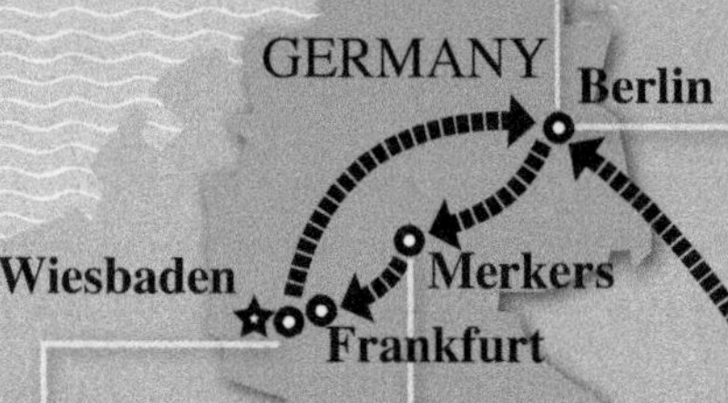

**April 1945**: the Monuments Men transfer the bust of Nefertiti to the Reichsbank (Central Bank) in **Frankfurt**.
**August 1945**: the bust is sent to the *Central Collecting Point* in **Wiesbaden**.
**1946 to 1956**: it is exhibited in the Wiesbaden Museum.

**Early 1945**: the bust is sheltered in the mines of the Werra-Fulda-Kalirevier near **Merkers**, in the Land of Thuringia, which later became part of the Soviet zone.

*Mediterranean Sea*

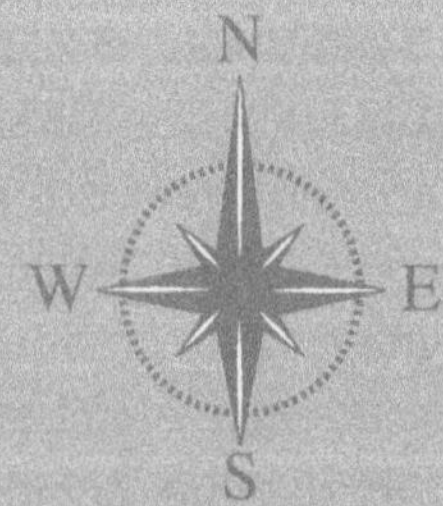


0 1 000 km

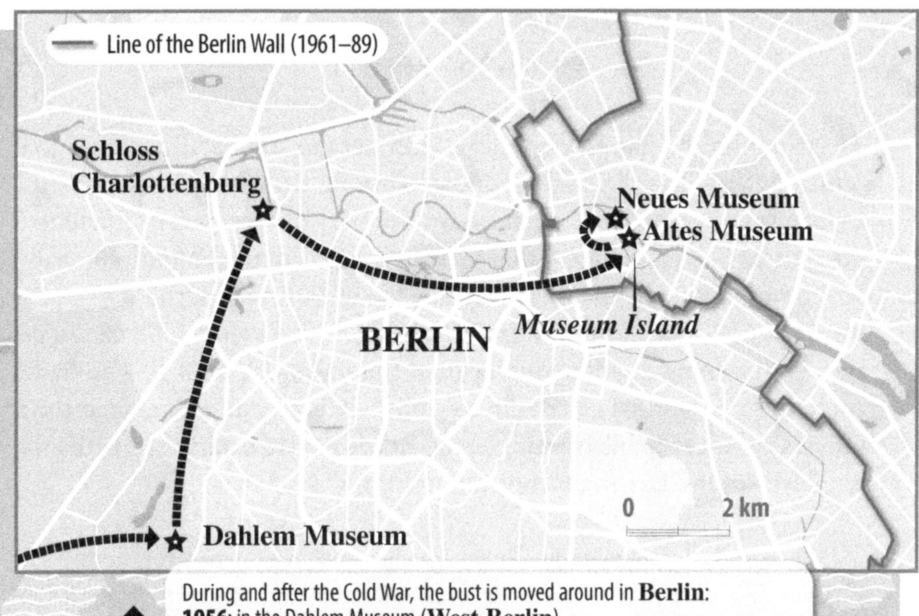


**5**

During and after the Cold War, the bust is moved around in **Berlin**:
**1956**: in the Dahlem Museum (**West Berlin**).
**1967**: in the Egyptian Museum in Schloss Charlottenburg (**West Berlin**).
**2005**: the bust is sent to the Altes Museum (on Museum Island).
**October 2009**: the bust is moved to the Neues Museum (on Museum Island).

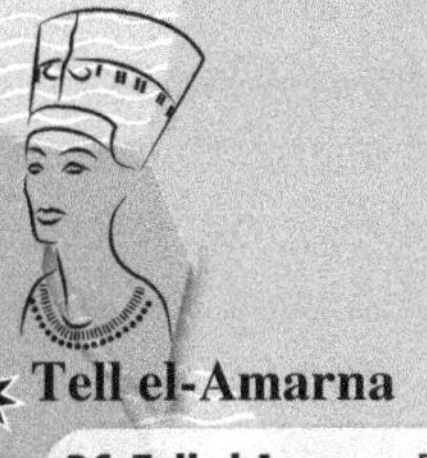

Tell el-Amarna

**1**

**BC: Tell el-Amarna**, Egypt, Thutmose has the bust of Nefertiti created.
**December 1912**: Ludwig Borchardt discovers the bust.
**20 January 1913**: the finds are shared out; the bust is earmarked for Berlin.

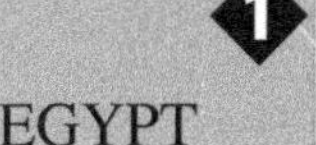


Nil

declaring that he has fallen in love with her, he stubbornly refuses to return her to Egypt.'[19] And it added: 'Nothing would have been more welcome to Egypt than a gesture on the part of Germany, returning the bust of Queen Nefertiti that Germany holds in the conditions that are common knowledge.' In the 1930s, the melancholy of the tone and the demand for restitution were far from new in Egypt: half a century earlier, the young Egyptian intellectual Ḥasan Tawfīq al-ʿAdl, who had come from Alexandria to Berlin to study, while teaching Arabic at the university, noted in his travelogue the words he had exchanged with an employee of the Egyptian Museum in Berlin:

> 'So,' he asked me jokingly, 'how do you find your treasures here?' 'They're very well presented, Sir, and you have made a great effort to preserve so much beauty. I'm glad they are in your country, so that you can keep Egypt in mind. And yet, clearly, it is we who have the more legitimate right to preserve them.'
>
> He retorted: 'In that case, why are you currently banning the export of antiquities from your country? It would be better if you increased the number of them in our country, so that we would remember you even more kindly.'
>
> I replied with a laugh: 'That's true, but in a sincere friendship, even a single object is enough to keep a memory alive.'[20]

During and after the Second World War, the bust of Nefertiti shared the fate of the tens of thousands of works protected from bombing by German museums, found and gathered together at collecting points by American army experts in the aftermath of the conflict, and returned in the 1950s to their respective museums. Those in Berlin were now divided between a western sector (where the bust of Nefertiti would be exhibited) and an eastern sector (which preserved Akhenaten): the couple remained separated by the Cold War until their belated reunification in the rooms of the Neues Museum on Museum Island in 2009, twenty years after the fall of the Berlin Wall.

*

Who does beauty belong to? To those who 'fall in love' with it? To those who, as children, teenagers, or peasants from Middle Egypt, had kept it under their feet for several thousand years and helped to excavate it a century ago? To their descendants – the women of Egypt, for example, some of whom see beauty as a symbol of freedom and autonomy? To Egyptologists? To the rising generation of young researchers who, like Monica Hanna – Professor of Archaeology at the Arab Academy of Sciences, Technology and Maritime Transport – are working in Egypt to rewrite the history of Western excavations based on the archives of the Ottoman Empire and Cairo? To the people of Berlin who, from generation to generation, for a hundred years, have visited the colourful queen in her various exhibition spaces? Or to the 'Prussian Cultural Heritage Foundation', named after the organization that now owns her in Germany? And, more generally: who does Antiquity belong to in our museums today? To the Egyptian, Persian, Turkish, Greek, and Ethiopian peoples who, during the colonial era, were employed by the international community of excavators on archaeological sites and then politically forgotten and robbed of their cultural heritage? Or to our European ancestors and to ourselves, who for decades have been fired by enthusiasm for these treasures, from which we draw part of our aesthetic, intellectual, scientific, and even political identity? The question is complex and it deserves, as the present example has made clear, to be treated in all its historical and cultural complexity, and not only in terms that are often partisan, politically correct, corporatist, or dryly legal. One fact is certain: the Nefertiti affair is and remains a collateral consequence of the old Franco-German antagonism. Germany, with France (and, in many other cases, Great Britain and the United States), bears a common historical responsibility towards the Egyptian state. Reducing the current debate to an antagonism between Cairo and Berlin offers no hope of progress. It is important to inform the public of the contexts that have allowed European museums to become what they are today: the repositories of world art, certainly – but also, and at the same level of importance, of the history and geopolitics of the nineteenth and twentieth centuries.

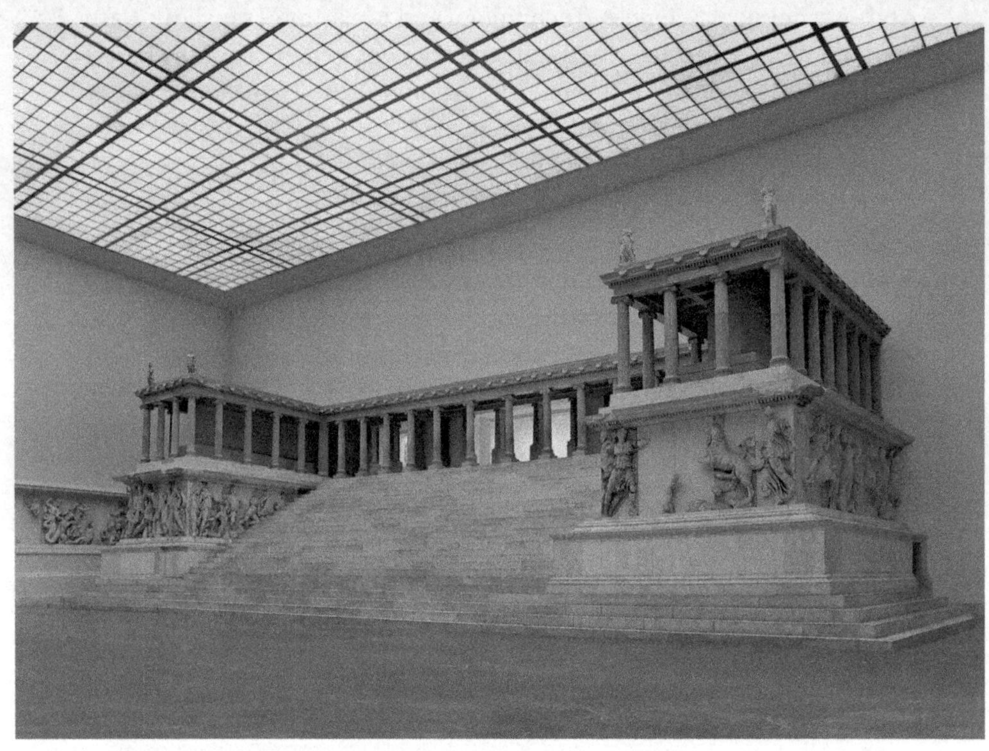

Unknown artists, Great Pergamon Altar (Altar of Zeus), second quarter of the second century BC (modern reconstruction and original marble fragments), approx. 34 × 36 × approx. 10 metres. Bergama, Turkey; Berlin, Pergamon Museum, Staatliche Museen zu Berlin – Preussischer Kulturbesitz. Photo © Scala, Florence / bpk, Bildagentur für Kunst, Kultur und Geschichte, Berlin.

# 2

# THE PERGAMON ALTAR

The Great Pergamon Altar is a monumental Hellenistic work that was erected on the acropolis of the ancient kingdom of Pergamon in Asia Minor – today called Bergama, on the west coast of present-day Turkey. Formed after the death of Alexander the Great, the kingdom of Pergamon continued to prosper until its peak in the second century BC, when this altar was built.

Also called the 'Altar of Zeus', this building, made entirely of white marble, is mainly impressive for its dimensions: a large square of about 30 metres on each side, surrounded by a wall decorated with bas-reliefs, some twenty steps leading to a platform surrounded by an Ionic colonnade – without doubt the courtyard intended for sacrifices – rising to a height of about 10 metres, and, on either side of the monumental staircase, two wings, also surrounded by a colonnade.

But what catches the attention of all those who look at this work is found mainly on the bas-relief frieze that surrounds it: the 'gigantomachy', the battle between the gods of Olympus and the giants, sons of Gaia, the Earth. Across 120 metres, this masterpiece of Hellenistic baroque offers the spectacle of an intertwining of characters with bodies and faces tense and twisted with effort, fury, and pain. This battle of the gods against the giants, according to some, is to be taken in a metaphorical sense: it is the fight of a kingdom (Pergamon) against its enemies (the Galatians). If we still do not know who created the frieze or the exact date when it was sculpted, it has been the object of considerable research since its discovery at the end of the nineteenth century by German archaeologists.

The 'object of desire' here is therefore not a piece, nor a statue, nor a chest, nor a painting, nor a fragment, but an entire monument that was moved from its original location to its current exhibition location – from Pergamon to Berlin. How was the altar identified at the end of the nineteenth century by the German architect in charge of building new roads in the Ottoman Empire? And where did the idea of moving such an 'object', and the technical means to do so, come from? Who now wishes they still had it? After being the focus of political debates in the nineteenth century, the altar was shipped from Berlin to Moscow at the end of the Second World War before being returned ten years later to the GDR, which viewed it as the flagship object of its ancient collections. How are the 'translocation' and the complex, long, and spectacular reconstruction of this building emblematic of the museographic policy of Europe around 1900, and of its long-term consequences in terms of memory?

Among what we could call the 'unthought aspects of heritage', the idea that these objects, found underground, belong to everyone, that they are part of a *shared* heritage, is widespread in Europe. Some believe – on the contrary, but for the same reason – that these objects belong to no one. Still others draw attention to the fact that, even if we assume that these objects belong to everyone, they are after all in the hands of a single, very specific institution, in Berlin, in a museum that has been closed to the public for renovation since 2014 and will remain so, according to the latest estimates, until 2037. On the other side of the Mediterranean, in what is now Turkey, calls have been increasingly voiced in recent years requesting the return of the altar to its original site, some 30 kilometres from the sea, on a height that, in Antiquity, overlooked three cities set one above the other, connected by an interlacing pattern of stairs and terraces, where many large buildings once stood. The ensemble is now classified as a UNESCO World Heritage Site.

In the twenty-first century, different logics clash, and many different claims are made. Who owns the Great Pergamon Altar? How, under the *Kaiserreich*, did this spectacular monument arrive in Berlin, at a time when the German capital was intoxicated by its archaeological conquests and the progress of orientalist sciences in its universities? What were the relations between the Ottoman Empire and the representatives of European archaeology in Asia Minor? In what way did museums play, in Berlin as elsewhere, a key role in the systematic movement of items from ancient times found in this region of the world, and in the self-assertion of a Europe better equipped than anywhere else to preserve them? Also – and perhaps above all – how can we take into account this history of domination today, and envisage the future of the heritage that arrived in our museums in the nineteenth century?

## A translocation in spare parts

A short flashback to the second century BC: we need to imagine the majestic city of Pergamon at its peak under the builder king Eumenes II. The city – all in rising levels, belvederes, and fortifications, clinging to the hillside – is surmounted by the Great Altar and surrounded by a prosperous countryside. A political, cultural, and economic centre, Pergamon was, according to Pliny the Elder, the 'most famous city in Asia.' In the heart of the city, parchment factories (the Latin *pĕrgamēna*, from the Greek *περγαμηνή*, means 'skin [prepared in] Pergamon') stand alongside libraries, temples, gymnasiums, schools, manufactories of fine cloth, and sculpture and ceramics workshops. It is even mentioned in the New Testament: a passage from the Book of Revelation, composed towards the end of the first century AD, links it to Satan, and some have deduced that the Pergamon Altar itself could have been his throne: 'And to the angel of the church in Pergamos write; ... I know thy works, and where thou dwellest, even where Satan's seat is.'[1]

In fact, there are many hypotheses as to which divinity this Altar was made for, none of which has been verified. Over time, Pergamon was successively a Hellenistic, Roman, Arab, Christian, and then, in the fourteenth century, Ottoman city. According to experts, it was in the sixth century that the Great Altar was dismantled and used for the construction of a fortified wall intended to protect the city from invasions. As is often the case, this partial destruction and the integration of fragments of the altar into a fortification wall probably helped protect its ruins from later pillaging.

The gigantic translocation of the Pergamon Altar to Berlin took place at the end of the nineteenth century. On the political and economic levels, the Ottoman Empire was losing its influence, while Western Europe (Great Britain, France, the German Empire, the Kingdom of Belgium, and the Netherlands) was in the midst of a colonial conquest, gradually annexing vast regions of the world. The Industrial Revolution and the improvement of means of transport – steam navigation in the 1830s, railways and steam locomotives around 1840 – encouraged this expansion and the transport to European museums of monumental pieces, even entire buildings, from distant climes. The transporting of the friezes of the Pergamon Altar in several stages between 1878 and 1886 benefitted directly from this progress. To move the fragments of the altar, the German excavators first had a road built, then a jetty on the Aegean Sea: this allowed the fragments to be successively embarked on German navy vessels to Smyrna (now Izmir, Turkey). They were then transshipped onto liners, then into railway wagons from Trieste, the last fragments being shipped directly from Smyrna to Hamburg.

This translocation took place in the context of great archaeological excitement in different regions of the world, whether or not they were colonized by European powers at the time. The rich and vast territories of the Ottoman Empire were particularly affected by the appetite of European museums. From Xanthus, for example (in the southwest of present-day Turkey), a British archaeologist had the massive fragments of a temple-shaped tomb transported in the early 1840s: the Nereid Monument, later 'reassembled' at the British Museum in London, where it now occupies an entire room. Also in the 1840s, in Nimrud, in Mesopotamia, in the north of present-day Iraq, British excavators unearthed an immense palace built during the reign of Ashurbanipal II, and transferred entire sections of its ornaments and sculptures to the same British Museum. In 1870, the German Heinrich Schliemann unearthed what he believed to be 'Priam's Treasure' at a site he identified as Troy, south of the city of Çanakkale (in present-day Turkey), and a few years later donated it 'to the German people to possess it forever and to keep it intact in the capital of the Empire',[2]

Berlin, where it was confiscated by the Red Army in 1945. It is now kept in Moscow. From 1875, the German archaeologist Ernst Curtius excavated the site of Olympia in what was then the Kingdom of Greece, a constitutional monarchy long ruled by a German king, Otto, Prince of Bavaria; here, the archaeologists took the unusual and highly political decision to leave the original ancient fragments in place, in a museum specially built on the site, and to transfer only casts to Berlin. In 1899, however, when, in another geopolitical context, the famous Ishtar Gate in Babylon, in present-day Iraq, was discovered by German archaeologists, it was transported and then 'recomposed' in Berlin to rub shoulders a few decades later with the Pergamon Altar in the museum of the same name (inaugurated in 1930). In 1903, the great market gate of Miletus, in Asia Minor (in the southwest of present-day Turkey), was unearthed by a German team, transferred to Berlin, and also placed in the Pergamon Museum.

One last example of the translocation of an entire building or large fragments: in 1902, the facade of the palace of Qasr Mushatta, one of the Arab castles often known as the Umayyad desert castles, about 30 kilometres from Amman (in present-day Jordan), was offered by the Ottoman sultan to the German emperor as a token of gratitude for his support in the construction of several railway lines: the one from Damascus to Medina, designed by German engineers, lay in the immediate vicinity of the palace, which was then dismantled to be reassembled in Berlin. Reconstructed to be 33 metres long and 5 metres high, the facade of the Mushatta Palace today constitutes one of the most spectacular examples of Arab architecture in a Western museum, the Museum of Islamic Art in Berlin, itself installed in the heart of the Pergamon Museum on Museum Island.

When the excavations of the Pergamon site began in 1878, the Ottoman Empire had already had regulations on antiquities for about ten years, as Greece had done in 1834: they stipulated the prohibition of exporting antiquities without prior official authorization, but these regulations, amended several times, were little respected, if at all – and remained ineffective until their amendment in 1906. In Western countries, even if some archaeologists helped to formulate these new laws, many took a dim view of them, convinced that they alone held the knowledge, the techniques, the finances, and the museums capable of accommodating and understanding the ancient remains omnipresent on the territory of the Ottoman Empire. To put it briefly, their syllogism was as follows: archaeology can be practised only by professionals, but there are no archaeologists in the Ottoman Empire, so it's up to us, Western archaeologists, to take charge of this activity. And intellectual appropriation went hand in hand with a material appropriation of the relevant works.

The idea was not new: from the beginning of the nineteenth century, the idea spread in so-called 'enlightened' Europe that this scientific research was much more fruitful if the objects were moved to the heart of European cultural and university centres, in the immediate vicinity of the great libraries and academies. Whereas, in the eighteenth century, scholars had travelled to the works to study them, it was now the works that were brought to the scholars. The trend became more pronounced throughout the nineteenth century – witness Salomon Reinach's 'Chronique d'Orient', published in the *Revue archéologique* in 1883, in which the great French archaeologist, renowned for his vehemence, not only described the discoveries and acquisitions related to his profession, but also expressed his hostility to the efforts of the 'excavated' countries to regulate the presence of foreign archaeologists on their territory.[3] In 1884, he again expressed his annoyance upon reading the new regulations on antiquities and excavations in Turkey, more radical than the previous one (1874) since it seemed to give the country of origin a monopoly on excavations. These regulations read:

> Art 1. – All remains left by the ancient peoples of the regions that today form the Ottoman Empire are considered objects of antiquity….
> Art. 3. – All objects of antiquity that exist in the Ottoman Empire, that are now unearthed, will subsequently be unearthed by the execution of excavations, will be removed from the bottom of the sea, lakes, rivers, or watercourses, belong by right to the State.
> Art. 5. – It is absolutely forbidden for owners to destroy without authorization the antiquities that will be discovered on their lands or to break into pieces and destroy the remains of buildings and ancient roads, walls of forts, ramparts, fortifications, baths, ancient cemeteries, etc.… It is absolutely forbidden … to use these monuments, either in part or in their entirety, as a dwelling, as a storehouse of grain, straw or

> hay, as well as as water reservoirs, troughs, fountains, etc., even if these uses would not damage them.
> Art. 8. – It is absolutely forbidden to export abroad antiquities discovered in the Ottoman Empire.
> Art. 9. – An official permit to carry out excavations and extract antiquities may be granted to an individual or on behalf of a scientific society. – This permit will be granted under the limited conditions set out in these regulations.
> Art. 10. – The permit to carry out excavations and to extract ancient objects will be granted by the Sublime Porte, under the conditions indicated in article 3, at the request of the Ministry of Public Education, following the approval of the council of this ministry and on the advice of the management of the imperial museum.[4]

As we can see, the protective measures were aimed at both the domestic populations (article 5) and foreign archaeologists. Salomon Reinach commented:

> During our five-month stay in Tunisia, archaeological discoveries followed one another in the Orient with extraordinary rapidity. There is hardly a week in which the newspapers of Athens and Constantinople, and the correspondence addressed from these cities to the various learned journals of Europe, have not reported the beginning of new excavations or the successful results of the explorations begun.... Today we must confine ourselves to making known a completely modern document, but one that may have a very considerable influence on the discoveries of ancient documents: we mean the new regulations concerning excavations in Turkey, a translation of which appeared in a French newspaper in Constantinople (*La Turquie*, 1, 3, and 4 March 1884). It will be seen that the archaeological advisers of the Sublime Porte did not put themselves to the trouble of imagining anything new: they were content to reproduce, with insignificant modifications, the restrictive and prohibitive laws applied in Greece for more than half a century. We will not waste our time dwelling on the drawbacks, on the disastrous effects of these measures: this is a task that we have carried out elsewhere, without hesitation or reluctance, because we knew that these measures were about to be adopted, and because we wanted to

> make an effort to interest the scholars of Europe in the defence of their heritage, one that is equally threatened by the regime of laissez-faire, that is to say, of pillage, and by that of prohibition, which hinders only regular research. Our hopes have been disappointed: the regulation drawn up by Hamdi-Bey has not triggered the slightest diplomatic protest, and the learned press of Europe has even refrained from reporting it. We will not imitate this silence, which may seem like tacit approval, and, without questioning the purity of the intentions that inspired the Ottoman antiquaries, we will regret, on their behalf, and on our own, the fact that they were able to impose systematic ideas that are, as we have proved, so contrary to the interests of archaeology and art.[5]

Drawing on his academic prestige and speaking in the name of knowledge, archaeology, and progress, Reinach here denounces a Turkish regime that not only would be incapable of 'properly protecting' its own works of art from pillage, vandalism, the recycling of materials, and smuggling, but also would hinder by prohibitive decrees the 'regular research' carried out by Western scholars. It is certainly no exaggeration to sense beneath his words not only the neutral and disinterested point of view of a man in search of knowledge (for example, nothing could prevent him from saluting the initiative of his colleague, the painter and archaeologist Osman Hamdi Bey, then engaged in Constantinople – as Istanbul was still called – in the latter's improvement of the Ottoman Empire's legislation on heritage, and more generally in the establishment of local structures to promote the birth and professionalization of the archaeological professions), but also, and perhaps above all, the opinion of a typical representative of his discipline, which in Europe at that time was deeply rooted in the logics of international competition, between London, Paris, and Berlin. And, to add to it all, the prospect of having to deal with a new protagonist was worrying.

These regulations, intended to correct the defects of the previous ones written by European scholars in 1869 and 1874, were therefore drawn up by Osman Hamdi Bey in 1884 – that is, several years after the discovery of the first fragments of the Pergamon Altar, the transfer of which took place completely legally, with the approval of the Ottoman authorities. Indeed, the latter did not initially oppose the translocation of the monument.

In any case, it is always very instructive to understand the translocations both from the point of view of European archaeologists, captivated by and passionate about *their* research subject, and from the point of view of the Ottomans, notably through the well-documented and accessible testimonies of eminent intellectuals such as Osman Hamdi Bey, a trained lawyer, talented painter, and architect of the draft law on the protection of the cultural heritage of the Ottoman Empire.[6] But the point of view of ordinary people who had often lived for several generations in the immediate vicinity of ancient ruins, or sometimes even in the middle of them, deserves no less to be taken into consideration.

## To take and to understand

Let's go back to Bergama in 1878, when the first fragments of the Pergamon Altar were extracted from their original context to be moved to Berlin. Why was a German national in this region of the world just then, inspecting Ottoman soil to find these improbable remains? An engineer by training, Carl Humann had been living in Asia Minor for several years, where he was counting on the mild climate to improve his fragile health and taking advantage of the activities and professional networks of his brother, Franz, one of the many German civil engineers working in a region that maintained close political and economic ties with the *Kaiserreich*. Carl Humann was soon being tasked by the Ottoman government with several cartographic missions, before being entrusted with road construction. Between 1867 and 1873, he and his brother supervised the creation of roads in Anatolia that would link Constantinople to Smyrna.

Strictly speaking, Humann never studied archaeology. Like many others at the same time, he was a 'self-taught archaeologist' when he identified, among the ruins of the city of Pergamon, large sculpted fragments that caught his attention and whose presence he reported to the Berlin museums – initially in vain. These museums, their energy absorbed by the prestigious and spectacular excavations of Olympia, paid little attention to Humann's efforts: without financial and scientific support, he could not undertake any large-scale projects. He had to wait several years before – thanks to a change of director at the head of the Antiquities Department of the Berlin museums – people finally took an interest in his discovery. Alexander Conze, appointed in 1877, felt that the fragments found in Bergama corresponded to the gigantomachy scene described by Lucius Ampelius in the *Liber memorialis* in the second century AD. Thanks to the financial and intellectual support of Conze and the museums, as well as the official permit from the Ottoman government to undertake excavations on the site of Pergamon, Carl Humann established an archaeological site on the Acropolis on 9 September 1878.

When he set up this site, Humann was not the first to take an interest in this locality. Before him, in the seventeenth century, an English traveller had already picked up at least two fragments there (rediscovered in Great Britain in the 1960s), and several European visitors of the same period had mentioned the site in their travelogues. But no further studies or archaeological excavations had been undertaken.

Carl Humann's excellently documented excavations were the subject of a major exhibition in Berlin in 2011.[7] Thanks to the notes of the engineer and his team, their scientific reports, correspondence, drawings, and sketches, as well as the detailed inventory of the sculptures sent to Germany or left in Pergamon, it is easy today to reconstruct not only the extent of the dislocation inflicted on this heritage site, but also the concrete conditions of the excavations: infrastructure, transport, the teams involved, the budgets that were committed, etc.

Hundreds of workers, oxen, and carts were deployed, tons of earth and stones were moved, and years of extraction were necessary to clear the different fragments of the altar, which has retained none of its initial form. We learn from the documentation of the excavations that it took no fewer than thirty to forty men, and three days of labour, to transport a single marble panel from the Acropolis to the lower city. Each panel, fragment, or statue brought down from the hill on sleds built for the purpose was then placed on a cart pulled by oxen to the sea, over a difficult road, built by Humann himself a few years earlier but made impassable by rains and seasonal river floods. Although all these archives are purely scientific in aim, they tell us about the taking and moving of the pieces found – in other words, about the gestures, both metaphorical and real, of appropriation.

What drove German archaeologists in those years was not so much the excavation as the prospect of a possible reconstruction of the altar, in particular the famous frieze. Like a child faced with a giant jigsaw puzzle, Humann tried from the first to think of the pieces found as a whole: he attempted to fit them together, to try out associations, and to make connections, looking for faces, legs, arms, bodies, human figures, and entire scenes. In his notebooks, he sketched the altar as he imagined it. And he already envisioned it quite accurately: a large square altar, a frieze at a certain height above the ground, and a monumental staircase leading to the sacrificial platform. The architect-engineer gradually became an archaeologist. He wanted more than just the pleasure of conquest: he was in search of meaning. He sought to take and to understand.

In parallel with this work of reconstruction, the question of sharing the excavations arose. According to the regulations then in force at the time (i.e. 1874),[8] it was not yet forbidden to take antiquities out of their country of origin, and so arrangements for sharing needed to be made between the excavators and the Ottoman Empire. Negotiations began between Berlin and Constantinople. An initial agreement stipulated that the finds would be shared out into three equal lots: one third for the owner of the land, one third for the home state of the discoverers, one third for the Ottoman state. Then an amendment specified that two thirds would go to the German state. Finally, the German embassy in Constantinople managed to get the Ottoman Empire, weakened by its defeat against Russia in 1878, to sign a definitive agreement: it was decreed that Prussia would recover all the pieces found in exchange for a modest sum (20,000 marks) paid to the Ottoman Empire.

## A model of reconstruction with a universalist vocation?

By 1878, Berlin had been the capital of the German Empire for seven years; the country was unified for the first time in 1871 – before that, it had been merely a juxtaposition of states of varying sizes, where Prussia, Saxony, and Bavaria stood out for their size and power alongside a marquetry of small kingdoms, city-states, and principalities. This late unification, compared to the situation in France and England, explains why Berlin lagged behind somewhat in centralizing its institutions in the capital – particularly art museums. There were only three in Berlin at the end of the nineteenth century, all located on the famous Museum Island: the Altes Museum (the 'Old Museum') inaugurated in 1830, the Neues Museum (the 'New Museum') which opened its doors around 1850, and the Nationalgalerie ('National Gallery') which, from 1876, had the mission of collecting and presenting contemporary German works of art.

At the end of the nineteenth century, Berlin, having become the capital of the Empire, was also in close competition with London and Paris for the acquisition of antiquities, with the thirst for accumulation naturally leading to a race for archaeological excavations. For the Western European powers of the time, increasing their collections of antiquities was a way of asserting their national greatness and legitimizing their status as heirs to a glorious past. Yet when the fragments of the Pergamon Altar arrived in Berlin, no special museum awaited them and they were initially stored – and partly displayed – among other ancient statues in the entrance rotunda of the Altes Museum. It was only in the following years that the project of a gigantic archaeological museum began to take shape in Berlin – one that could rival the British Museum and the Louvre, which had invested staggering sums in the preceding decades to expand their surface area (the Louvre) or to move their entire collections to a spectacular building (the British Museum). In 1884, six years after the arrival of the first fragments from Pergamon and while excavations on the original site were still ongoing, Berlin launched a major architectural competition to design a fourth building on Museum Island intended to house not only the finds from Pergamon, but also (in the form of casts) those from Olympia. This building was meant to live up to the national and scientific ambitions of the German Empire. In 1884, all the professional firms and architects in Germany at the time took part in the competition, which generated a fantastic number of plans, each more monumental than the last: some imagined not just presenting the Pergamon Altar in the rooms, but also building a giant copy of it on the roof of the future museum, from which in winter, thanks to a modern thermodynamic system, the heated air from the exhibition rooms would emerge, as if the altar were still smoking from some sacrifice. None of these plans would ever be realized. It was not until half a century later, after the altar had been exhibited in a temporary building, that what is now known as the Pergamonmuseum (Pergamon Museum) was inaugurated in 1930.

From their first exhibition at the Altes Museum in the early 1880s onwards, the effect of these second-century BC Hellenistic fragments on the public and on the world of art history was considerable. The Pergamon style, so different in its expressiveness from what was then known of classical Greek art, made a great impression on visitors. For the first time, they could see fiery, convulsed, untrammelled faces and bodies. The art historian Jacob Burckhardt, one of the authorities of the time, judged that the discovery of the Pergamon friezes ought to lead to a complete rewriting of the history of art: 'Everything is full of a furious vehemence and the grandest style. It all turns the history of art upside down', he wrote in 1880.[9] The same year, the Russian writer Ivan Turgenev took advantage of a trip to Berlin to devote some remarkable pages to the fragments that were being exhibited on the ground: according to him, they would bring the Prussian government 'more glory than the conquest of Alsace and Lorraine'. Overwhelmed by their 'millennial beauty' and the 'tumultuous freedom' that emanated from them, he wrote a lengthy description of

> those figures, sometimes radiant, sometimes threatening, living, dead, triumphant or dying, with those twisting rings of snakes' scales, those outstretched wings, those eagles, those horses, those weapons, those shields, those fluttering clothes, those palm trees, and those bodies, those superb bodies of men in all positions, audacious to the point of improbability, as harmonious as music, all the most varied expressions in the faces, those movements of indomitable limbs, that triumph of fury, and the despair and the gaiety of the gods, and the cruelty of the gods – all this heaven and all this earth – but it is the world, the whole world, at the revelation of which an involuntary shudder of joy and passionate veneration stirs you to your very entrails.[10]

The text ends with these sentences: 'As I left the Museum, I thought: "How happy I am not to have died before having experienced these last impressions, to have seen all this."'[11]

As soon as the first fragments from Pergamon arrived, a need was also felt in Berlin to use the various blocks that had been found to reconstruct the altar as it must have originally stood on the Acropolis of the city of Asia Minor. A temporary museum was built in 1901 with exactly the right dimensions to contain the altar. It admittedly had a short life, just seven years, but the reconstruction attempted by the Berlin archaeologists caused a sensation in Germany and Europe: the altar and the frieze were for the first time reconstructed and staged as if the building were standing in its original state. The museum was covered with a glass roof that let in daylight to make the inside seem as if it were outside. It was an architectural and archaeological feat that also expressed the desire to make visitors 'forget' that they were in a museum in northern Europe. Among them was Guillaume Apollinaire, then twenty years old, still quite unaware of his destiny as a man of letters. To earn a living, the young man was giving French lessons to the daughter of a good German family. The latter's parents took him to visit Berlin. Overwhelmed by his visit to the Pergamon Altar in its temporary museum, Apollinaire wrote his first art review; it was quickly published in the prestigious *Revue blanche*:

> Berlin is a dreadful and convenient city. Everything that tends to give it the appearance of a capital is in detestable taste. Besides, any of the cities of the empire is more interesting than this city without churches. Were it not for the surrounding castles, a few paintings in the old museum, and the recently opened Pergamon, a trip to Berlin would be pointless. The building called Pergamon, located behind the old museum, contains the finds brought back from the excavations of Pergamon, especially the famous gigantomachy that decorated the altar of Jupiter. This altar has been reconstructed – the work cost the Berlin scholars twenty-three years' effort.
>
> But how beautiful it is! What a magnificent poem in stone! The Olympian gods, terrestrial, marine, and infernal, the animals, the giants, and the monsters furiously intertwine their sometimes mutilated limbs, the torsos of the goddesses rear up on the heroes' arms, faces tense up,

> mouths bite. This work, which craftsmen carved in very coarse-grained stone, emits such a sense of divinity that the traveller, forgetting the crowd of visitors with hooked moustaches and ugly women, eagerly awaits the hour when the bulls of the hecatombs will roar.[12]

Despite what one could call its aesthetic and didactic 'effectiveness', this first Pergamon museum turned out to be too cramped. The lack of space meant there was not the necessary perspective to contemplate the altar in all its proportions. Thus, seven years later, the building was destroyed and a new construction site was opened on Museum Island. Slowed down by the First World War, the change of political regime (the transition from the Empire to the Weimar Republic), economic crises (1923, 1929), and a subsoil that was very unsuitable for the construction of heavy buildings, the work dragged on and it was not until 1930 – the centenary of Museum Island – that the (current) Pergamon Museum finally opened its doors. Once again, this inauguration was followed by the whole of Europe and widely publicized, at a time when press photography – and, even more, film newsreels – allowed for a wide dissemination of information beyond national borders. In addition to the Pergamon Altar, the museum presented, life-size, the Ishtar Gate and the Processional Way from Babylon, as well as the monumental market gate from Miletus in Asia Minor, the original fragments of which had also been excavated by German archaeologists and transferred to Berlin.

The gigantic proportions of the new Pergamon Museum made it possible to reproduce in real size the originals of a dreamt-of Antiquity in which you could move around as if on a film set. According to the archives of the Berlin museums, Charlie Chaplin had his photo taken nonchalantly sitting on the steps during a visit to Berlin in 1931. At the time, there were no other reconstructions of ancient monuments from fragments found on their original sites anywhere else in Europe. The only similar examples of 'immersive' stagings were Egyptian temples and other architectural structures made of papier-mâché or plaster at the World's Fairs. Neither in London nor in Paris did anyone think at that time of simulating Antiquity with original fragments in their great national museums. For example, London presented the famous Parthenon Frieze from Athens in a juxtaposition of isolated fragments.

In the case of the Pergamon Altar, this simulation appealed to the public's imagination. In order to allow visitors to contemplate the frieze as a whole, and because the room was still not deep enough to offer a complete tour of the altar, it was only half reconstructed. Also, the 'back' half of the frieze of the gigantomachy was deployed on all the walls of the room, in order to create continuity for the eye. The effect produced was unprecedented. Opinions diverged, of course, and art critics had a field day, both admirers and detractors. In *L'Illustration*, which devoted a long report to the new museum, the French art historian Louis Gillet wrote:

> The effect is incredible; it is perhaps excessive, because you take it in at a glance and receive all at once, so to speak, the total shock of a sculpted mass that was once distributed over the four faces of the altar. Ancient spectators had to go around the monument, of which they could not take in more than a quarter at a time. Here, the four faces add up, simultaneously deluging the tottering spectator in one accelerated movement with their gust of wind, their storm of gods and Titans.
>
> At first, you remain dizzy, as if caught in the wind of an avalanche. However, I must admit: I had never found these sculptures so beautiful. It seemed to me that I was seeing them for the first time. Seen thus, in the thunder and tumult of their episodes, in the tangle of their forms, in the furious movement of the drama which sweeps them away, you forget all criticism; you are no longer sensitive to detail, you yield as if to a whirlwind under the weight of this heroic force, of this divine rabble where Olympus and Earth, the dazzling Ouranians and their deformed children of Ge, collide and jostle with each other. In this duel between celestial beings and rebellious elements, where Hellenic gods fight creatures in animal forms, pythons with human torsos crawl on reptile-jawed coils, and winged spectres, half human, half bird-like, you think you can see Greece, as in the time of its origins, grappling with Asia and its monstrous swarm of chimeras, dragons, wyverns, and griffins, which in their impure cloud populate the dreams of the Orient.
>
> In any case, this staging is a revolution in museography: no longer are masterpieces just lined up like so many objects for display: rather, their monumental life and their physical power are restored. All museum directors will now have to take lessons from Berlin. The British Museum

will no longer be allowed to exhibit the remains of the Mausoleum in a cellar and to present in a musty gallery, like the detached bones of a fossil, the august debris of the Parthenon ... It will be a source of embarrassment if the gods are relegated to a storeroom....

This system has been applied with stylish boldness by Professor Wiegand. Gone is the time when people unabashedly mutilated a monument, tearing out a figure or a decorative detail! Here, entire monuments have been transported in one piece to Berlin.... Architecture has become *museumfähig*, an object in a museum – or its prey. One day, the colonnade of the Louvre will be exhibited! ... Professor Wiegand, however, insists to me that he is innocent of all vandalism: he has not destroyed or damaged any existing monument. These are ruins exhumed from the earth, ruins that he has resurrected and patiently recomposed, much as was done for the new excavations of Pompeii where the ash, sifted on site, has brought to light the elements of domestic life and even the atmosphere of the buried city.[13]

Not only was the reconstruction spectacular, triggering intense visual emotions, but it also affirmed the national greatness, and even the scientific superiority, of Germany. The reconstruction project led by Theodor Wiegand, who then headed the Antiquities Department of the Berlin museums, was a museographical model that also served the national discourse.

In contrast to the glowing review published by *L'Illustration*, the French art critic and novelist Albert Flament was exasperated. As he wrote in 1932:

In the rooms on the ground floor, so vast that only a surveyor could measure them, with their completely glazed ceiling four or five storeys above, the remains of the Pergamon frieze have been reconstructed, in exactly the same spirit as the horizons and the brasseries or terraces of the Haus Vaterland.[14] Using a fragment of cornice just a few centimetres wide, whole metres of cornice have been *reconstructed*. Titanic columns have been remade, of which only a fragment of the base and part of the capital were extant. The famous frieze of fighting warriors and horses has been restored in the same spirit on a Cyclopean stone base, under an oversized entablature. Egregious 'doctors' have not put back the arms

> and legs carried away by the gusts of past centuries blowing through the ruins, but they have embedded them in a composition intended to give the whole ensemble, right from the entrance, a primitive appearance. To blend the different tones of these remains with that of the new materials, it was necessary to wash them with all kinds of detergents and acids. Deprived of the patina of time, the warriors have been given some kind of coating, always with the aim of masking the restoration. Behind, a colossal staircase, with steps that are too narrow, supports a colonnade that is too low. The effect is unbearable, disproportionate, without grandeur, and without meaning. This room seems to have been arranged for a performance of some tragedy staged by a reinforced concrete contractor....
>
> We have just touched on the great fault of the German. He believes in what he reconstructs in the same way that he believes in numbers. He remakes the centuries. He camouflages the past; he illuminates with a harsh spark of magnesium the night of ages that have been swallowed up in death, and he sincerely imagines that he is restoring sunshine and life to them.[15]

This aesthetic and political discourse, manipulated for or against the reconstruction of ancient monuments – without, moreover, a single mention of the regions from which they had been taken a few decades earlier – shows to what extent the museums of Europe and their museographic choices were able, at the beginning of the twentieth century, to crystallize national, and even nationalist, issues via a 'museumized' Antiquity. During the 1936 Berlin Olympic Games, moreover, the Museum Island in general, and the Pergamon Museum in particular, would become a major site for staging the Nazi regime.

Sheltered during the Second World War along with all the other important items in the Berlin museums, the Pergamon Altar was spared by the Allied bombings but confiscated by the Red Army in May 1945. It was taken in pieces to the USSR as a military trophy and as compensation for the heritage destruction inflicted by Germany on Soviet territories.

Thirteen years later, the altar was returned ... not to Turkey, but to the 'socialist' half of the now divided Germany: the GDR. The monument taken from Asia Minor returned to the Pergamon Museum in 1959. This was an important political act: having taken care of the collections – as it did not fail to emphasize in propaganda brochures accompanying the return of the Berlin collections of antiquities – the Soviet Union staged the generous restitution of these remains to its vassal.

It is obvious how each translocation, whether it is an appropriation or a restitution, is part of a political gesture. By returning the Pergamon Altar to East Berlin, the USSR imposed a sense of gratitude on the GDR and maintained a relationship of domination. In the East German capital, the altar was immediately symbolically adopted by the Communist regime. This was demonstrated, for example, by its reproduction on a 1959 postage stamp which, on a blue background, showed the tiny black and white photograph of the monumental altar in its Berlin museum, and just below this inscription in black capital letters, 'DEUTSCHE DEMOKRATISCHE REPUBLIK'. It would have been difficult to demonstrate more clearly, by postal means (i.e. destined to circulate throughout the world), to whom the ancient monument belonged.

The history of the successive movements of the Pergamon Altar illustrates with great clarity the mechanisms by which the ideology of the national museum with a universalist vocation was established in the nineteenth century. International rivalries over antiquities played a determining role in the imperial policy of the new European nation states. This race to acquire masterpieces was accompanied by intense museographical reflection, which shows how much the museum had become a key element in the architectural imagination of capital cities. In London, Paris, and Berlin, the creation and development of large museums led to an ideological investment in the collections. The cultural policy of individual states was based on a nationalistic use of museums, one that depended on a financial, scientific, and political capacity to accumulate these new symbols of Western universalism. It was also in museums that the community of citizens wrote its history, ordered its past, and organized its memory. However, this narrative was created at the expense of the regions from which the works historically came.

Since 2014, in Berlin, the Pergamon Altar has no longer been accessible to the public due to restoration of the museum that houses it.

Scheduled for 2023, the reopening has been postponed several times; it is now announced for the 2030s. Initially, 261 million euros were to be invested in this restoration, which, halfway through, has already risen to half a billion euros. These considerable sums remind us that reunified Germany, in a concern for conservation but also in a gesture of national reaffirmation, is using the museum to show the whole world its newfound scientific, cultural, and financial power.

On the other side of the Mediterranean, on the Acropolis overlooking the modern city of Bergama, at the exact location of its ancient site, a model of the altar was installed in an open-air display case in 2014. That same year, 2014, marked the inclusion of 'Pergamon and its surroundings' on the UNESCO World Heritage List. Paradoxically, the absence of the monument did not prevent this nomination, because it was the entire site – 'Pergamon and its multi-layered cultural landscape', to borrow the title of the application filed by the municipality of Bergama[16] (that is to say, a vast archaeological complex) – that was designated. In its assessment report, the International Council on Monuments and Sites (Icomos) praised the innovative nature of the ancient urban and landscape planning of Pergamon, which, it noted, decisively paved the way for the formation of the Eastern Roman Empire. Within this ensemble, the Pergamon Altar constituted a missing and yet ultra-present piece. Although absent from the site, it was mentioned in all UNESCO documents and described by all parties involved in the accreditation process as a key argument in favour of its inclusion on the list of World Heritage Sites. Thus, in the 550-page application submitted by the municipality of Bergama, we read: 'In the middle of this landscape, the Great Altar is the most precious and unsurpassable sculptural work of art. This work of art, which is no longer in Bergama but is exhibited in the Pergamon Museum in Berlin, is extremely powerful proof of the sociocultural superiority of this region at that time.'[17] The presence of absence: at the Bergama Müzesi, the archaeological museum of the city of Bergama inaugurated in the lower town in 1934, it is a model, surrounded by a few black-and-white photos, that welcomes visitors. And these discreet words, in Turkish and English, on an explanatory panel: 'Rebuilt in 1930, the altar is now in Berlin.... In our museum, there is only the torso of a horse statue and two or three architectural pieces that perhaps decorated the altar.'

Even absent, this piece of 'exceptional universal value', according to UNESCO terminology, thus remains fictionally linked to the original site. It is as if, in 2014, the parties concerned (the municipality, Icomos and UNESCO) had mentally added the altar to Bergama's candidacy, not considering its absence as an attack on the integrity of the site (even though integrity is a *sine qua non* factor for inclusion on the UNESCO World Heritage list). The municipality itself, in a perhaps provocative nudge, merely notes in parentheses and in italics in the middle of the file: '*Although the Great Altar is exhibited in Berlin, the Pergamon Museum is not today part of the property proposed for inclusion on the World Heritage List.*'[18]

*

Who owns the beauty of the Pergamon Altar? The Ottoman Empire, which had abandoned it for centuries to wear and tear and pillage? The descendants of this ancient city in Asia Minor that was not swallowed up by the earth and by time but still exists in Bergama? Those German archaeologists who undertook scientific excavations authorized by the Ottoman authorities? The Ottoman scholars who, by drafting laws, tried to prevent the Sublime Porte from authorizing its export? The *Kaiserreich*, which has not existed since 1919 and sought by all means available to demonstrate its power – and especially its financial, scientific, and cultural capacity to compete with France and England? The Foundation for Prussian Cultural Properties (Stiftung Preussischer Kulturbesitz), which has managed the Berlin museums since the dismantling of Prussia in 1945? Turkey? Greece?

In any case, the delay in reopening the Pergamon Museum would certainly have made it possible to consider the possibility that the altar (which, after all, is accustomed to travel) could have made an extended stay in Bergama ...

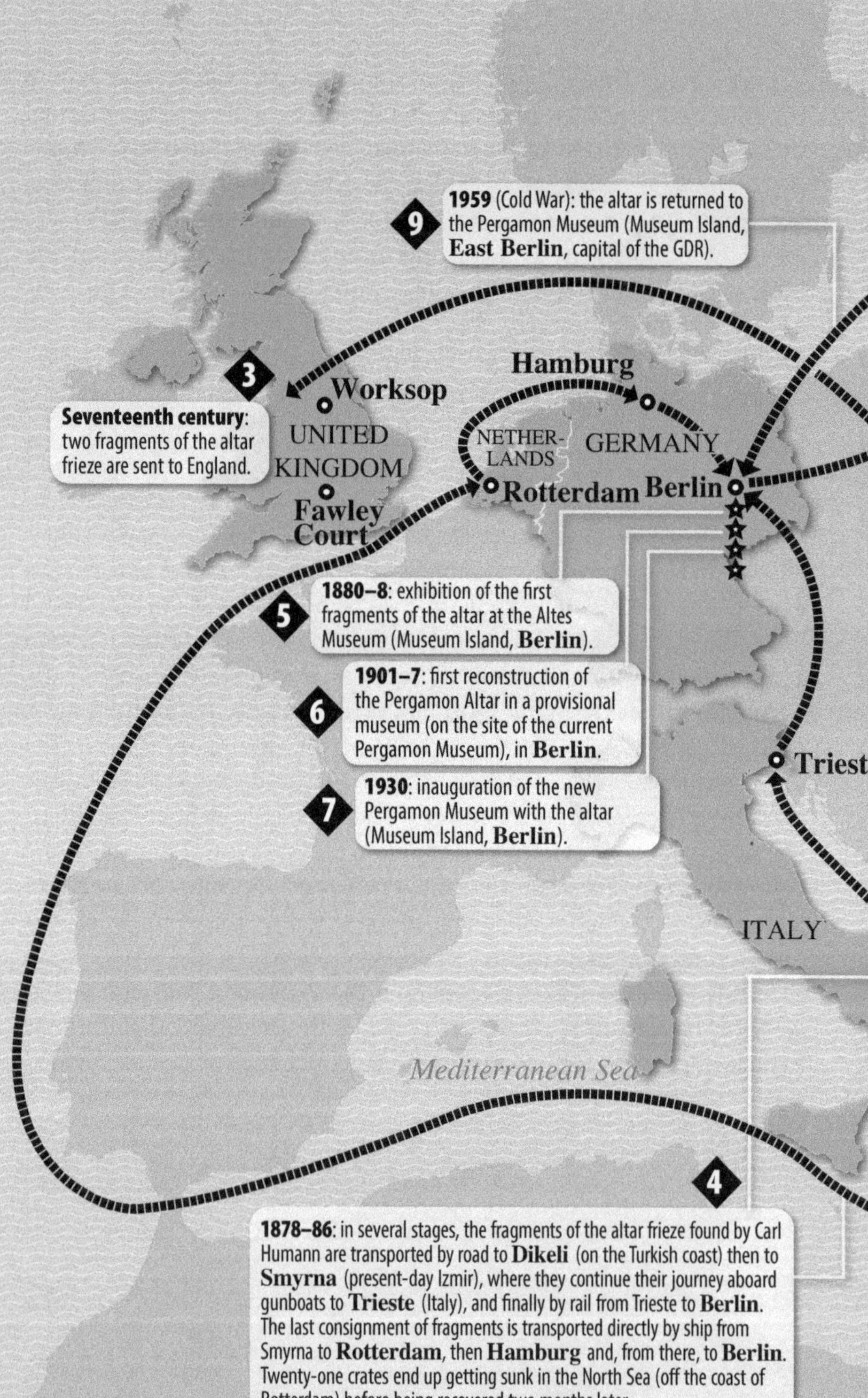

9
1959 (Cold War): the altar is returned to the Pergamon Museum (Museum Island, East Berlin, capital of the GDR).
3
Seventeenth century: two fragments of the altar frieze are sent to England.
Worksop
UNITED KINGDOM
Fawley Court
Hamburg
NETHER-LANDS
GERMANY
Rotterdam
Berlin
5
1880–8: exhibition of the first fragments of the altar at the Altes Museum (Museum Island, Berlin).
6
1901–7: first reconstruction of the Pergamon Altar in a provisional museum (on the site of the current Pergamon Museum), in Berlin.
7
1930: inauguration of the new Pergamon Museum with the altar (Museum Island, Berlin).
Trieste
ITALY
Mediterranean Sea
4
1878–86: in several stages, the fragments of the altar frieze found by Carl Humann are transported by road to Dikeli (on the Turkish coast) then to Smyrna (present-day Izmir), where they continue their journey aboard gunboats to Trieste (Italy), and finally by rail from Trieste to Berlin. The last consignment of fragments is transported directly by ship from Smyrna to Rotterdam, then Hamburg and, from there, to Berlin. Twenty-one crates end up getting sunk in the North Sea (off the coast of Rotterdam) before being recovered two months later.

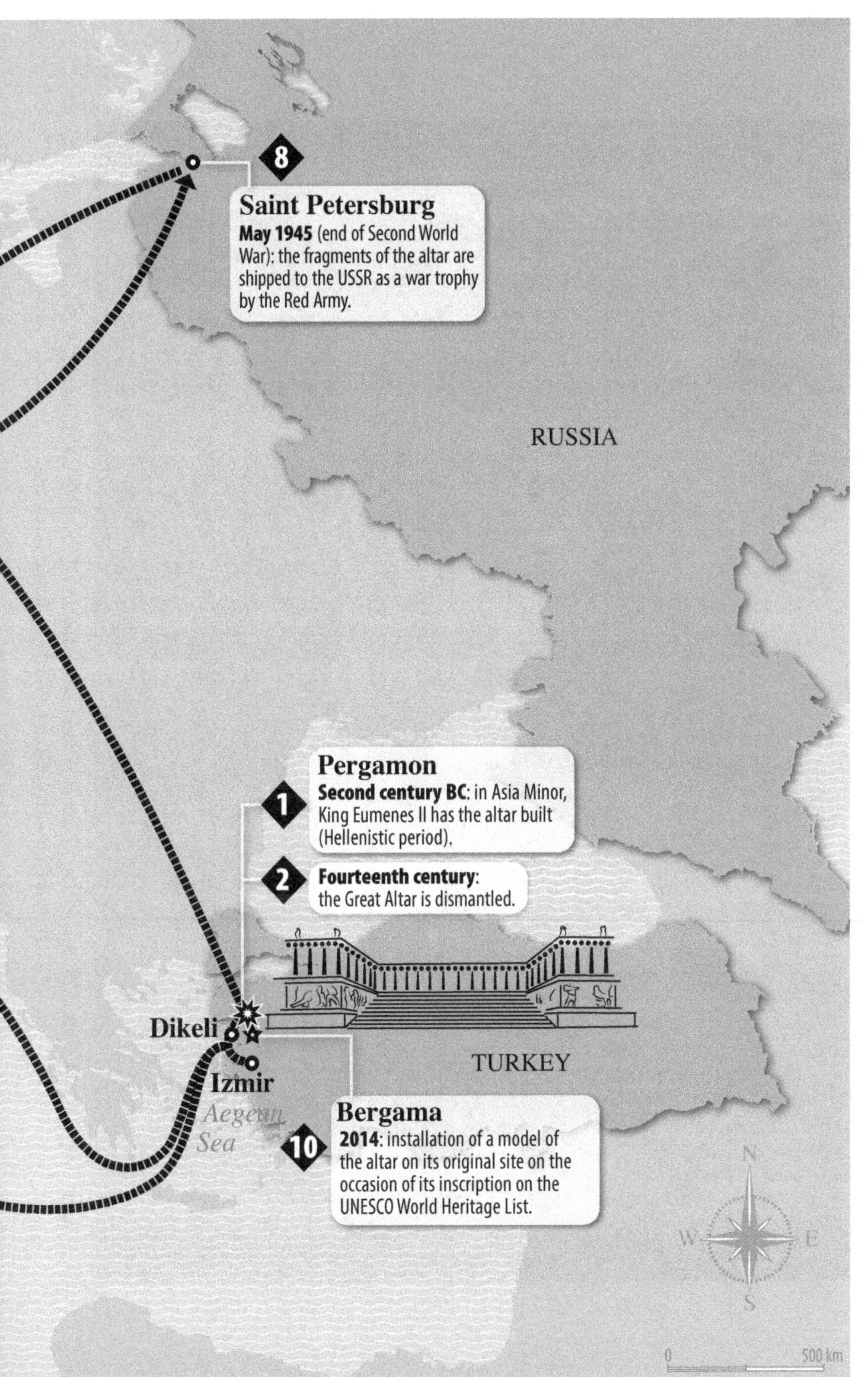
8
Saint Petersburg
May 1945 (end of Second World War): the fragments of the altar are shipped to the USSR as a war trophy by the Red Army.
RUSSIA
Pergamon
1
Second century BC: in Asia Minor, King Eumenes II has the altar built (Hellenistic period).
2
Fourteenth century: the Great Altar is dismantled.
Dikeli
Izmir
Aegean Sea
TURKEY
Bergama
10
2014: installation of a model of the altar on its original site on the occasion of its inscription on the UNESCO World Heritage List.
N
W
E
S
0
500 km

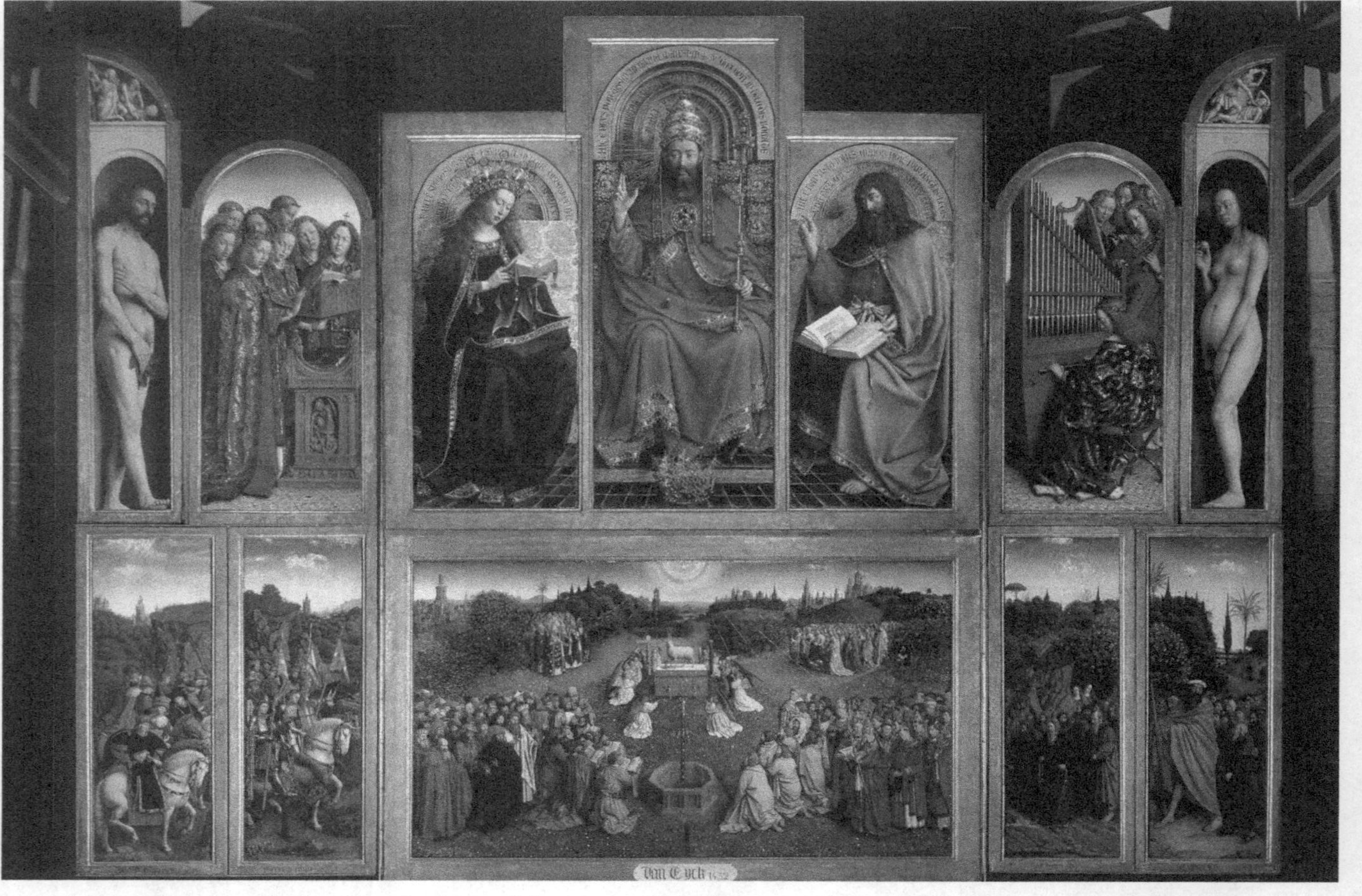

Hubert and Jan Van Eyck, *The Adoration of the Mystic Lamb*, completed in 1432, oil on wood, 375 × 520 cm. Saint Bavo's Cathedral, Ghent. Photo © Scala, Florence.

# 3

# THE ALTARPIECE OF 'THE MYSTIC LAMB' BY THE VAN EYCK BROTHERS

This is one of the most desired, stolen, moved, and publicized objects in the history of European art. What an amazing fate befell these wooden panels depicting biblical scenes of astonishing precision and naturalism, dating from the fifteenth century, and which became the subject of a Hollywood blockbuster! In the film *The Monuments Men*, a small group of art experts are sent by the American authorities during the Second World War to protect and save artistic and historical monuments in war zones, including the altarpiece of 'The Mystic Lamb'.

This fascinating artwork from the Flemish school, painted by the Van Eyck brothers around 1430 on oak panels covered with thin layers of a mixture of chalk and glue, was designed for a special place: Saint Bavo's Cathedral in Ghent, in what is now Belgium. Composed of two sides, each 3.75 metres high, this monumental polyptych is doubly visible to the eye, with one 'closed' side (it is then 2.60 metres wide) and another side (more than 5 metres) that is 'open' on rare liturgical occasions. The transition from one to the other is a moment of grace. At the heart of the work is a small white sacrificial lamb.

During the French Revolution, the central panels of 'The Mystic Lamb' were seized and dismantled by France, then at war with the Austrian Netherlands in Flanders, and partially transported to Paris. To legitimize the removal of the work from its context, the idea of 'liberated heritage' was deployed: as art is a product of freedom, it is necessary, according to a subtle rhetoric developed around 1792, to repatriate its masterpieces to the land of freedom – that is, France. Returned after the fall of Napoleon, the central panels were placed back in Saint Bavo's Cathedral after 1815. But, at the same time, thanks to the political and economic chaos caused by the end of the Empire, six side panels were sold on the art market. They were finally purchased by the museums of Berlin in 1821 and exhibited for a hundred years in the heart of the city, like stars of the show, on Museum Island opposite the castle of the kings of Prussia. In the aftermath of the First World War, defeated Germany was condemned by the Treaty of Versailles to return these panels to Belgium, where they were duly sent back. The altarpiece was then restored to its original state. But the respite was short-lived. One panel was stolen in 1934. At the start of the Second World War, the entire polyptych was dismantled and transported far from Ghent to escape the covetousness of the Nazi government, which nevertheless ended up locating it and having it taken, in the middle of the war, to Bavaria. The Monuments Men recovered it in 1945 and sent it back to Brussels, which in turn returned it to the city of Ghent and its original cathedral. It is still there today, but in a 'museum-like' manner, behind a secure display case: it is no longer immediately integrated into worship, as it was for centuries. In addition to these successive moves, the altarpiece has therefore been transformed in its very meaning – symbolic, religious, artistic – and in its unity since the stolen panel, never found, was replaced by a copy.

How can we rediscover the sources of a memory attached to a cultural asset when it has been damaged, dismembered, restored, rebuilt, copied, stolen, and moved many times before going back to its place of origin? How can we think about the 'return of the same-but-different'? The history of this translocation invites us to enter into the complexity of the history of European heritage, inseparable from its varied political, military, religious, and cultural contexts, but also to observe what is at stake on the emotional side. Alongside the feeling of collective loss experienced by those who were deprived of their altarpiece in Ghent, we must remember the anger of certain enlightened circles in the late eighteenth century, the covetousness of art historians, the impact of various wars, the aesthetic wonder and the fertilizations triggered by people's encounters with a masterpiece, and the art market. Who owns the amazing beauty of the altarpiece of 'The Mystic Lamb'?

*

It is an exceptional object of worship and an *objet d'art*: closed most of the time, the altarpiece reveals its sacred heart only on certain occasions in the Christian calendar. On ordinary days, it shows, in luminous shades of white and grey barely enhanced with blue, red, pink, and green, a scene of the Annunciation in four compartments: the archangel Gabriel, on the left, delivers his message to the Virgin Mary who, on the right, replies. Between them we see the blue of the sky through a window and some utensils in a niche. Just below are painted, in imitation marble or alabaster, two statues of Saint John the Baptist and John the Evangelist, whose tunic folds rival in their virtuosity those of the living people who inhabit the other panels. To their right and left, in colour, are depicted the rich donors of the polyptych. The upper part is occupied by prophets and sibyls wrapped in ribbons bearing texts announcing the coming of Christ. When the altarpiece opens, it reveals, in all its shimmering glory, another story, set in a landscape of dazzling luminosity and precision, where a crowd of the faithful, joined on either side by cohorts of knights and saints, witnesses the sacrifice of the white lamb mounted on a red altar. Its blood flows into a golden chalice. The scene unfolds on a large rectangular panel and four side panels; the colours and details are of a subtlety that only a then-unequalled mastery of oil painting techniques could have made possible. Above the lamb, immense and majestic, God, in the centre, Mary on his right, and John the Baptist on his left dominate the painting.

It is the central panels (God, Mary, John the Baptist, and the sacrificial landscape) that have attracted the covetousness of the centuries. I will now detail their journey through space and time. Unlike the previous works, found in the sands of Egypt or on the heights of a now Turkish city before being exhibited in European museums, the altarpiece by the Van Eyck brothers has not changed cultural sphere during its tribulations. It bears witness to the heritage wounds that Europe has long inflicted on itself.

## An annexed heritage

The altarpiece of 'The Mystic Lamb' was commissioned by the wealthy Ghent patrician Joos Vijd, and his wife, Elisabeth Borluut. It was designed for the side chapel of Sint-Jans, today's Saint Bavo's Cathedral, also founded by Vijd. Commissioned around 1420, the work was probably completed in 1432. Between that date and the French Revolution – that is to say, for more than 350 years – the polyptych did not leave Ghent. It was, however, endangered twice over by the Protestant iconoclastic campaigns of the mid sixteenth century, which hunted down images – deemed impious – and systematically vandalized statues and paintings in churches. The work was first hidden, for its own protection, in the cathedral's bell tower (1566), and then, after being put back in place, for a second time in the Ghent town hall (between 1579 and 1584). At the very end of the eighteenth century, it was confiscated *manu militari* and transferred on large carts to Paris. This was in 1794.

At that time, revolutionary France claimed to be the country of liberty. It deployed impressive military and intellectual resources to gather in its capital all the works of 'art and science' found in the regions of Europe occupied by its troops and likely to enrich its collections: precious manuscripts and books, paintings, antiques, and specimens of natural history. Even exotic animals were taken from the princely menageries of northern Europe, such as the famous elephant couple, Hans and Parkie, captured on the island of Ceylon (today Sri Lanka) in 1784: transported to the Netherlands in 1786, they were brought on foot to Paris nine years later. In this sense, the French Republic extended outside its borders the policy of nationalizing the property of the clergy and aristocracy already conducted after 1789 within its national borders. The precious books and rare manuscripts were intended to enrich the Bibliothèque nationale (formerly the Bibliothèque royale) in Paris. The natural history collections and living mammals joined the Museum at the Jardin des Plantes. The paintings and sculptures were sent to the Musée central des arts (the future Louvre Museum) created in 1793. The doctrine of 'liberated heritage' made it possible to justify to a world shocked by this policy of aggressive cultural appropriation the accumulation and centralization in Paris, in successive waves, of objects that came first from what is now Belgium, the Netherlands, and certain German cities (1794–5), then from Italy (1796), and finally from several German-speaking regions: Bavaria, Austria, Prussia, Poland, and other smaller states with rich art collections (1801–9), as well as Spain (1808). The period that interests us here is the first, the years 1794–5, which can be considered a 'test phase' of the French policy of heritage translocation.

On the orders of the Convention, special commissioners, deployed with the armies of the Republic, selected from the churches and convents of the occupied territories, from libraries, from rich Jesuit colleges, from botanical gardens, and from the collections of foreign princes, works deemed useful to the public institutions of the French capital, whose collections were to be 'complemented'. These commissioners systematically criss-crossed the occupied regions and proceeded with the spectacular removal of dozens of altar paintings from the very rich and powerful towns on the left bank of the Rhine: Antwerp, The Hague, Ghent, Cologne, and Aachen, to name just a few. In the months that followed, convoys arrived in Paris loaded with internationally renowned masterpieces: works by Rubens and Van Dyck, Dutch and Flemish paintings, drawings by masters and other prints, even architectural items such as the famous monumental Carolingian columns of Aachen Cathedral, prised away and transported at great expense to the Louvre. In one of these convoys were the central panels of the altarpiece of 'The Mystic Lamb', whose creators, the Van Eyck brothers, were at the time considered to be the inventors of oil painting. An increasingly sophisticated discourse and ever improved transport techniques accompanied these forced displacements.

Officially, this heritage had been freed from the yoke of religion and of despots, whose gaze, it was said in France, sullied the paintings. Inflamed by its own ideals, the assembly of the representatives of the people decided in Paris that these confiscated art objects were now part of a heritage placed at the universal service of public education and knowledge. It was obviously not a question of looting or injustice, even less of any juridical legitimacy, to possess this or that work, but of universality, of progress in the arts and sciences, and of cross-border influence. The French Republic did everything possible, from its point of view, to promote the flourishing of culture and knowledge, dissociated – by an abstract mental operation – from their places and contexts of production. In a spirit of centralization and international competition, the rhetoricians of French-style heritage saw Paris as the capital of a singular universalism: 'Let Paris therefore be the capital of the arts ..., the refuge of all human knowledge and the repository of all the treasures of the mind.... It must be the school of the universe and the metropolis of human science, and it must exercise over the rest of the world this irresistible empire of instruction and knowledge', as the lawyer François-Antoine Boissy d'Anglas, a central political figure of the Convention, wrote in 1794.[1]

Several hundred paintings, hundreds of other ancient items, art objects, drawings, books, and manuscripts were moved to Paris in the space of a few years. This annexed heritage was sorted upon arrival and the various works were either distributed among the public establishments of the capital, or sent on to the newly created provincial museums, or simply inventoried and never presented to the public. When it opened its doors in 1793, the Musée central des arts de la République, in the Louvre Palace, initially appeared as a confused collection of often prestigious works, most of which came from the royal collections or those of the great French aristocracy, but were poorly organized: their number soon doubled, tripled, or quadrupled thanks to France's 'artistic conquests' abroad. This ultra-rapid accumulation was accompanied by massive state investments that, with a great deal of work, transformed the palace into a true 'experience' of the history of European art, whose periods and regions visitors could soon explore on foot, and for free. In 1803, the museum was renamed the Musée Napoléon. At the fall of the Empire in 1814–15, its catalogue listed nearly 1,400 masterpieces of European painting from the thirteenth to the eighteenth centuries on display – all the rest remaining invisible. According to the museum's internal records, the Louvre then had 4,400 paintings, 1,808 ancient statues and 61 vases, plus 6,500 drawings and several hundred *objets d'art* and curiosities.

Let's have a look at the *Notice des tableaux exposés dans la Galerie Napoléon* from 1813. This small-format catalogue was published by the museum itself. It was intended, at a very modest price, for visitors, who could use it to make the connection between what they saw in the museum's rooms and the history of art as a scholarly discipline – one that was starting to become more democratic and better structured. Thus, the *Notice* contains 'scientifically correct' information for the time on the works, their authors, their materials, and their dimensions, and sometimes some scholarly indications on attribution or theme. Two centuries later, these notices are valuable because they inform us about the history of taste, cultural consumption, the layout of the rooms and the staging of this or that work, and about the knowledge (and lack of knowledge) of art historians. Here, the altarpiece of 'The Mystic Lamb' appears under the heading 'German School' – a surprising category (I shall come back to this). It is not presented as a single, two-sided work, but is broken down into several distinct numbers: '299, God the Father. 300, the Virgin. 301, Saint John the Baptist, etc.' Number 302 corresponds to the panel of the 'spotless lamb, the symbol of Jesus, [who] receives the homage of the virgins, the martyrs, the Fathers of the Church, and the entire celestial hierarchy'.

By thus individualizing the panels of the altarpiece number by number, by exhibiting its inner face, usually hidden, to the public eye, and by not mentioning the existence of side panels, the museum managers subjected it to a significant transformation. From being an object of Christian worship, it became an object of scholarly study, a desacralized aesthetic experience of dissociated and immobilized fragments, or even the object of a new cult – no longer the worship of 'God the Father', but that of the arts. In other words, the sacred power of the altarpiece was, as it were, 'neutralized' by its entry into the museum, and replaced by a secular and scientific cult.

But how can we accurately assess the effect produced around 1800 by the presence of such an uprooted object in a public museum open to all, in the middle of a politically and socially eruptive capital city, among several hundred other paintings? At the very end of the eighteenth century, Paris attracted a considerable number of visitors, men and women from all over Europe, drawn by the political, urban, and cultural 'laboratory' that the French capital had become, but also by a host of professional and economic opportunities. Among these visitors, many not only went to the Louvre, the

Bibliothèque nationale, the Jardin des Plantes, etc., but also devoted long and valuable descriptions to them in the travel accounts that they published on their return home. For others – and in particular a whole section of European youth (those who were twenty years old in 1789) – swept up in the new social, geographical, and psychological mobility induced by the French Revolution, Paris became a place where people could settle for several years. For artists, finally, the French capital, where one could now study the history of European art united in a single museum, became a privileged school, replacing Rome, until then the undisputed capital of the arts in Europe. Numerous written traces, drawings, sketches, and letters allow us today to measure the effect produced by the altarpiece of 'The Mystic Lamb' in Paris – the effect or, more precisely, the effect*s* in the plural, each of which would 'activate' the work for singular needs and uses, as demonstrated by the following three examples. They concern a philosopher, a painter, and certain professionals of ancient art.

The philosopher is the German Friedrich von Schlegel. Aged thirty when he settled in Paris, he intended to start a new life there and launched himself into a career as a public intellectual and journalist. He gave lectures to his friends and acquaintances, examined all the paintings in the Louvre one by one, described and evaluated them during long hours of work, and founded and almost single-handedly edited a German-language journal, aimed at informing his compatriots of cultural and political developments in France – a journal that he significantly entitled *Europa*. It was here, from Paris, that in many articles Schlegel developed his famous aesthetic of German Romanticism, which would have a considerable impact across the Rhine. The philosopher-journalist devoted a long passage in his journal to the altarpiece of 'The Mystic Lamb.' He said not a word about its forced dismantling, its original location and function, or the idea of a 'closed' and 'open' liturgical mode. In fact, the staging of the panels in the Louvre, as seen by Schlegel, clearly suggested to visitors that they were separate works. This, at least, is what we gather from the pages in *Europa* that set up a rivalry between the central panel of the sacrificed lamb, on the one hand, and, on the other hand:

> three church paintings by the same painter, which form an infinitely more moving whole, even if they are no more interesting. They represent God the Father, the Virgin and Saint John the Baptist. The elegance and the Egyptian rigidity of these divine figures, so severe, as straight as in the most remote Antiquity, inspire a profound respect; they seduce us in spite of their frightening severity, like the enigmatic monuments of an ancient, vaster, and harsher world.[2]

This surprising association between a fifteenth-century Flemish painting and Egyptian Antiquity, between Christianity and hieroglyphics – praised here for their impenetrable austerity – is typical of German Romanticism. But, significantly, in the rest of the text, it is a form of national identity that Schlegel associates with this element of mystery; it leads him to affirm the German-ness of the Van Eyck brothers, both born in a small Flemish town between Antwerp and Cologne, one of whom died in Ghent while the other died in Bruges. 'Since Holbein was inspired by Van Eyck, ... it would be natural to consider Van Eyck as a representative of German painting, whose history and evolution appear with great clarity and simplicity when one considers its three major stages: Van Eyck, Dürer, Holbein.'[3] And, further on, he insists: 'The edifice formed by German painting can be satisfactorily reconstructed from an analysis just of the three painters cited above: Van Eyck, Dürer and Holbein.'[4] Schlegel here is intent on establishing, thanks to the works gathered at the Louvre – of a kind barely visible elsewhere, or dispersed in churches or private collections – a singular Germanic lineage, ideally free of French or Italian influences. In Paris, around 1800, the altarpiece by the Van Eyck brothers was transformed, in the eyes of the German philosopher, into a patriotic and romantic screen, a surface onto which could be projected a taste for what was 'impossible to understand', mixed with political aspirations.

At the same time, a very young French painter was also tarrying in front of the Ghent panels exhibited at the Louvre: Jean-Auguste-Dominique Ingres, twenty years old, originally from Montauban. A highly gifted figure, he went to Paris at sixteen to study painting. His studies and sketches at the Louvre testify to his interest, unusual for the time, in the works of the old German and Flemish schools that had just arrived in Paris. He copied paintings by Hans Holbein and, according to some experts, was directly inspired by the altarpiece of 'The Mystic Lamb', adopting Van Eyck's depiction of God (or Christ) in his purple cloak, his right arm raised in blessing, and whose head, seen from the front, seems to be haloed by the golden back of his throne. We find almost the same composition in one of Ingres's most famous portraits: *Napoleon I on the Imperial Throne*, painted by the young artist in 1806, which seems to be striving to elevate the emperor to the rank of a god, his hyperrealistic face a little grey, floating as if set on an abstract body.

At the time, critics immediately spotted the connection between this imperial commission, with its disturbing result, and the aesthetics of the Van Eyck brothers. Some congratulated Ingres 'for having dared to paint a fourteenth-century painting (*sic*)'; others accused him of having 'set art back four centuries', of being 'bizarre', or 'gothic',[5] which in turn delighted the younger representatives of the European public, who saw in Van Eyck and Ingres the heroes of a revolution in the artistic gaze – especially since Ingres had 'customized' the imperial portrait by inserting a multitude of mysterious signs (stars, zodiac, globes) that intrigued the younger generation then in search of new visual experiences. The gathering in Paris of works such as the altarpiece of 'The Mystic Lamb', which disturbed the public's artistic habits, was a major source of aesthetic regeneration. The fact remains that the bizarre portrait of Napoleon, although officially commissioned, would be kept out of sight until the fall of the Empire, when, in 1815, it entered the Louvre – at the very moment that Van Eyck's panels were returned to Belgium. An astonishing cross-pollination – and a no less astonishing fertilization between a masterpiece of fifteenth-century Christian iconography and an icon of propaganda-by-image under the Empire.

My last example of the effect produced by the polyptych of the Van Eyck brothers on the art world in Paris around 1800 is its valuation, by experts of the art market, within the framework of the general inventory of the Louvre. At the height of the establishment's renown, when successive military campaigns had made it the 'most beautiful museum in the world', as some liked to call it at the time, the Louvre had to submit to a new exercise: that of the monetary valuation of its collections.

> Sir,
> I came to your establishment to submit to you the attached model report. We can describe in one line any painting, however beautiful and picturesque it may be ... Our work will not have any picturesque beauty, but it will have administrative beauty: clarity and brevity. By this means, despite the small number of our clerks, we can hope to see the end of our labours.[6]

With this note, the young Henri Beyle – the future writer Stendhal – attempted, in October 1810, to encourage the director of the Louvre to get on with his task of establishing, as soon as possible, an inventory of all the works of art in the possession of French *châteaux* and museums: so the Senate had decided. This involved a systematic census of the works of art seized in France and abroad since the Revolution and proclaimed to be national property – in other words, the unitary classification of an extremely heterogeneous set of objects of the most diverse provenances, kinds, and manufacture. But, above all, the establishment of their value in money. It was not the symbolic, artistic, or aesthetic capital accumulated at the Louvre that interested the state, but financial capital, that most real of values. All of this was part of the new administrative spirit established in France under the Consulate, with the systematic and regular official collection of statistical data on a territorial scale. As in a population census, it was thus the works of the Louvre that now needed to be counted, including our altarpiece of 'The Mystic Lamb.'

Such a statistical and monetary approach, as one might expect, did not correspond to the museum management's idea of an inventory. But, as a temple of Beauty, the establishment had to comply with the administrative logic of the centralized state. The spiritual and the aesthetic realms, 'picturesque beauty,' mystery, enigma, and wonder had to yield to a scheme where accuracy and objectivity, comparability and completeness, prevailed – with extraordinary consequences for research in art history, at the crossroads of aesthetics, economics, and the history of taste. But how was such an enterprise organized, in concrete terms? Who was responsible for the monetary valuation of works that, in many cases, had not changed owners a single time between their creation and their forced transfer to Paris? So how was their value to be determined? Who could decide the sum, expressed in francs, at which the antiquities confiscated from the Vatican, the Raphaels, Dürers, Rembrandts, Titians, the Van Eyck brothers or the *Mona Lisa* would be valued?

On all these questions, administrative correspondence and archival material provide valuable resources for an answer. We learn from them that the museum management entrusted the valuation of the works to external experts, renowned dealers in the Parisian art world. The invitation that the Louvre addressed to them deserves to be quoted in full, because it demonstrates the museum's pragmatism. Here is the letter received by one of these experts in the autumn of 1813:

> The general inventory of the paintings, drawings, statues, and precious objects contained in the Napoleon Museum and the imperial palaces is finished; it is now a question of setting a price for each of the objects described. I am reluctant to rely solely on my knowledge and that of the curators of this establishment for this highly important operation, and I thought that you would be kind enough to help me with your knowledge. I therefore invite you, Sir, to come to the museum on Wednesday 13 October to begin this work together with certain other people whom I have also summoned so that the discussion of the price to be assigned to each item can determine the latter's real value.[7]

What a wonderful letter! We can hear the vibrancy of the various elements that express, beyond all uncertainties, the director's confidence in the possibility of assigning a 'real value' to the artistic treasures of the Musée Napoléon – perhaps in opposition to a 'felt value'. Producing objectivity regarding beauty by confronting subjectivities – it would be difficult to imagine a clearer admission of the irrational nature of such an undertaking. In any case, the experts' work was completed very quickly and the result is impressive: thousands of numerical estimates now fill the columns of the Louvre inventory, with sums ranging from 1.5 million francs to 1 franc. Everything that the history of European art has produced since Antiquity that is gathered in the museum now has not only a symbolic value, but also a price value that can be read as a numerical fixation of its symbolic value. On this price scale, the four panels of the altarpiece of 'The Mystic

Lamb' occupy a choice place. To be sure, they come after the painters of the Italian Renaissance who occupy the top of the table, with three Italian paintings coming first, with an astronomical level, for the time, of at least 1 million francs: Correggio's *Saint Jerome*, confiscated from Parma; and Veronese's *The Wedding Feast at Cana*, a Venetian work that entered the Louvre following Napoleon's First Italian Campaign. The absolute record was Raphael's *Transfiguration*, taken from a church in Rome and estimated at 1.5 million. By way of comparison, Rubens' *Descent from the Cross*, confiscated from Antwerp Cathedral, was valued at 600,000 francs. But, on its own, the central panel of the Ghent Altarpiece, valued at 100,000 francs, was placed above Leonardo da Vinci's *Mona Lisa* (90,000 francs) and the great paintings of Rembrandt, the most expensive of which came in at around 60,000 francs. Even though it was not for sale, the polyptych by the Van Eyck brothers now had a market value, and its subsequent fate shows to what extent, over time, this value – just as much as its religious or aesthetic value – would determine its life.

In 1815, after Napoleon's abdication and subsequent final defeat at Waterloo, the Louvre Museum was dismantled. The works taken from foreign collections were mostly returned to their cities of origin and to their rightful owners. The altarpiece of 'The Mystic Lamb' returned to Ghent, where it arrived in the spring of 1816. However, it was not reconstructed.

## From dismantlement to reconstruction

After spending twenty years in Paris, including ten years of great international visibility, the central part of the polyptych of 'The Mystic Lamb' was reinstalled in Saint Bavo's Cathedral. The altarpiece, an object of religious worship, had also become, in the meantime, the object of a patriotic and romantic aesthetic cult whose basis was theorized by Friedrich Schlegel. The taste for the 'primitives', as these fifteenth-century painters were then called, was accentuated by the Parisian sojourn of their works, which fed the appetite of young generations of artists and enthusiasts for new forms. It also aroused the appetite of dealers: barely had the central section of the work returned to Ghent in 1816 than the cathedral's managers sold six of the eight side panels to a Brussels dealer, who resold them to a very rich English merchant, Edward Solly, who managed to sell them, along with 3,000 (!) other paintings from his collection, to the Prussian government in 1821. Wars, crises, and revolutions have always been conducive to the art trade. From this date onwards, the altarpiece of 'The Mystic Lamb' was split between two, or even three, locations: Berlin had the largest part of the original work, with six double-sided side panels (out of a total of eight), while the single-sided central panels that remained in Ghent represented only a smaller surface area of the work, further diminished by the modesty of the monks, who considered the nudity of Adam and Eve, on the two side panels that remained at home, too obscene for a church and hid them away before later sending them to the Museum of Fine Arts in Brussels. In both Ghent and Berlin, the missing pieces of the polyptych were replaced with copies. This did not prevent the Flemish painter Pieter Frans De Noter, in 1829, from depicting the altarpiece open and complete, peacefully displayed in its original chapel, topped with a Gothic canopy and admired by visitors in mediaeval costume, in a gentle and idealized historical atmosphere – witness, in the middle of the nineteenth century, to a revival characteristic of European romanticism.

An object of identification and desire: the altarpiece, of course, interested the Flemish, who restored its religious value by putting it back in its church – but who also intended, from now on, to affirm the national roots of its authors, Hubert and Jan Van Eyck, in the turbulent context of the creation of a new state – present-day Belgium – founded only in the 1830s. But the national identity of the Ghent painters was disputed. Were they Belgian, Flemish, or German? And did their works have a nationality? Was the ownership of a painting linked to its place of origin, creation, or exhibition? Or did it belong to those who claimed possession, or who recognized the work as representing them, to those who studied it and 'understood' it, as Schiller's poem put it (see Introduction, above)? Or was it the law of the strongest, the richest, or the best endowed that defined ownership?

Throughout the century, in any case, Berlin's museums would strive to highlight 'their' Van Eyck, both from a museological point of view (for example, by inventing techniques facilitating the simultaneous exhibition of both sides of the same panel), and from an academic and scholarly point of view (by making the work one of the best explored in the history of northern European art). Incidentally, it was a woman, Johanna Schopenhauer, a painter and writer – and mother of the philosopher Arthur and the novelist Adèle – who published in Frankfurt the very first major study of the Van Eycks. This was followed in Germany by countless other scholarly works. A few years before the First World War, Berlin's passion for the Ghent Altarpiece culminated in the creation of a room entirely dedicated to it in a brand new museum at the tip of Museum Island: room no. 72 of the Kaiser-Friedrich-Museum (now the Bode Museum). On the eve of the declaration of war, of the twenty panels that make up the work (sixteen of which have side panels), two (double-sided) belong physically to the Brussels museum, four (single-sided) to Saint Bavo's Cathedral in Ghent, and twelve to the museums of Berlin. To whom does it belong intellectually and in terms of spirituality? The dismantled altarpiece is a religious object and a museum object, an object of patriotic esteem and an object of instruction, and even an erotic object in the eyes of some; during the war years, it underwent a new transformation: it was turned into an object of propaganda and reparation.

In August 1914, the German army violated Belgium's neutrality and invaded its territory, bringing the United Kingdom into the war. A few days later, the burning of the rich and very old university library in Louvain aroused disgust throughout Europe. The international press mobilized to denounce German barbarity, publishing a great number of war photos as evidence. In June 1915, the well-known magazine *Mercure de France* wrote:

> Fortunately, there is every reason to hope that the principal treasures of the Royal Museums of Brussels, the masterpieces preserved in Antwerp, Ghent, and Bruges (the gentle and melancholic Bruges of Memling, today trampled underfoot by brutal mercenaries!), have been consigned to safety, and Mr Bode, director of the Berlin Museums, has denied the rumour that he has transported the two Van Eyck panels, Adam and Eve, from the Brussels Museum to Berlin: the precaution, in fact, might well have been deemed useless, since Germany doubtless intends to annex these panels, along with the altarpiece of 'The Mystic

> Lamb', together with the whole of Belgium. Let us hope that, on the contrary, it will be the panels of this same altarpiece kept at the Berlin Museum that will return after the war to their place in the Saint Bavo polyptych.[8]

From the beginning of the war, the Ghent Altarpiece was thus at the heart of an aggressive campaign regarding the future of heritage objects in the zones occupied by Germany, a discussion fuelled by the plans of certain German intellectuals: the director of the Berlin museums intended to recover *manu militari*, in Belgium and France, the works of art, manuscripts and books seized under the French Revolution and the Napoleonic Empire that had not been returned in 1815. A hundred years later, in the midst of the First World War, 'The Mystic Lamb' was on everyone's mind – as was, more generally, the idea that the confiscation or forced return of works of art to the future victor could serve as compensation for the crimes against heritage (amongst others) committed by the parties involved. Very early on, the *Mercure de France*, raising the danger of German confiscations, envisaged the recovery of the Berlin panels of the Ghent Altarpiece, which had been acquired completely legally a century earlier. But, reciprocally, the German press imagined how, if Germany were to win the war, it could compensate itself with works of art from its defeated enemies. More than ever during this bloody conflict, despite the then recent adoption of international conventions intended to protect places of culture and worship in times of war, the idea that compensation or reparations could be demanded for atrocities committed in the form of works of art (as if they were the equivalent of sums of money) was on the agenda. When the conflict ended in 1918 with the defeat of Germany, the idea took legal form: the Treaty of Versailles, signed on 28 June 1919, determined the sanctions taken against Germany, which lost certain territories in Europe and was deprived of its colonies, as well as being required to pay heavy economic reparations and forced to disarm. In addition to these measures, there was this one, formulated in Article 247:

> Germany undertakes to furnish to the University of Louvain, within three months after a request made by it and transmitted through the

> intervention of the Reparation Commission, manuscripts, incunabula, printed books, maps and objects of collection corresponding in number and value to those destroyed in the burning by Germany of the Library of Louvain. All details regarding such replacement will be determined by the Reparation Commission.
>
> Germany undertakes to deliver to Belgium, through the Reparation Commission, within six months of the coming into force of the present Treaty, in order to enable Belgium to reconstitute two great artistic works:
>
> (1) The leaves of the triptych of the Mystic Lamb painted by the Van Eyck brothers, formerly in the Church of St. Bavon at Ghent, now in the Berlin Museum;
>
> (2) The leaves of the triptych of the Last Supper, painted by Dierick Bouts, formerly in the Church of St. Peter at Louvain, two of which are now in the Berlin Museum and two in the Old Pinakothek at Munich.[9]

In this treaty, seen as a humiliation by the Germans, the question of the initial legality of the acquisitions made on the art market in the nineteenth century is ignored in favour of a moral approach to the question, implying that the immeasurable harm committed must be repaired with equally immeasurable values: dismembered paintings. One could comment at length on the symbolic scope of this idea that war reparations (reparations in the metaphorical sense of the term) must take the form of very real reparations (those of polyptychs quartered like living organisms). This treaty caused a trauma in the German museum community, which, to this day, struggles to come to terms with the loss of such cherished and studied works. In the same spirit, but with reference to the heritage translocations that took place outside Europe in the colonial context of the nineteenth century, Article 246 of the Treaty of Versailles stipulates that 'Germany shall return to His Majesty the King of Hejaz the original Koran that belonged to Caliph Osman and was taken from Medina by the Turkish authorities to be offered to the former Emperor William II.' The question of restitutions, which seems so contemporary to us today, is in fact part of a long military and diplomatic history.

Berlin complied. The altarpiece was reassembled in Saint Bavo's Cathedral, Ghent, in 1921. Once again, it was the return of the same difference, the question of the physical integrity of the work now echoing the suffering of the millions of men and women killed, disfigured, or disabled in the conflict. In this logic, the arts and bodies, culture and humanity, go hand in hand – the unified altarpiece, so to speak, alleviates the pain of the wounds. And it became, more than ever, a symbol of free Belgium.

Photographed, filmed, reproduced, taught in schools, and even exported abroad – at least virtually – the altarpiece of 'The Mystic Lamb' was transformed in the interwar period into a quasi-advertising medium for the country that gave birth to it. In 1939, for the New York World's Fair, the Belgian government commissioned a report from the young director André Cauvin. He was among the first, in the (still young) history of cinema, to experiment with moving the camera close to the pictorial surface, with tracking shots and other macroscopic shots of tiny details of the painting. His film *The Mystic Lamb* was screened for the inauguration of the Belgian pavilion, where it made a strong impression. The cinema camera begins outdoors, shows Saint Bavo's Cathedral, enters and approaches the closed altarpiece in the half-light, but finally keeping a discreet distance. The cinematographic experience is visual and auditory, offering spectators an almost supernatural dive into details that escape the naked eye, complementing the image with an almost celestial music. Finally, the altar comes to life – it opens. A ray of external light illuminates the face of God for a moment; the angels on the side panels seem to sing, and Adam and Eve breathe. Like all the pavilions at the World's Fairs of the 1930s, the Belgian pavilion had a cinema where the film continued to be shown as an ambassador for Belgium, with the painting playing a symbolic role similar to that which the *Mona Lisa* might play for France or Nefertiti for Berlin. The mystic lamb, God, the angels, and the saints now had a 'diplomatic mission': to promote Belgian culture beyond its borders. André Cauvin's documentary was subsequently presented at various festivals, including the Venice Film Festival on 31 August 1939, where it was one of the award-winning films. The following day, the German army invaded Poland. This marked the start of the Second World War and the end of a short period of unity for the Ghent polyptych.

## Evacuation, looting, restoration

The story of its evacuation far from Belgium, its abduction by a Nazi agent, its underground exile in a mine in Bavaria, its reunion with the 'free world' in 1945, and with Saint Bavo's Cathedral a few months later, has been described, filmed, and broadcast many times – it partly serves as the screenplay for the American–German blockbuster *The Monuments Men* (2014) mentioned above. So I will not here repeat this story in detail, but broadly set this 'segment of life' of the work, now almost 500 years old, within the more general field of Nazi heritage looting, and draw attention to a lesser-known event in this story: the filming, again by André Cauvin, of a second exceptional documentary on the (umpteenth) return of the precious painting.

A few weeks after entering Poland, the German army invaded the Netherlands, Belgium, and Luxembourg. Ghent was taken on 23 May 1940. On the 27th, on the eve of the capitulation, the director general of the Berlin museums, the infamous Otto Kümmel, rather insistently requested that the German Minister of Propaganda, Joseph Goebbels, return to Berlin the six side panels of the altarpiece of 'The Mystic Lamb', returned to Belgium twenty years earlier, as well as the other works ceded under the Treaty of Versailles. A few days later, the German military commander of occupied Belgium was informed by his artistic department that a large number of works seemed to have been taken to safety, including the famous altarpiece, although their location was not yet known. 'We are continuing our quest', noted the author of the letter.[10] In fact, since 17 May, the original panels of the polyptych then kept in Ghent (one of them, as mentioned above, had been stolen in 1934) had been packed into ten large wooden crates and transported to Pau in the Pyrenees, at the farthest point from the military front and the zone occupied by the German army. They remained there despite a vast campaign of artistic recovery undertaken by the German authorities – at least on paper – which, if implemented, would have consisted in the confiscation from the occupied zone of all 'religious cultural property stolen by France from Germany since 1500', in particular revolutionary and imperial appropriations not returned in 1815, but also, more generally, all 'Germanic' works. This explains the presence of the Ghent Altarpiece in the very first pages of this unrealized action plan, known as the 'Kümmel-Bericht' (Kümmel Report).

It was a year later, on the occasion of the commemorations accompanying the 500th anniversary of the death of Jan Van Eyck, that the plan to find the altarpiece and add it to the collections of the Führermuseum – the monumental museum planned by Hitler in Linz, Austria – assumed a clearer shape. Publicly announced in 1941, it was accompanied by an intellectual plan: that of proving, with the support of precise historical sources, that the Van Eycks were painters of German inspiration. In any case, the Nazi authorities agreed that the recovery of the side panels 'stolen' in Berlin was legitimate and desirable, even if it meant overcoming 'likely resistance'.[11] At this time, there was some confusion among the various Nazis involved about locating the polyptych and getting it out of Pau, with the military government of occupation in Belgium wanting to return it to Ghent, and Hitler's entourage seeking its 'return' to Berlin or its transfer to Austria. Finally, in the middle of the war, the director general of the Munich museums was personally tasked with organizing the transport of the altarpiece to Bavaria – mainly to prevent it from being reinstalled in Ghent, but officially to protect it from possible bombings in the legendary, magical castle of Ludwig II of Bavaria in Neuschwanstein, to where the precious collections of the Munich Pinakothek had already been evacuated.

With the express agreement of Pierre Laval and the Vichy government, the altarpiece of 'The Mystic Lamb' left Pau at the end of July 1942 and, under French military escort, was accompanied to the German border. The action did not remain secret; the press seized on it. The *New York Herald Tribune* headlined in early 1943 'Vichy Gift to Goering'. In Bavaria, after several months spent in Neuschwanstein, the polyptych from Ghent was finally evacuated to the Altaussee salt mine, where Hitler's private collection was also stored away, secure from bombing. The rest of the story is well known: the paintings, and several thousand other works of art illegally seized from Jewish families in Europe, were recovered by the Monuments Men from German museums that had sheltered their collections of works intended for Hitler's museum in Linz; gold from the Deutsche Bank, along with other treasures, had also been stashed away. The polyptych was repatriated to Brussels by plane in August 1945, inspected, photographed, restored, and exhibited at the Museum of Fine Arts, then returned to Saint Bavo's Cathedral, Ghent, in October of the same year.

*Le Retour de l'Agneau Mystique* (*The Return of the Mystic Lamb*) is the title of André Cauvin's second documentary on the work, and its restitution in 1945. The soundtrack of the film seems to be lost, and is replaced in the version currently available by Beethoven's grandiose 'Eroica' Symphony. The film mixes news footage shot by the American army in the mines of Bavaria with coverage of the arrival of the panels, which we see entering the Museum of Fine Arts in Brussels, and mounting the stairs leading to the restoration workshops, borne like survivors by the museum staff. Then the director focuses on detailing the precise movements of a handful of men in white coats who, like doctors, examine the paintings with various modern tools, including X-rays, as if they were carrying out scans on seriously injured people. The camera enlarges the details and slowly caresses the painted surfaces of the panels placed on the ground; the characters in the painting acquire an unprecedented volume and intensity. With a magnifying glass in his hand, the bespectacled museum director scrutinizes the naked bodies of Adam and Eve lying flat on an operating table. Another orderly in a white coat wraps the panel showing the donors in an immaculate sheet, as if he were tucking in a patient. In a fraction of a second, the relationship between the work of art and the human being is revealed in all its mystery through the staging of the motif of care and repair, of love lavished as proof of real belonging ... And what if the person who knows how to observe, care for, and restore the work was, above all, its legitimate owner? At any rate, André Cauvin's film suggests as much.

In 1986, the altarpiece of 'The Mystic Lamb' was installed in the former baptistery of Saint Bavo's Cathedral, transformed into a glass vault resembling an aquarium, which allowed the work to be exposed to view and no longer to danger. Between 2012 and 2020, it underwent a large-scale restoration campaign, which mobilized the most advanced technologies and expertise, in a similar glass room in the Museum of Fine Arts in Ghent. Before the eyes of the public, the painting regained its unity and its light thanks to the meticulous

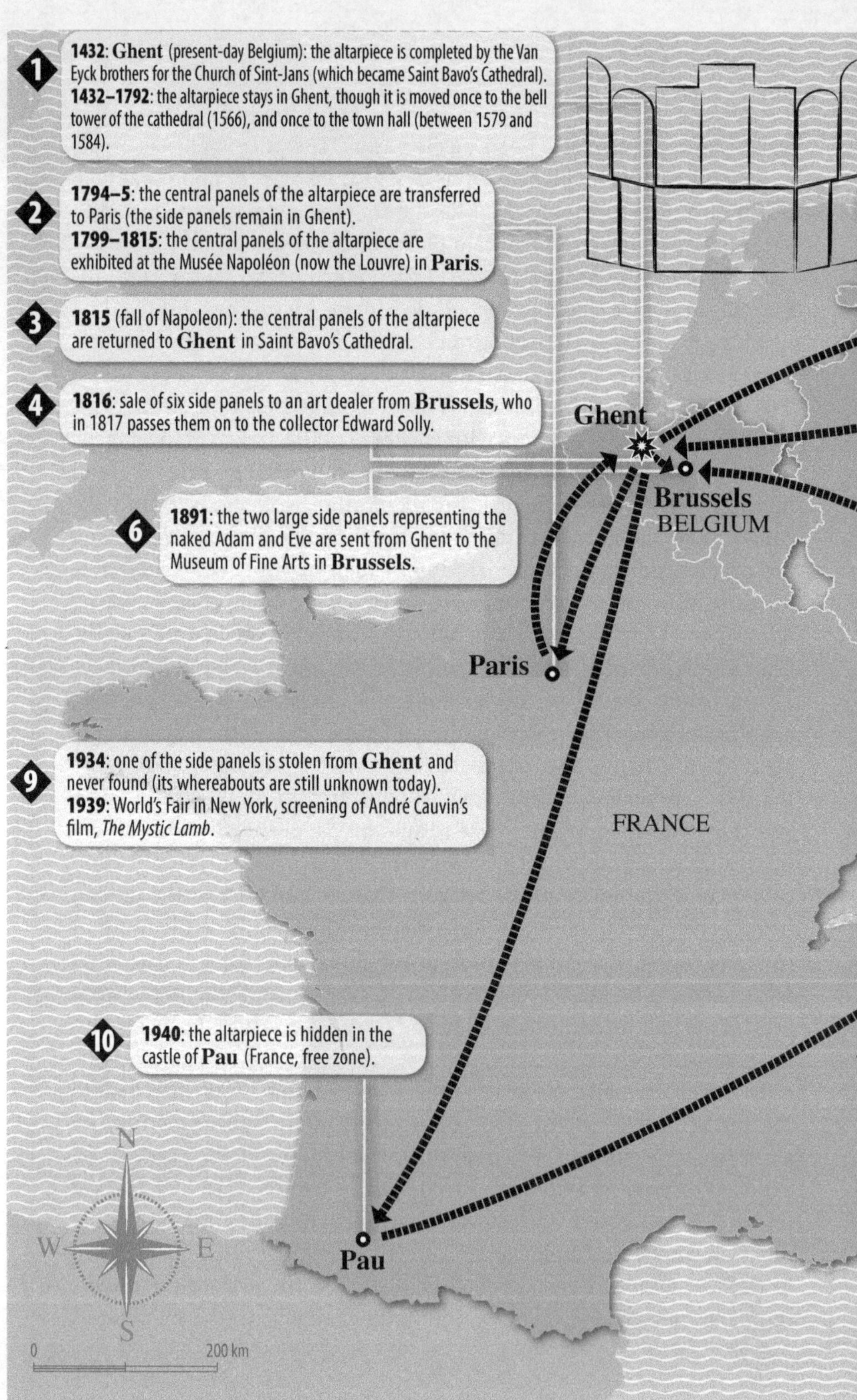
1 1432: Ghent (present-day Belgium): the altarpiece is completed by the Van Eyck brothers for the Church of Sint-Jans (which became Saint Bavo's Cathedral).
1432–1792: the altarpiece stays in Ghent, though it is moved once to the bell tower of the cathedral (1566), and once to the town hall (between 1579 and 1584).
2 1794–5: the central panels of the altarpiece are transferred to Paris (the side panels remain in Ghent).
1799–1815: the central panels of the altarpiece are exhibited at the Musée Napoléon (now the Louvre) in Paris.
3 1815 (fall of Napoleon): the central panels of the altarpiece are returned to Ghent in Saint Bavo's Cathedral.
4 1816: sale of six side panels to an art dealer from Brussels, who in 1817 passes them on to the collector Edward Solly.
6 1891: the two large side panels representing the naked Adam and Eve are sent from Ghent to the Museum of Fine Arts in Brussels.
9 1934: one of the side panels is stolen from Ghent and never found (its whereabouts are still unknown today).
1939: World's Fair in New York, screening of André Cauvin's film, The Mystic Lamb.
10 1940: the altarpiece is hidden in the castle of Pau (France, free zone).
Ghent
Brussels
BELGIUM
Paris
FRANCE
Pau
N
W
E
S
0
200 km

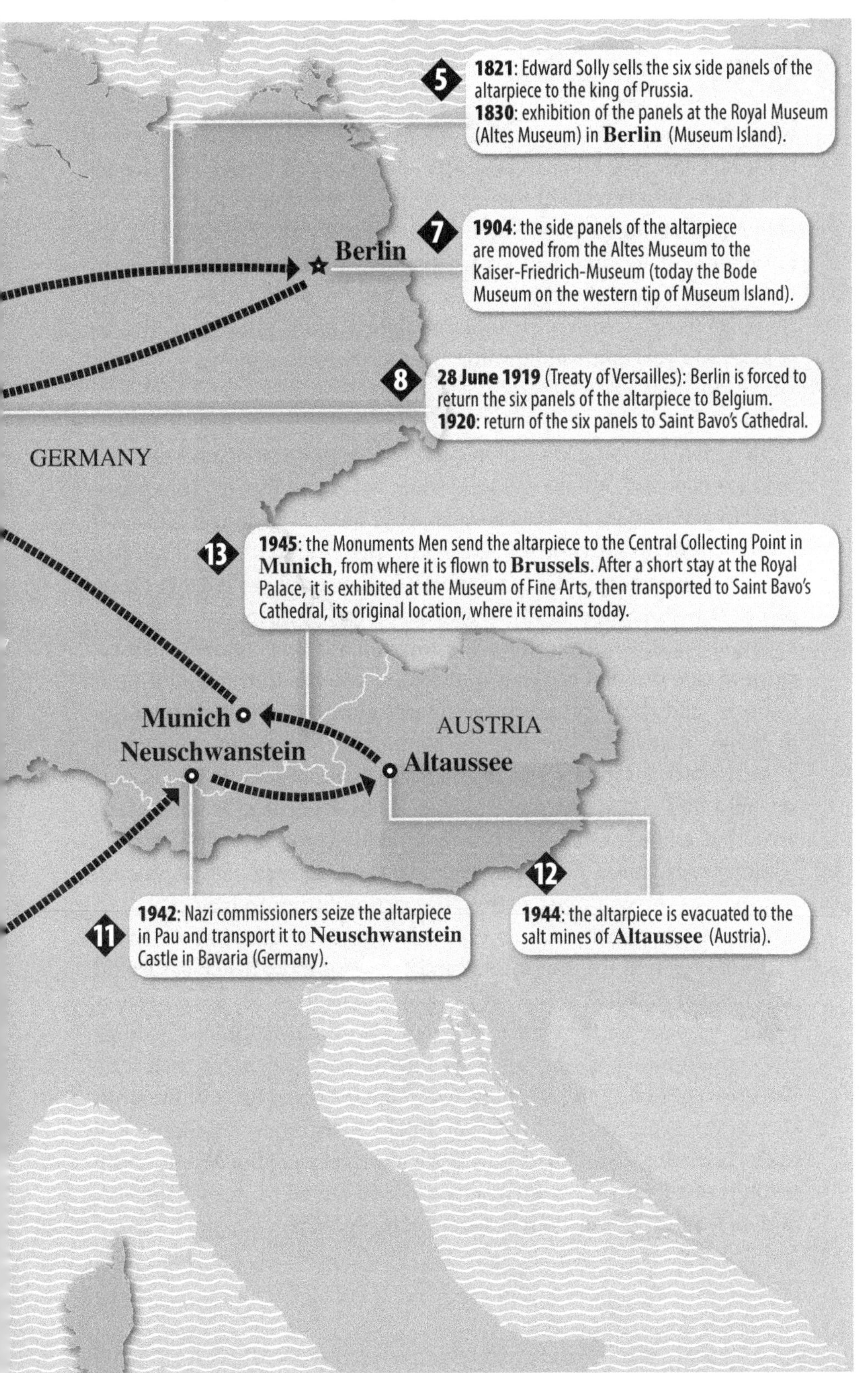

5
1821: Edward Solly sells the six side panels of the altarpiece to the king of Prussia.
1830: exhibition of the panels at the Royal Museum (Altes Museum) in Berlin (Museum Island).
Berlin
7
1904: the side panels of the altarpiece are moved from the Altes Museum to the Kaiser-Friedrich-Museum (today the Bode Museum on the western tip of Museum Island).
8
28 June 1919 (Treaty of Versailles): Berlin is forced to return the six panels of the altarpiece to Belgium.
1920: return of the six panels to Saint Bavo's Cathedral.
GERMANY
13
1945: the Monuments Men send the altarpiece to the Central Collecting Point in Munich, from where it is flown to Brussels. After a short stay at the Royal Palace, it is exhibited at the Museum of Fine Arts, then transported to Saint Bavo's Cathedral, its original location, where it remains today.
Munich
AUSTRIA
Neuschwanstein
Altaussee
12
1944: the altarpiece is evacuated to the salt mines of Altaussee (Austria).
11
1942: Nazi commissioners seize the altarpiece in Pau and transport it to Neuschwanstein Castle in Bavaria (Germany).

work of a team of restorers. Each detail is now heightened with a new brilliance: the sparkling foliage, the snow-capped peaks, the slender bell towers and turrets of the city of Ghent, the drapes in flamboyant colours, the mother-of-pearl reflections of the water flowing from the fountain as if nothing had ever happened ... But, above all, it is the rediscovered gaze of the lamb with his halo of golden lines that grabs the spectator's attention. He looks straight at us. He has been alive for at least 500 years and will live for an eternity to come.

*

Who owns 'The Mystic Lamb'? What will happen to it (and to us) in the next century? Where will it be when we are no more? From generation to generation, mortals have appropriated it, opened it, closed it, assembled it, disassembled it, staged it, sheltered it, moved it in order to hide it or, on the contrary, to exhibit it; they have packed it in boxes, placed it behind glass, and so far it has always returned, the same as ever and yet different, to the place for which it was created. A sacred work in this original context, a historical witness to the 'evolution of the arts' and their 'progress' in the museum, an object of erudition in books, a stake in the military conflicts of the twentieth century, a tourist attraction, a focus of scientific experiments, the subject of several films ... the altarpiece teaches us how heritage is not a stable asset, but a living value. Over time, its value is formed and deformed while encapsulating the memory of the past, as many layers that are now part of the work just as they are part of European history.

One last image: the frame of the polyptych emptied of its panels and wide open in front of the sea and the sky, on the beach at Ostend. The Belgian artist Kris Martin installed it there in 2014, as a way of paying homage to the Van Eycks, but also of questioning, perhaps, the contemporary springs of a spirituality that is content with little, like an architecture full of emptiness. Like the great texts of literature that never cease to fertilize other works – through variations, new takes, rewritings, and hijackings – the altarpiece of 'The Mystic Lamb' belongs to all who allow themselves to be affected by it, by its history and its wounds – which are also, collectively, ours.

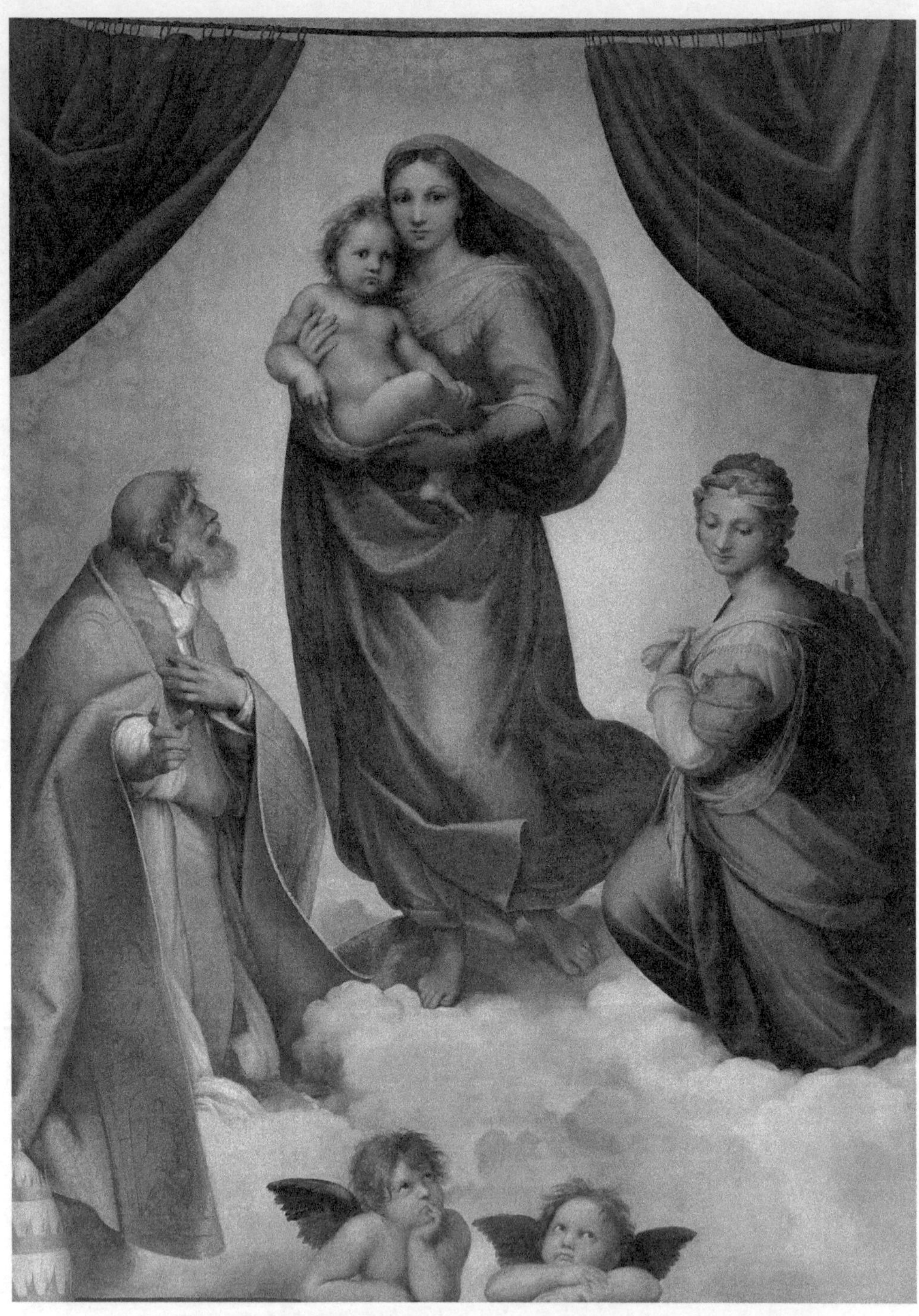

Raphael, 'Sistine Madonna', 1513, oil on canvas, 265 × 196 cm. Piacenza, Italy; Dresden, Gemäldegalerie, Staatliche Kunstsammlungen. Photo © Fine Art Images / Bridgeman Images.

# 4

# RAPHAEL'S 'SISTINE MADONNA'

The 'Sistine Madonna' is the last Virgin painted by Raffaelo Sanzio, known as Raphael, before his premature death in 1520. Right from the start, the arts and the arms of war were linked to the history of the painting: Pope Julius II commissioned it from Raphael to commemorate a military victory over the army of the king of France. Painted in 1512–13, it was then offered to the church of San Sisto on the occasion of the incorporation of Piacenza into the Papal States. When he completed the painting, Raphael was not yet thirty years old. Born in 1483 in Urbino, not far from the Adriatic coast, he distinguished himself very early on, picking up a series of prestigious contracts while still in his teens – first in his native region, then in Florence, and finally Rome. When he died there at the age of thirty-seven, from an unknown cause, he was buried like a god, in an ancient sarcophagus in the Pantheon.

One detail of the 'Sistine Madonna' is firmly etched in the collective visual memory of Western societies: the relaxed pose of two angels in attendance, leaning in *trompe-l'oeil* on the lower edge of the frame, their eyes raised to the sky. Behind them, weightless on a cloud, stand the Virgin and the baby Jesus in her arms, venerated by, on their knees, Saint Sixtus on the left, in the guise of Pope Julius II, and Saint Barbara on the right, her eyes lowered. In the sky, the pale, barely outlined faces of an abstract multitude of cherubs are turned towards the scene, half-hidden by the folds of a double green curtain. The gazes of the Virgin and Child seem to be filled with a dark foreboding: that of their own destiny, the death of Christ on the cross, but perhaps also of the fate to which history will subject this large canvas painting, more than 4 metres by almost 3.

The first translocation of the painting came after a 250-year sojourn in Piacenza, where it belonged to the Benedictine monks of the monastery of San Sisto. It is not known how it was originally presented, but, from the end of the seventeenth century, it was set in an impressive baroque frame about 10 metres high, plated with gold leaf, decorated with volutes, angels and giant acanthus leaves. After the departure of the 'Sistine Madonna', the frame would remain in Piacenza and the void left by the absent painting was immediately filled by a copy. It is this copy and the baroque frame that welcome you to Piacenza if you visit the church today. Raphael's original crossed the Alps around 1750 and joined the collections of the prince-elector of Saxony in Dresden, in what is now the Federal Republic of Germany (FRG), where it still remains. Half a century after its spectacular move, the Madonna attracted the keen interest of Napoleon I's envoys, who, crossing Saxony on the road to Berlin in the train of the Grande Armée, suggested that the painting – and a few other masterpieces from the Dresden museum – could well be demanded as a war tribute and sent to Paris, like the works of art I mentioned in the previous chapter, to enrich the collections of the Musée Napoléon (the Louvre). The manoeuvre failed. The painting remained in Germany, where the proliferation of processes for the reproduction of images (engraving, lithography, photography, etc.) ensured it a growing international reputation in the nineteenth century. After 1830, people came from all over Europe, Russia and even the United States to admire the painting, which gradually acquired the status of a secular icon and was never loaned or removed from the museum – until the horrors of the Second World War and the Allied bombings that reduced Dresden to ashes in February 1945 and caused the death of 35,000 civilians.

Along with all the other paintings in the Dresden Gallery, the 'Sistine Madonna' was sheltered during the war. Then it shared the fate of the collections located in 1945 in the zone liberated by the Red Army and was shipped as a war trophy, with tens of thousands of other pieces, to the USSR. It was not until 1955 that the Soviet authorities decided to return the 'Sistine Madonna' to Dresden, after a final free exhibition lasting for ninety days at the Pushkin Museum in Moscow. Dresden was then one of the most important cities in the GDR, a satellite country of the Soviet Union and a tourist attraction for visitors from the 'Eastern bloc' – Russians in particular. The 'Sistine Madonna' became an instrument of propaganda, then of marketing after the fall of the Berlin Wall, as the museums of Dresden accounted for much of the region's economy.

Who owns Raphael's 'Sistine Madonna', a painting created in Italy that has become, in Dresden, an icon for the Germans, for Europe and for the world? Does it belong to the church of San Sisto in Piacenza, even though the Italians have not staked a claim to it? To the *Land* of Saxony, to Germany, to the 'Dresden State Collections' which hold the title of ownership and physically conserve the original whose image rights they exploit? Does it belong to Russian culture which, since the nineteenth century, has devoted a major cult to it through its literature and the number of its admirers who come from that country? Or is it an object that, through its translocations and reproductions in countless derivative products, has become, in the broad sense of the term, a work belonging to the heritage of humanity?

From Italy to Germany, from Dresden to Moscow, this work allows us to scrutinize a case that is both singular and typical of the process of translocation. Typical because its removal from Piacenza, around 1750, was the result of an asymmetrical relation of economic power: the transaction was made possible by the extreme poverty of the community of monks who owned the work, aggravated at that time by poor harvests, and by the extreme wealth of the elector of Saxony, one of the most industrious and prosperous regions of Europe. Singular because, over time, this church work was 'resacralized' into a museum icon; this Italian work became, in its new home in Germany and thanks to the latter's 'museum apparatus', an object of desire and identification for a whole swathe of Europe, and indeed the world. The 'Sistine Madonna' is thus an example not only of a locally rooted heritage, which it bears in its name ('Sistine' refers to the church for which it was painted), but also of a global heritage, or at least one felt to be 'shared' in certain parts of the world.

## The advent of the public museum

Around 1750, like other enlightened princes of the European courts, the elector of Saxony (a role that for several generations had come with being king of Poland), Augustus III, planned to open to the public the prestigious collection of paintings and antiquities formed by his ancestors – one of the richest collections of its kind in Europe. This project was accompanied by major development work and a vast campaign of purchases of works of art, mainly paintings, on the European market, in Paris, London, and Amsterdam, but especially in Italy, where the elector maintained many agents touting for masterpieces. Not only was the future Dresden Gallery to provide the international public and local artists with the works most likely to educate their taste and advance their talent, but also it was to demonstrate to Europe that Dresden was one of the most powerful artistic capitals on the continent. In 1753, after tough negotiations with the Italian ecclesiastical hierarchy, Augustus III finally secured the purchase of the 'Sistine Madonna' for a colossal sum.

Contrary to the very French idea that the public museum was an invention of the Revolution, there were in fact, as early as the 1750s and 1760s – and even more so from 1780 – galleries open to the public at large in Europe. At the end of the nineteenth century, the French encyclopaedic dictionary the *Grand Larousse* stated: 'It was the republican France of 1789 that, in this as in so many other things, had the honour of setting an example to other countries: the Louvre was the first truly national museum in Europe. In every respect, the Louvre can be considered the first of the national museums.'[1] However, in reality, from the eighteenth century onwards, many European capitals had museums open to the international public. They admittedly did not have the term 'national' in their names, since the idea of a nation state was not on the agenda in Germany or Italy, for example. They were princely galleries that functioned as public museums, with catalogues in several languages in inexpensive pocket formats available for purchase on site; they also provided facilities for artists. At the Royal and Imperial Gallery in Vienna, considered by experts, even before the French Revolution, to be the most 'revolutionary' museum in Europe, admission was completely free from 1783 onwards. In Dresden, in 1786, the 'Japanese Palace' was inaugurated; its pediment bore the Latin inscription: 'Museo Usui Publico Patens' ('Museum for public use'). In many cases, even before 1789, these museums were housed in independent buildings dedicated to welcoming visitors, such as in Kassel with the Fridericianum museum inaugurated in 1779, but also in Düsseldorf, Munich, and Vienna in the German-speaking world. In Italy, the Uffizi in Florence, the Pio-Clementino museum in the Vatican, and the first archaeological museum in Naples, exhibiting the excavations from Pompeii, were widely open to the European public. Ironically, in fact, the only people not to have a public or national museum at the time of the French Revolution were ... the French. Hence the energy deployed by the latter to 'catch up', as well as the revolutionary and republican propaganda effort put in from 1793 to create a public museum in Paris, and to establish France as the homeland of the arts and freedom.

In Dresden, the Gemäldegalerie, soon to become famous throughout Europe, was established around 1745 in a remarkable building in the heart of the city: the former royal stables, which had been renovated at great expense a few years earlier to accommodate visitors and artists. The rich collection of paintings, mainly Flemish and Italian, occupies the first floor, with its area of approximately 2,000 square metres, and the collection of antiquities takes up the ground floor. According to visitors, the Dresden Gallery was a veritable journey to Italy. In its early days, it attracted German art historians, artists, intellectuals, and writers – the young Goethe, the young Winckelmann, the Schlegel brothers, and Johanna Schopenhauer, to name just a handful – as well as European visitors on the Grand Tour: the latter, including the French painter Jean-Honoré Fragonard, waxed enthusiastic about their visit. The friend who accompanied Fragonard noted in his travel diary:

> In Dresden, Tuesday, August 23 (1774). – We have to start again every morning at eight o'clock, reviewing the galleries: they are always new and quite live up to expectations, and are an inexhaustible resource for practitioners and connoisseurs of art; both groups waste a great deal of time in Italy, which you need to have seen, of course, but more

> superficially, before immersing yourself in the beautiful galleries of Dresden, Düsseldorf, and Mannheim.[2]

Not only was the Dresden Gallery accessible to the public, but it gave everyone the opportunity to discover in comfort, without the cost and the labour of a journey across the Alps, the magnificence of the Italian schools of painting, in particular those of the Renaissance. For the museum also assumed a social function: in the catalogue of the Dresden Gallery, published in pocket format and in several languages in 1765, the foreword stated:

> The great aim of these precious assemblages of Paintings, to which the name of Galleries is attached, is less to make a pompous display of what is in many ways a quite respectable magnificence than to ennoble it by exhibits that have as their object the Public Good. These Treasures serve as much to honour and perpetuate the memory of men, who have made themselves famous by their genius and distinguished by their talents, as to preserve the monuments of Art, which adorn the mind by forming the taste of the Nation.[3]

The message is clear: by forming one's gaze and taste through contact with beauty, society collectively grows and flourishes. 'It is through beauty that one arrives at freedom', Schiller would write a few years later in his *Letters on the Aesthetic Education of Man* (1795). And it is in this aesthetic and political context that the first years of the 'German' life of the 'Sistine Madonna' must be placed.

But how, exactly, was this unique painting acquired? How were the monks of Piacenza convinced to part with it? When the Gallery opened to the public in the 1740s, the 'Sistine Madonna' was not yet exhibited there, nor any other major work by Raphael. But owning a Raphael seems to have been, for a gallery of that period, a *sine qua non* for equalling the collections of the greatest princes of Europe: the king of France owned some of his works, and the Medici and the Pope had been collecting them from very early on. Thus, since the 1740s, the elector of Saxony had pursued an intense policy of acquisition on the international art market, where he was also in competition with other crowned heads, such as Catherine II of Russia. In 1746, he acquired en bloc the hundred most beautiful paintings in the collection of the duke of Modena, among which were several by Correggio, Titian, and Velázquez. But how was one to obtain a major work by Raphael, an artist who had died young and none of whose authentic paintings, at the time, was in circulation on the art market? For months, even years, emissaries sent from Dresden to Italy or recruited locally would scour, on behalf of the elector of Saxony, the convents, churches, and other Italian religious establishments to convince the abbots and monks to sell one of those rare pieces. In 1752, an Italian emissary was dispatched to Piacenza where, since its creation, Raphael's masterpiece had not left the great church of San Sisto. It certainly had not acquired the international fame that its move to the museum would bring it. Nevertheless, it was sufficiently well known to be spotted by a man sent from Dresden, where it then became the sole object of desire. For two years, the emissary tried to convince the monks of the monastery adjoining the church to sell him their Madonna.

Luckily, archives preserved in Dresden and Piacenza allow us to reconstruct the negotiations. The correspondence was conducted in Italian.[4] In the spring of 1742, the name of the elector of Saxony still did not appear anywhere. In order not to excite the financial appetite of the monks, who had been financially ruined by several years of poor harvests and accumulated debts, Dresden first attempted an incognito purchase. But the monks resisted. In July 1742, the abbot of San Sisto explained to the intermediary of the anonymous elector that he had made a huge effort to convince his brotherhood to accept the 'extraction' (in the sense of 'separating, dissociating') of the Madonna, but that this might be considered for an extremely high sum, if a buyer agreed to pay it. Another requirement was the production of a copy to replace the original. In Dresden, the price was initially considered too high. The negotiations got bogged down, then resumed. In December, a representative of the ecclesiastical hierarchy conceded that the sale of a painting of such quality, one that was 'precious but brought no material advantage' ('prezioso ma infruttifero')[5] could allow accounts to be settled, but he would prefer that another economic arrangement be found. Moreover, everyone at the time knew that the duke of Parma, on whom Piacenza depended, would oppose any attempt to export the painting. The monk then suggested that authorization from the Pope could make things easier. This was obtained: the monks described their misery to the sovereign pontiff, detailing the decrepitude of their monastery and the church – and they obtained the Pope's authorization to sell their Raphael. In March 1753, the contract was signed. There remained one final step: authorization from the duke of Parma. When asked, the latter described the operation as 'a looting with considerable consequences that would cause irreparable damage to the city' ('uno spoglio di tanta conseguenza e danno irreparabile di quella Città'),[6] and firmly opposed it. In June 1753, the elector of Saxony decided to lift the incognito to convince the duke to accept the deal. He succeeded. The work was taken down from the high altar. But, at the last moment, customs officers prevented it from leaving the country. It was not until 21 January 1754 that the exhausted intermediary informed Dresden of the departure of the work, which he 'firmly hoped' would arrive at its destination 'in the same state in which he had found it' in Piacenza. Thus, in the middle of winter, the 'Sistine Madonna' crossed the Alps on a large cart, travelling via Cremona, Brescia, Trento, Innsbruck, and Augsburg. The journey lasted six weeks. The work, unscathed, was presented with great pomp to its new and happy owner on 1 March 1754.

## The Dresden 'Madonna'

At the Dresden museum, despite its immense aura and the considerable sum of money it had cost, the 'Sistine Madonna' was hung at eye level, surrounded by other paintings, in the 'Italian' section, the heart of the museum, nestled inside a 'Flemish and Dutch' gallery. In this context, the 'Madonna' seemed almost drowned out by the other works, far from its original uniqueness, when it was perched 5 metres above the ground on its high altar. By tradition, but also for simple reasons of space, the collection of the elector of Saxony was at that time presented as a 'skin of paintings' covering the walls of the room, without any pedagogical, chronological, or thematic considerations. This did not prevent the 'Sistine Madonna' from becoming, in a few decades, the centrepiece of the Gallery.

Its fame increased greatly in the 1780s, thanks to the distribution of an excellent black-and-white reproduction made by one of the most gifted German engravers of his generation. This was the first time in 270 years that the painting had been copied in engraving, and this reproduction was itself imitated, reduced, and adapted. The 'Sistine Madonna', whose beauty could until then be admired only in person, now circulated beyond the museum and transcended borders. A double process was set in motion: on the one hand, the museum desacralized the original by mingling it with other paintings and by authorizing the production and distribution of reproductions; on the other hand, it valorized this same original which, by contrast with the black and white of the reproductions and their reduced format, could alone guarantee the aesthetic experience of the unique work, and above all of its colours. One of the most frequent comments made after a visit to the museum by visitors familiar with the engravings was the difference between the shades of grey and the colours – the purple, the flesh tints, the blues, the green, and the violet shadows of Raphael's painting formed a dazzling spectacle. The more the reproductions circulated, the more the desire to *see* – or even to *have* – the original grew.

By 1800 at the latest, the priceless painting acquired from penniless monks by the extremely wealthy court of Saxony dethroned Correggio's *Holy Night*, until then the flagship work of the Dresden museum, in the collective imagination and public taste. The history of taste is inextricably linked to that of economic conditions and reproductive technologies. However, against all expectations, the work – torn from its religious context, lowered to eye level and set in competition with hundreds of other paintings – was resanctified in the museum. Unlike the altarpiece of 'The Mystic Lamb' in the previous chapter, presented in separate pieces as an object of study, Raphael's painting invites contemplation and silence: forms of secular prayer that have been described by many visitors. 'Every time I entered this gallery, I spent whole hours in front of the only Raphael in the collection, the mother of God, her lofty gravity, her quiet grandeur', recalled the writer Heinrich von Kleist in 1801.[7]

To look and be silent. To let oneself be affected by art as by a religion. To give the eyes time to connect with the soul. In Dresden, the museum is a temple of Beauty, as theorized and desired by the Romantic generation:

> Picture galleries ... ought to be temples where, in serene and self-effacing silence and in solitary exaltation, we may admire the great artists, those most sublime of mortals, and warm ourselves in the sunshine of rapturous thoughts and sentiments in prolonged and tranquil contemplation of their works.
>
> The appreciation of sublime artworks is akin to prayer.[8]

But they were forgetting France. Around 1800, its aggressive policy of cultural appropriation conducted in the name of republican universalism, described in the previous chapter, was on the verge of destroying the historical fabric of museums in Europe. The great collections of the Dutch sovereigns were dismantled for the benefit of Paris around 1794 and 1795, then those of northern Italy and the Pope in Rome in 1796; Venice paid its tribute in 1797, Munich and Bavaria did likewise around 1801, and then Vienna. As the Musée Napoléon (Louvre) grew, the galleries in the rest of Europe became poorer, or disappeared. Then, in the autumn of 1806, the Grande Armée came to the gates of Dresden. It had just inflicted a severe military defeat on Saxony and Prussia. Following the French army, the famous director of the Louvre, Dominique-Vivant Denon, was preparing to make Germany yield an 'ample harvest of superb things',[9] as he put it – in other words, one of the most vast and systematic campaigns of artistic confiscation since the Revolution. Of course, the 'Sistine Madonna' was on his list. Denon wrote to Napoleon to convince him to make it part of the peace treaty being drawn up with Saxony:

> I thought, Sire, that I was a nuisance for the Elector of Saxony; I had not tried to see him, but Count Marcolini, director of his museum, came to meet me. The Elector sent word that he wanted to meet me. I could see in his conversation that he had no particular taste for the masterpieces that he knows he possesses; but he will never offer any of them to Your Majesty.... However small the number of objects that Your Majesty would require, it would still be of great value. – A single painting by Raphael from the Dresden collection was purchased for

> 9,000 louis by King Augustus: it is worth twice as much to Your Majesty. Correggio's 'Night' is worth at least as much; two other Correggios and a Holben [*sic*] are in the same rank. This last painter is missing from your museum. It is not any artistic spoils that I am proposing Your Majesty appropriate by asking you to demand four or six paintings from a collection that contains 2,000 of them, 200 of them capital works – a collection that also contains heaps of gold, diamonds and pearls; but I must repeat to Your Majesty that in conquering the rest of Europe you will never find the opportunity that Saxony is offering you at this very moment. It is not mere enthusiasm on my part that speaks to you, Sire; but the awareness of my duty.[10]

It was a classic procedure: Denon intimated that the legitimate owner of the works was incompetent – devoid, in his view, of any taste for the arts – in order to justify their possible transfer to Paris. To convince the emperor, he argued in terms of capital, real and symbolic, shedding light once again on the inseparable historical link between museums and money. But he was not granted his wish. In his *Memoirs*, Talleyrand, Minister of the Empire, described the arrival of Denon's letter at headquarters:

> [Napoleon] was reading it when I entered his office, and he showed it to me. – 'If Your Majesty,' I said to him, 'has some of the paintings removed from Dresden, you will do more than the King of Saxony has ever allowed himself to do, because he does not believe he has the power to have any of them placed in his palace. He respects the gallery as national property.' – 'Yes,' said Napoleon, 'he is an excellent man; we must not upset him. I will give the order not to touch anything. We will see later.'[11]

The Dresden Gallery remained intact. The 'Sistine Madonna' would not travel to Paris to join the impressive collection of works by Raphael already confiscated from Italy or taken from the French royal collections nationalized in 1789. We still have to go to Dresden to see it. But the almost complete reunion, over a period of ten years, of the young painter's works in Paris unleashed an unprecedented international craze, a veritable 'Raphael cult' which impacted on the painting in Dresden. From the 1820s onwards, the 'Sistine Madonna' became one of the most copied works in Europe. Going beyond black-and-white engravings, an army of young painters now set about reproducing it in oil and in colour in order to decorate the rich salons of the aristocracy of northern Europe, particularly in the Germanic and Russian world. The 'Sistine Madonna' and its angels could now be found in the winter palace of Elisabeth Alexeevna, empress of Russia by marriage to Alexander I, in Saint Petersburg; in the Anichkov Palace of Duchess Nikolai, also in Saint Petersburg; in Berlin, in the study of King Frederick William III of Prussia, and in the Green Salon of Prince William and Princess Marianne. At the same time, an abundant scholarly literature was produced on the subject, notably in the very first 'scientific' monograph devoted by an art historian to a painter – that by Johann David Passavant at the end of the 1830s.[12] In the Germanic space, this craze could also be explained by an extreme politicization of aesthetics and religion, at the crossroads between a Protestantism embodied by Dürer and a Catholicism embodied by Raphael. In this configuration, museums played a central role. One only has to observe what happened to the 'Sistine Madonna' in Dresden during the nineteenth century. First, in 1843, a huge protective glass pane was installed inside its frame. In 1855, it was moved. To adapt to the museographic developments of the time, when the museums of Berlin, the Louvre in Paris, and the British Museum in London were investing considerable sums in the development of their collections, Dresden equipped itself with a huge and functional new gallery of paintings. Significantly, the 'Sistine Madonna' was now hung alone, far from the bustle of the other paintings, in a room specially designed for it, which symbolically bore the letter A. It was given a new, monumental, carved wooden frame inspired by Renaissance tabernacles, whose base bore in gold letters a quote from Vasari, considered at the time to be the 'father of art history', the first scholar to have mentioned the painting's existence. In a way, this new setting was the very materialization of what, on the immaterial level, was happening to the work: desacralized (unsuccessfully) during its first 'museumization', it was now resacralized, reisolated, re-elevated – but in the name of art history and erudition. The museum, through its architecture, through the choice of room, setting, lighting, and even floor, prescribed to visitors the physical and psychological attitude they should adopt in front of the painting.

They were reminded of the lost original function of the painting; it was made physically perceptible to them. Some, indeed, were all too aware of it and even irritated by it. Thanks to the development of the steamship and the railways, more and more people came from the United States and Russia to see the painting in its new setting. This fact is more significant than it seems: after seeing the painting, Leo Tolstoy questioned the obligation of devout contemplation that the museum imposed on its visitors: 'The "Sistine Madonna" awakens no emotion in me, but merely an agonizing uneasiness as to whether I feel the required feeling.'[13] Devotion cannot be summoned up to order.

Nor could the effects produced by the painting in nineteenth-century literature and art. We know that Dostoevsky kept a partial reproduction of the 'Sistine Madonna' above his sofa in the study of his apartment in Saint Petersburg. He cherished in it – if we are to believe Svidrigailov's words in *Crime and Punishment* – her face, which had 'something fantastic in it, the face of mournful religious ecstasy.'[14] It was the half-mad woman who interested him here, not the purity of features in which others detected a trace of the divine. In *The Demons*, Stepan Trofimovich defends the Madonna against Varvara Petrovna, calling Raphael's figure 'that very Queen of Queens, that ideal of humanity, the Sistine Madonna, who to your thinking is inferior to a glass or a pencil.'[15] And a few years later, in an aphorism entitled 'Honesty in Painting' from the collection 'The Wanderer and His Shadow' (1879), Nietzsche congratulated Raphael for his vision of the 'Sistine Madonna' as a perfectly normal woman: 'Here for once he wished to paint a vision, but such a vision as even noble youths without "faith" may and will have – the vision of the future wife, a wise, high-souled, silent, and very beautiful woman, carrying her first-born in her arms.'[16]

And Nietzsche responded to the child's gaze with this beautiful observation: 'The reunion of two different ages expressed in the same face.'

In the last quarter of the nineteenth century, while visitors flocked to Dresden to try out for themselves the effect that the original of this much discussed, much reproduced, much interpreted, and much venerated painting would produce, chromolithography – which allowed for colour reproductions – and then photography added an additional dimension to its virtual omnipresence. Everyone could now buy for just a few pence a postcard of the Madonna or of the two winged children leaning at the bottom of the painting; later, they could be found as fridge magnets or bookmarks. The democratization of the painting was consummated on the eve of the First World War. By now, it was difficult to say to whom the 'Sistine Madonna' belonged. In any case, almost no one associated it with Piacenza any more. It was everywhere, and the original was in Dresden. More than ever, it belonged to the king of Saxony – until his abdication and flight in 1918, when revolutionary republics were proclaimed throughout Germany.

The German Empire came to an end. Under the Weimar Republic, the princely collections – those of the kings of Prussia in Berlin (the Hohenzollerns), the kings of Bavaria in Munich (the Wittelsbachs), the kings of Saxony in Dresden (the Wettins), etc., all of which had been accessible to the general public for at least a century – passed into the domain of the state. The 'Sistine Madonna' became the property of the people and continued to be copied, reproduced, and adapted – now well beyond European borders, as evidenced by the chromolithographic printing made at the famous printing house of the brothers Shrinathdasji and Shyamsunderlal Brijbasi, in Uttar Pradesh in India, depicting a child Krishna (blue all over, as the tradition required) and his foster mother, Yashoda (in a purple and gold sari), in a pose closely modelled on the Dresden Madonna and the Christ child. In the 1920s and 1930s, Raphael's Madonna entered the hybrid, shimmering, and widespread repertoire of popular Hindu imagery. An original local and global diffusion formed a dialectic inextricably linked to the painting.

During the Second World War, like the bust of Nefertiti, the Pergamon Altar in Berlin and the other treasures of the Dresden museums, Raphael's 'Sistine Madonna' was sheltered from the American and British bombings that reduced the city to ashes. First hidden in a fortress in the region, it was placed in late 1943 in a padded carriage parked under a railway tunnel whose two entrances were walled up. At the beginning of January 1944, worried specialists measured a temperature of 8 °C and an air humidity of between 80 and 84 per cent. It was here, in May 1945, the day after fierce fighting, that the Red Army and a handful of Russian experts, including art historians, found the painting. Like the rest of the Dresden and Berlin collections, it was confiscated as a war trophy, compensation for the destruction inflicted by the German army on Russia's architectural and artistic heritage. The Madonna was taken to the USSR with several tens of thousands of other pieces, then kept until 1955 in a secret location in Moscow. In the mid-1950s, the USSR decided to return the Red Army's trophies to what had in the meantime become a sister republic of the USSR – namely, the GDR. Before its return to East Germany, the 'Sistine Madonna' was exhibited for ninety days at the Pushkin Museum in Moscow. In a country where writers and artists had venerated it since the nineteenth century, its public presentation was an unprecedented event, photographed, filmed, and widely commented on.

The writer Vasily Grossman – a Ukrainian Jew, a war correspondent for the Soviet army, and an eyewitness to the horrors of the Second World War, which he covered mainly in the Donbass region and in Stalingrad in 1942 – went to see the 'Sistine Madonna' at the Pushkin Museum in May 1955. It deeply moved him and inspired an essay, published in Moscow two decades after his death and quickly translated into several European languages. A long meditation on the irreducible humanity of mankind and the immortality of works of art, the text begins by describing the queue of visitors who have come to pay homage to the masterpiece, continues in front of the painting, and ends on Volkhonka Street with the poignant and unexpected evocation of the Treblinka extermination camp.

> This painting has been seen by twelve generations of people – a fifth of the generations that have lived on earth since the beginning of recorded history.
>
> Old beggar women have looked at this painting – as have European emperors and students, American billionaires, Popes, Russian princes. Young virgins, prostitutes, colonels from the general staff, thieves, geniuses, weavers, bomber pilots and schoolteachers have looked at it. Good and evil people have looked at it.
>
> During the centuries this painting has existed, European and colonial empires have risen and fallen, the American nation has come into being, the factories of Pittsburgh and Detroit have gone into production, revolutions have taken place and the world's social structure has changed.

During these centuries humanity has left behind it the superstitions of the alchemists, just as it has abandoned hand-driven spinning wheels, muskets and halberds, sailing ships and horse-drawn mail coaches. It has entered the age of electric generators, electric motors and turbines; it has entered the age of atomic reactors and hydrogen bombs. During these centuries great scientists have shaped a new understanding of the universe: Galileo has written his *Dialogue*, Newton his *Principia*, Einstein his *On the Electrodynamics of Moving Bodies*. During these centuries Rembrandt, Goethe, Beethoven, Dostoevsky and Tolstoy have enriched our souls and made our lives more beautiful.

What I saw was a young mother holding a child in her arms.

…

In his Madonna Raphael has revealed the mystery of maternal beauty. But the secret of the painting's inexhaustible life lies elsewhere. The secret of the painting's life, of the Madonna's great beauty, is that the young woman's body and face are – in fact – her soul. In this visual representation of a mother's soul lies something inaccessible to human consciousness.

…

The Madonna's beauty is closely tied to earthly life. It is a democratic, human and humane beauty. It is a beauty that lives in every woman … This Madonna is the soul and mirror of all human beings, and everyone who looks at her can see her humanity …

I believe that this Madonna is a purely atheistic expression of life and humanity, without divine participation.

…

The Madonna with the child in her arms represents what is human in man. This is why she is immortal.

Looking at the Sistine Madonna, our own epoch glimpses its own fate. Every epoch contemplates this woman with a child in her arms, and a tender, moving and sorrowful sense of brotherhood comes into being between people of different generations, nations, races and eras. Conscious now of themselves and of the cross they must bear, people suddenly understand the miraculous links between different ages, the way everything that has lived and ever will live is linked to what is living now.[17]

Raphael's painting finally returned to Dresden in 1956, after seventeen years of invisibility.

## Saving or appropriating a 'treasure of humanity'?

In the midst of the Cold War, this restitution was surrounded by energetic propaganda. Since Antiquity, all acts of 'voluntary' restitution have been privileged political moments – opportunities for a victor, or a 'possessor' state, to stage its loyalty or its 'friendship' by granting to a former enemy – or a country recently under its tutelage, a colony or a vassal – entire lost swathes of its cultural heritage. In 132 BC, Rome returned to Sicily, now one of its colonies, the treasures seized by Carthage during the Punic Wars; in 1815, the emperor of Austria returned to Venice, which had come under his rule, the horses and the lion of St Mark's Square confiscated by France in 1797; at the end of the Second World War, in 1945, the American army returned to Florence, in a carefully choreographed parade, the treasures of its museums taken from Nazi Germany. And in the 1950s, the USSR turned the restitution of the 'Madonna' to the GDR into a great moment of affirmation of the 'friendship of peoples'. Exhibitions, brochures, speeches, banners, and inscriptions engraved in marble hailed the USSR's action: 'Safeguarded for humanity'; 'Treasures of humanity saved by the Soviet Union'; 'The restitution of our paintings by the Soviet Union spurs our fight for peace'; 'The rescue of the Dresden Gallery by the Soviet army is a major act of socialist humanism, a historic event. We will forever be grateful to the peoples of the Soviet Union' – such was the tone of the discourse surrounding the return of the 'Sistine Madonna', unwrapped in Dresden in front of television cameras and photographers' flashbulbs.

One of the elements of this propaganda was a film that deserves a moment's attention, as it has remained unknown in France but is very famous in the former Eastern bloc. In its own way, it asks the question that concerns us: 'Who owns beauty?' It was the Dresden museums themselves that, in 2012, on the occasion of the 500th anniversary of the creation of the 'Sistine Madonna', brought this film back to light. Co-produced in 1960 by the East German studios DEFA and the Soviet firm Mosfilm, *Five Days, Five Nights* depicts, against a backdrop of fighting and concentration camps, what was then presented as the 'rescue' by the Red Army of Dresden's masterpieces in May 1945

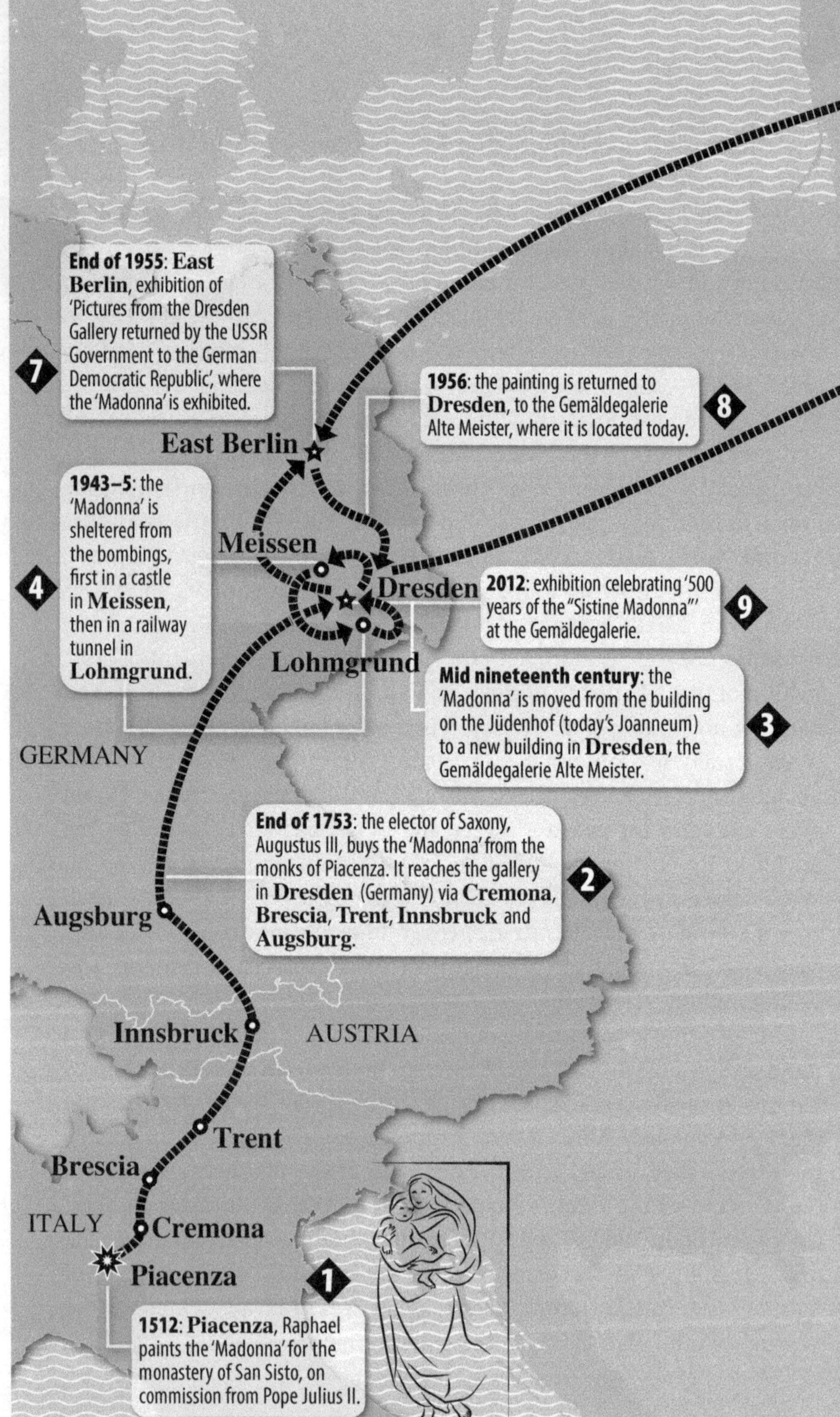
End of 1955: East Berlin, exhibition of 'Pictures from the Dresden Gallery returned by the USSR Government to the German Democratic Republic', where the 'Madonna' is exhibited.
7
1956: the painting is returned to Dresden, to the Gemäldegalerie Alte Meister, where it is located today.
8
East Berlin
1943–5: the 'Madonna' is sheltered from the bombings, first in a castle in Meissen, then in a railway tunnel in Lohmgrund.
4
Meissen
Dresden
2012: exhibition celebrating '500 years of the "Sistine Madonna"' at the Gemäldegalerie.
9
Lohmgrund
Mid nineteenth century: the 'Madonna' is moved from the building on the Jüdenhof (today's Joanneum) to a new building in Dresden, the Gemäldegalerie Alte Meister.
3
GERMANY
End of 1753: the elector of Saxony, Augustus III, buys the 'Madonna' from the monks of Piacenza. It reaches the gallery in Dresden (Germany) via Cremona, Brescia, Trent, Innsbruck and Augsburg.
2
Augsburg
Innsbruck
AUSTRIA
Trent
Brescia
ITALY
Cremona
Piacenza
1
1512: Piacenza, Raphael paints the 'Madonna' for the monastery of San Sisto, on commission from Pope Julius II.

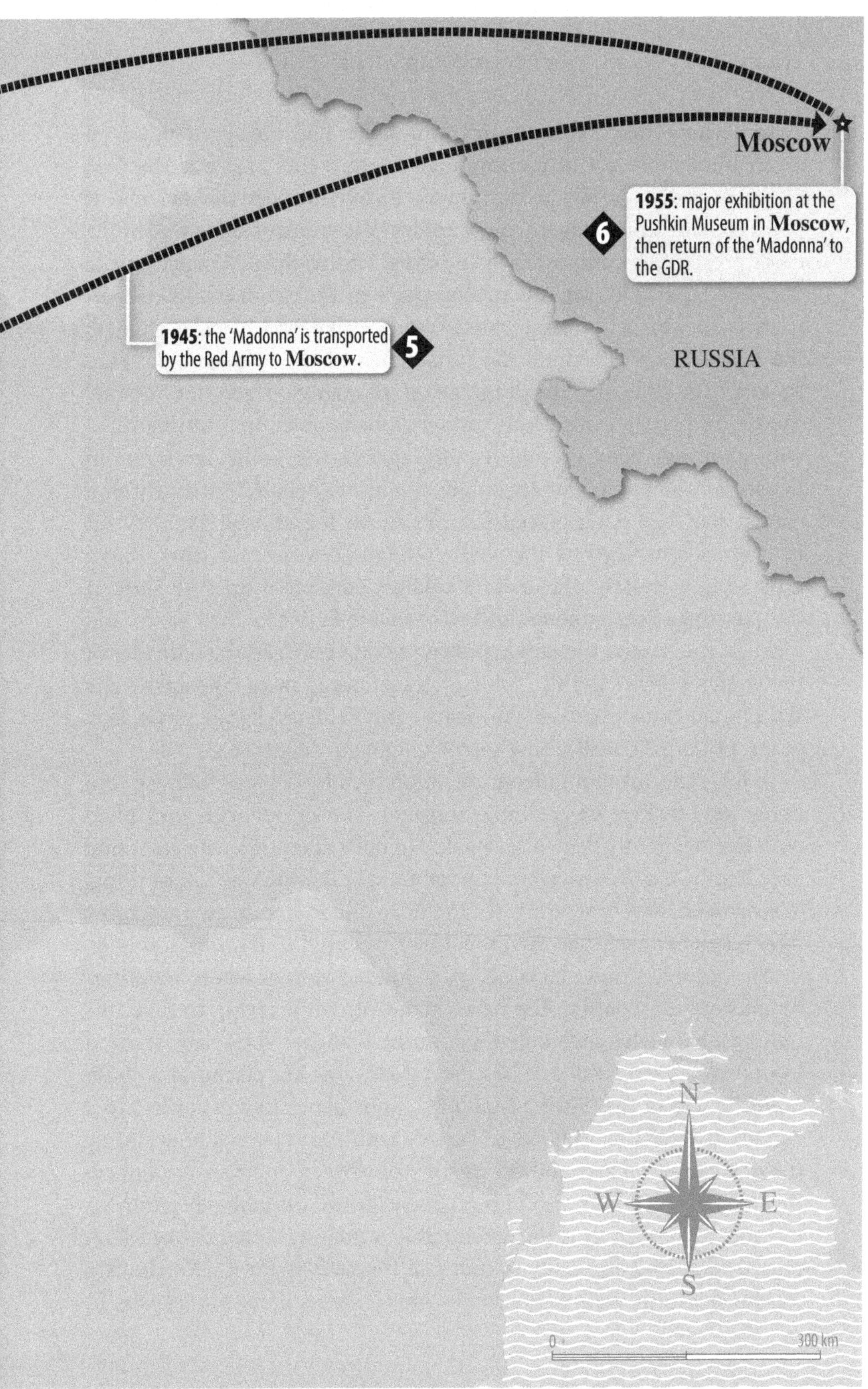

Moscow
1955: major exhibition at the Pushkin Museum in Moscow, then return of the 'Madonna' to the GDR.
6
1945: the 'Madonna' is transported by the Red Army to Moscow.
5
RUSSIA
N
W
E
S
0
300 km

– something that Western historiography had always denounced as an intolerable act of looting. Significantly, this film was the first German–Soviet co-production in the history of post-war cinema. It had a considerable budget. The soundtrack was entrusted to one of the most prestigious composers of the time: Dmitri Shostakovich. In the disjointed, perilous, and disturbing space of the depots, wagons, and tunnels to which the masterpieces of Dresden had been evacuated, the film set out to remind the inhabitants of the Eastern bloc what Russia had done for the heritage of humanity. Here, the 'Sistine Madonna' plays a central role: under ribbed vaults, in a setting filled with paintings piled up and leaning against the walls, one scene in particular shows two Soviet soldiers who very carefully straighten a canvas that had been placed face down on the ground. As they lift it, it reveals itself to be Raphael's 'Madonna.' Moved to tears, lining up as if in a church, officers and soldiers come to a halt. All stare at the painting. The camera slowly alternates between their faces and those of the Virgin, the child, and the saints; between the bare feet of the young woman and the soldiers' transfigured faces. Shostakovich's symphonic music pierces the heart. The soldiers' hands cross in a gesture of prayer: everything seems to hang in suspense.

In this scene of spontaneous devotion (beauty belongs to those who know how to love it), a simple sergeant, stocky but with eyes filled with feeling, gently begins to speak. He talks about his wife and child executed by the Wehrmacht: 'I understand … she too was a poor thing, like my wife. Barefoot, and with the little one in her arms. They must have taken her away like that, too, to be executed.' A few minutes later, in the dramatic blue darkness of a flooded tunnel where paintings by masters are floating, the brave sergeant, while trying to save this heritage, is mortally wounded by a mine that the Nazis had attached to one of the works of art. His mortal remains are placed in a coffin … at the feet of the 'Sistine Madonna.' Shostakovich's music rises to a climax. It would be difficult to convey with more pathos how closely the destiny of the arts and the destiny of women and men are linked. Beauty, the film says, belongs to those who, without education or fortune, recognize in it the 'irreducible humanity' often evoked with regard to it, and are ready to sacrifice themselves for it. Humans are mortal, art immortal. Whoever restores it, takes care of it, repairs it, retouches it, reframes it, cures it of the injuries of war, so that it may endure beyond generations, is its only worthy guardian. From there to appropriating art materially, as the Soviets did in 1945, there is only a short step. When it comes to translocating a work of artistic heritage, the rhetoric of care must also be handled with caution.

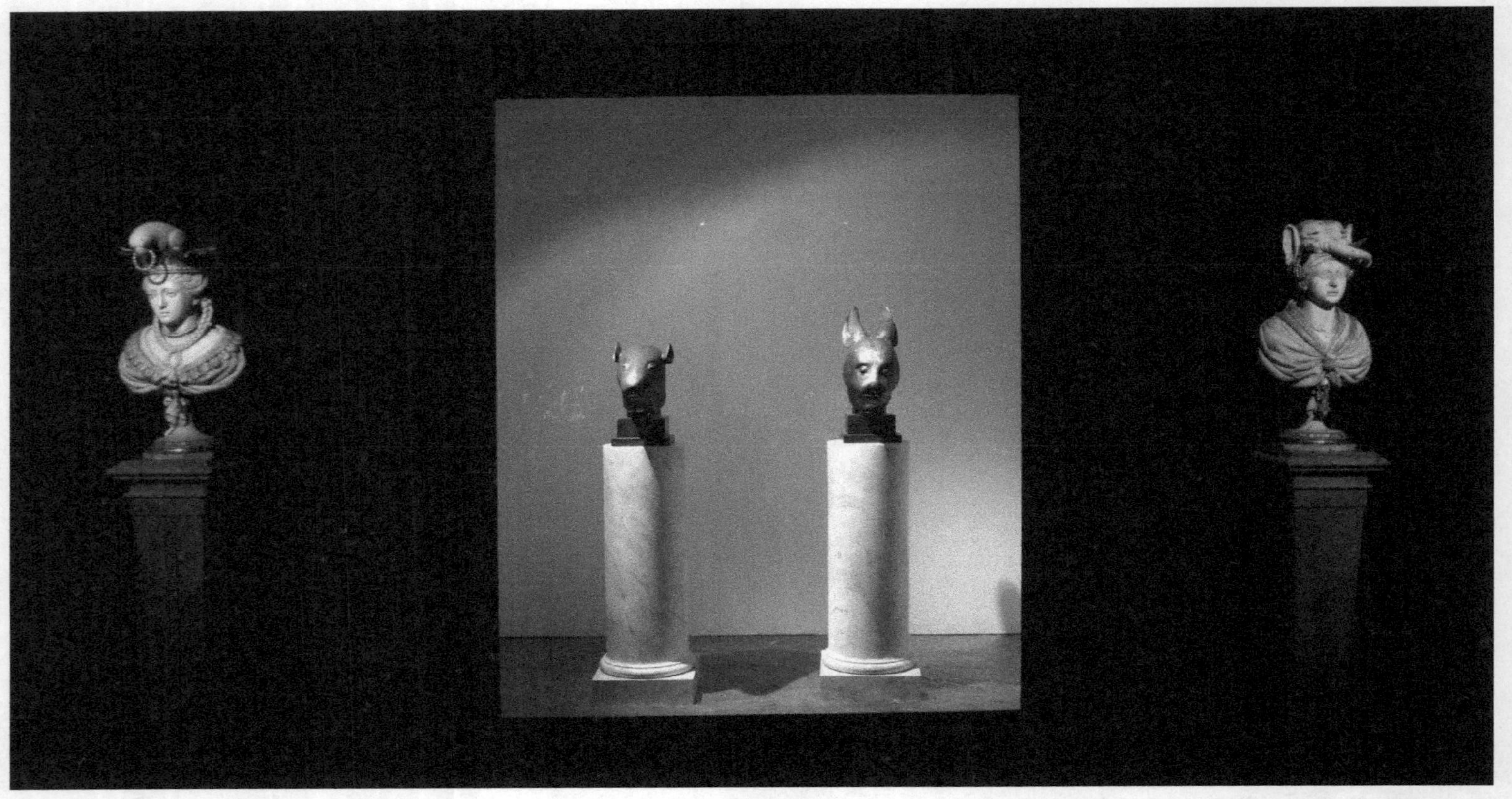

Giuseppe Castiglione (after drawings by), 'Heads of a rat and a rabbit,' Qian Long period (1736–95), bronze, h. 45 cm. Beijing, National Museum. Photo © Jean-Luc Luyssen / Contributor / Getty.

# 5

# THE BRONZE HEADS OF THE SUMMER PALACE IN BEIJING

In February 2009, the Grand Palais in Paris was the scene of an event that galvanized the art world, and that the international press called the 'sale of the century': that of the legendary collection of Yves Saint Laurent and his companion Pierre Bergé at a spectacular show orchestrated by the auction house Christie's. Blue and pink lighting illuminated the extraordinary glass dome of the prestigious Parisian exhibition space. The *Tout-Paris* of art and fashion was there. However, controversy cast its shadow over this fairy tale of glamour and money. Like the evil fairy in the story, the Chinese State Administration in charge of cultural heritage condemned the sale and demanded its cancellation, requesting the restitution of two eighteenth-century bronzes that had disappeared during the pillaging of the Summer Palace in Beijing (then Peking) by French and British troops in 1860–1. Pierre Bergé refused to return the disputed objects unless China agreed in return to 'apply human rights, to free the Tibetans, and to accept the Dalai Lama on their territory'.[1] Nearly a century and a half after the bloody looting of the Summer Palace, this very French response in a way echoed the universalist rhetoric of the Revolution: the arts are a product of freedom and must be preserved in the land of freedom. But Pierre Bergé's refusal triggered the wrath and indignation of the Chinese press. While in Paris the bidding for the heads rose, caricatures were circulating in China representing the statues in tears, with Chinese characters written in speech bubbles: 'I want to go home ... ', or even 'Homesick'.[2]

The episode reminds us, if we need to be reminded, that victims of the theft of works of art have long memories. Far from healing, the wounds caused by the trauma of dispossession seem to worsen over time. Who owns these bronze statues? Can we speak of a shared heritage in their case? How much did it cost to take them away? Can we separate the notions of belonging and identity from the economy and the market? To address these questions, we must go back to the creation of these animal heads in Beijing in the eighteenth century.

## Money, nation, heritage

The story began in Milan towards the end of the seventeenth century. It continued during the Second Opium War (1856–60) which pitted the Manchu Empire of the Qing dynasty, eager to end the narcotics trade orchestrated by the Western powers, against the French and British Empires, which were enriching themselves considerably from this traffic, and even seeking to extend their sphere of action northwards towards the interior of China. In December 1857, a Franco-English expedition landed in Guangzhou (Canton). Two years later, it was at the gates of the capital of the Empire. At the beginning of October 1860, the troops entered the Summer Palace, the Yuan Ming Yuan (literally 'garden of perfect clarity'), abandoned by the fleeing emperor. In this immense imperial domain, decorated with legendary gardens, the Chinese emperors had resided and governed since Qianlong in the eighteenth century. Soldiers and officers from both armies ransacked the palaces for several days. Some observed that the local population also took part. Once the looting was complete, the Yuan Ming Yuan and its gardens were set on fire, on the orders of the British army. According to witnesses, they burned for three days and three nights.

Several thousand items were taken to Europe: porcelain, cloisonné enamels, sculptures, furniture, silk paintings, screens, manuscripts, etc. Among them were twelve large bronze animal heads, representing the signs of the Chinese hourly cycle and calendar: rat, ox, tiger, rabbit, dragon, snake, horse, sheep, monkey, rooster, dog, and pig. Created a hundred years earlier and based on the drawings of a Jesuit missionary born in Milan in 1688, Giuseppe Castiglione, these pieces are the manifestation of an early, fascinating cultural transfer between Asia and Europe. Invited at the age of twenty-five to the court of the emperor of China along with other European Jesuit artists, such as the French astronomer, cartographer, engineer, and architect Michel Benoist, Castiglione adorned the imperial palaces with works of European inspiration. Among them was an ingenious system of fountains distributed throughout the large park, including a clepsydra ('water clock') in front of one of the European-style palaces. This was where the bronze heads had come from: in two symmetrical hedges, they framed an enormous marble shell. Seated and dressed like wise men on flat pedestals, the animals had human bodies sculpted in stone. Their bronze heads reproduce with gentle meticulousness, right down to the hair, the heads of idealized wise animals: the round, well-polished eyes of the rabbit and the rat seem to confer a high degree of intelligence on them. Originally, water flowed successively from each head for two-hour periods; at midday, it flowed simultaneously from the twelve heads.

Very active in China from the seventeenth century onwards, the Jesuit missionaries brought to the Summer Palace a Western semantics that they adapted to and combined with Chinese aesthetics, whose forms they appropriated in return. Castiglione, indeed, took the Chinese name Lang Shining ('Man of the Quiet World') upon his arrival. Finely chiselled and displaying great finesse, including in their psychological acuity, his zodiacal heads now seem to belong neither to an Asian aesthetic nor to the European aesthetic of the eighteenth century. They belong to a hybrid culture, at the crossroads of Asia and Europe, as astonishing testimonies of a culture not understood in the fixed sense of a national thing, but in the dynamic sense of common elaboration and co-production, of mixture and migration. It is an assembly of forms and ideas that have come from different regions and traditions to create something never seen before. The invitation extended by the emperor of China in the eighteenth century to European Jesuits to embellish the Summer Palace takes us to the very heart of these cultural transfers.

Some 300 years after their creation, other geographies and other transfers are still making their mark on their lives as objects. In 2009, when the rat's head and the rabbit's head were put up for sale in Paris, several other heads had already been sold on the international market: the pig's head (sold by Sotheby's in New York in 1987), the tiger's head (sold by the same auction house in Hong Kong in April 2000), the monkey's and the ox's heads (also sold in Hong Kong in April 2000, but by Christie's), and the horse's head, acquired by Stanley Ho, a Hong Kong multimillionaire active in Macao, who donated it to a Chinese museum in 2007. Today, the rabbit's and rat's heads are on display at the National Museum of China, which opened in 2003 on Tian'anmen Square in Beijing. It was the French millionaire François-Henri Pinault who 'restored' them to China in 2013.

Born of an artistic transfer carried out by Catholic missionaries operating between China and Europe, torn from their context by a war motivated by the opium trade, arriving thanks to the vicissitudes of private sales in the collections of wealthy Western art lovers themselves connected to global artistic creation and the world of high finance, bought by Asian or European tycoons, and finally exhibited on one of the most infamous squares in the history of the twentieth century, the bronze heads of the Summer Palace illustrate, as clearly as possible, on a global scale, the links between wars, empires, economy, heritage, and nations.

## The price of pillage

Until the beginning of the twentieth century, booty and the spoils of war were not prohibited by international military codes. It was still common practice in the nineteenth century. From a legal point of view, the 'right to ravage and pillage what belongs to the enemy' and the 'right to appropriate what has been taken from the enemy',[3] to use the terminology of the Dutch jurist Hugo Grotius (1625), were perfectly well recognized. After the trauma and the countless public debates caused in Europe by the 'artistic conquests' of the Revolution and the Empire, it is true that European nations spared each other this kind of outrage. But they systematically resorted to it during the colonial or commercial wars that they engaged in, first in Asia and then in Africa in the nineteenth century. It was not until 1899 and the Convention concerning the Laws and Customs of War on Land, signed in The Hague by twenty-four sovereign states, that the practice of pillaging and the taking of cultural property during military campaigns became illegal. But, significantly, these provisions only concerned the signatory states and did not include either Asia or Africa.

Thus, in China, in 1860, the joint military raid by the French and British armies was the occasion for an unprecedented ransacking of heritage. When the expeditionary troops looted and burned the Summer Palace to force China to open its market, the soldiers took what they found and what they could carry. Without any clear awareness of the economic, cultural, and symbolic value of the seized objects, they first traded them on the spot: the British and the French were distinguished by two very distinct cultures of pillage – one ordered, the other not. Several contemporary accounts, valuable for reconstructing the military practice of 'cultural booty', describe the management of the pillage in the immediate aftermath of the looting. On the English side, the *Narrative of the North China Campaign of 1860* by Robert Swinhoe, an eyewitness to the dismantling of the Summer Palace, devotes several pages to a description of the great success of the sale organized by the British army directly after the looting, where officers and soldiers thronged together for several days, 'caught up in the fever of bidding' and the lure of profit.[4] Mentioned in other military and colonial contexts of the nineteenth century, these internal sales within the British army were clearly an effective way to get the most precious pieces out of the hands of ordinary soldiers and into those of their officers. On the French side, however, as evidenced for example by the *Lettres intimes sur la campagne de Chine en 1860* (*Intimate Letters on the China Campaign in 1860*) by the military interpreter Armand Lucy, disorder, hubris, and lack of awareness of the value of cultural heritage seem to dominate:

> The army presents the most singular sight. We came without carriages, but there were more than 300 of them loaded just with loot. The soldiers replaced their white neck covers with red silk turbans for the grenadiers, yellow for the skirmish units, blue, green or pink for the centre. Then,

> on the sack, enormous bales. If they'd been made to carry half of all that, they'd have complained loudly.... Others, more ingenious, camp their booty on the back of a peasant, who has come to satisfy his curiosity or rather to steal. Then, holding the means of transport on a leash by his caudal appendage, off they proudly go, jeering at their comrade who, like the wise man of Greece, carries everything on his own back.[5]

Inserted in the text, an engraving reinforces the message: it shows a French soldier of small stature, protected from the sun by a delicate parasol and from the heat by a beautiful fan, as he leads along on a leash, like a horse or a donkey, a Chinese-looking man with long moustaches. The man on a leash is much taller than the soldier leading him. Like a beast of burden, he is bent double under a heavy load of various objects taken from the Yuan Ming Yuan. The caption states: 'Chauvin et Cie removal company, for the countryside and abroad.'[6]

On the ground, then, the two pillaging armies capitalized on the looted objects in accordance with different logics. At the other end of the chain, however, in Europe, both armies paid homage to their respective sovereigns, presenting them with the most spectacular pieces: both Queen Victoria in England and Empress Eugénie in France soon possessed impressive treasures from the Summer Palace. In London, many of them would end up at the Victoria & Albert Museum, where they are still to be found today. In Paris, a major exhibition offered them to the public gaze in the Tuileries Palace. *Le Monde illustré* (1861) described the exhibition in these terms:

> We have just visited the gallery on the ground floor of the Marsan pavilion, in the Tuileries Palace, which is currently offering the curiosity of art lovers a spectacle that is as splendid as it is strange. This is the gathering of precious objects found in the Summer Palace in Peking: enamel work exceeding all known dimensions, porcelain of all shapes from the different periods of Chinese art, jade stones of perfect workmanship and a rare size.[7]

A few months later, the masterpieces presented at the Tuileries were transferred to the Château de Fontainebleau, where they formed (as they still do) the 'Chinese Museum of Her Majesty Empress Eugénie.'

Among the objects brought back to Europe from the Summer Palace in the aftermath of the 1860 attack, those that did not end up in French or British public collections were dispersed at auction or remained for several generations in the families of the soldiers involved.

While research on provenance has apparently not allowed us to determine precisely through the hands of which French or British soldier or officer the bronze heads in question passed in 1860, we can, however, state without any risk of error that they began to circulate on the art market as soon as they arrived in Europe, like the thousands of other pieces looted in Beijing. In the city of Paris alone, between 1861 and 1863, no fewer than twenty-one sales devoted to the treasures of the Summer Palace were held at the Hôtel Drouot, created ten years earlier with a monopoly on auctions in France. In London, at Christie's, Sotheby's, and other dealers, dozens of similar sales contributed to the dispersal of Chinese imperial treasures. For example, the *Catalogue des objets précieux provenant en grande partie du palais d'été de Yuan Ming Yuan et composant le musée japonais et chinois de M. le Colonel Du Pin* (*Catalogue of Precious Objects from the Summer Palace of Yuan Ming Yuan and Composing the Japanese and Chinese Museum of Monsieur le Colonel Du Pin*), dispersed at the Hôtel Drouot in four sales in the winter of 1862, gives an idea of the rhetoric at work in France:

> It was necessary for diplomacy to give us access to Japan (1858), and for the sword to open the road to Peking (1860), for us to become aware of the artistic riches of the two greatest Empires of the Far East. Until then, only secondary specimens, generally modern, had come to Europe. Those presented in this catalogue are mostly ancient, and of a perfection whose secret seems to have been lost by contemporary native artists. Here we find pieces dating back to the fifth century AD; there are even a certain number that are unique.[8]

Admiration for, and recognition of, the high historical, aesthetic, and material value of the works are here combined with the feeling of superiority of the Europeans who already cultivated the received idea that the Chinese of the nineteenth century were incapable of producing works of art as refined as those of their ancestors. Further on, the same catalogue offers for sale a 'Large album representing the forty views of the palaces of Yuen-Ming-Yuen. Paintings on silk ..., unique pieces, and the only ones that preserve the image of the burned Palaces.'[9] Not without cynicism, the author of the brochure not only accepts the destruction of the Summer Palace by the European powers, he also prides himself that the memory of the place had been captured by this precious piece of evidence, now preserved at the Bibliothèque nationale de France.[10]

Meanwhile, in China, after 1860, the defeat in the Opium War and the damage to the native heritage inflicted on the Qing dynasty marked the beginning of a long series of military setbacks, economic dispossessions, and political concessions to foreign powers – Great Britain and France, Russia and Japan. Today, this long period is known and preserved in Chinese collective memory under the term 'century of humiliation' (百年國恥 *Bǎinián guóchǐ*). The looting of the bronze heads and the destruction of the Summer Palace occupy a central place in this highly political and politicized memory.

## Repairing history?

> In a certain corner of the world could be found a wonder of the world. This wonder was called the Summer Palace. Art has two principles: the Idea that produces European art, and the Chimera that produces Oriental art. The Summer Palace was to chimerical art what the Parthenon is to ideal art. Everything to which the imagination of an almost superhuman people can give birth was there. It was not, like the Parthenon, a rare and unique work; it was a sort of enormous model of the chimera, if the chimera can have a model.... This wonder has disappeared.... We Europeans are the civilized ones, and for us, the Chinese are the barbarians. This is what civilization has done to barbarism. In the view of history, one of the two bandits will be called France, the other will be called England. But I protest, and I thank you for giving me the opportunity to do so; the crimes of those who lead are not the fault of those who are led; governments are sometimes bandits, peoples never.... I hope that a day will come when a France liberated and purified will return this booty to a despoiled China.[11]

It was Victor Hugo who expressed himself thus, in 1861, in reaction to the sack of the Summer Palace. In Europe, he was not alone at the time in condemning the cultural violence inflicted on China. But the stories of the victor dominate, and few voices show their solidarity with the vanquished peoples far away. In terms of heritage translocations, the question of restitution, posed here by Hugo as a moral imperative, is generally formulated by the dispossessed; indeed, they speak less of restitution (since the term implies the point of view of the possessor) than of recovery, recuperation, or reparation. In the case of the bronze heads auctioned in Paris in 2009, this motivation was all-important on the Chinese side.

From the mid-1990s, in fact, successive Chinese presidents distanced themselves from the strictly Communist ideals of the early days of the People's Republic of China and adopted a political rhetoric of 'awakening', 'rebirth', and 'national renewal' – and soon, the 'Chinese Dream'. In this constellation, the memory of the 'century of humiliation' plays a central role. Far from being erased or repressed, the violence suffered in the nineteenth century, the wars, the 'unequal treaties', the heavy economic and political sanctions inflicted on China are remembered in deeds and words. Deliberately choosing not to restore the ruins of the Yuan Ming Yuan, the authorities transformed them into a giant memorial to European imperial aggression. Since 1994, the site has been used as a centre for national patriotic education, a place for festivities and official commemorations. A bust of Victor Hugo mounted on a high base engraved in gold letters recalls the position taken by the French writer: his words on that occasion are certainly one of the best-known and best-studied texts of French-speaking literature in China. Elsewhere, the text is reproduced in large characters, Chinese and Roman, on a wide-open stone book. Since its creation in 2011, the National Museum of China has also reminded everyone of this violent history. It is no coincidence that the official slogan of the 'Chinese Dream' was launched within the museum itself. In the display entitled 'The Road to Rejuvenation', which among other things discusses the looting of the Summer Palace, the current secretary of the Chinese Communist Party, Xi Jinping, declared, on a highly publicized visit on 29 November 2012, that the time for renewal had come. Referring explicitly to Western military aggression in the mid nineteenth century, he noted that 'the Chinese people have never given up' and that they have 'succeeded in becoming masters of [their] own destiny'[12] – formulas that were then constantly repeated, for example on the occasion of the centenary of the Chinese Communist Party in 2021, when Xi declared:

> After the Opium War of 1840, however, China was gradually reduced to a semi-colonial, semi-feudal society and suffered greater ravages than ever before. The country endured intense humiliation, the people were subjected to great pain, and the Chinese civilization was plunged into darkness. Since that time, national rejuvenation has been the greatest dream of the Chinese people and the Chinese nation.[13]

Attention to Chinese history, the memory of the 'century of humiliation' and its gradual overcoming, and an increasingly uninhibited nationalism were henceforth closely intertwined.

It is no surprise, in this context, that the bronze heads of the Summer Palace, and more generally the heritage looted from China, have been a major focus of attention in the media and popular culture of Asia. In 2012, Jackie Chan devoted an entire film to the history and future of the bronze heads taken from the Summer Palace, *Chinese Zodiac*, which he produced and in which he played the lead role. Although almost no one in the West paid attention to this curious moment in cinematography that combined martial arts, historical reconstructions, and contemporary issues of heritage justice and restitution, it broke box-office records in many countries in Asia and the Middle East. Thanks to an incalculable number of stunts, which also earned him an entry in *The Guinness Book of Records*, Jackie Chan himself, playing an agent of modern China, manages to infiltrate the castle of a group of extremely rich French people, where he finds the famous bronzes and sets out to bring them back to his country.

In contrast to this nationalist heritage rhetoric, dissidents accuse the Chinese government of using the case of the bronze heads to distract the population from China's 'real' problems. This is what the artist Ai Weiwei suggested in the statements and interviews surrounding his 2011 creation of his spectacular installation *The Circle of Animals / Zodiac Heads*, which embarked on a world tour in 2013. The work, of which there are several versions, shows gigantic reproductions of the twelve animal heads originally grouped around the water clock of the Summer Palace. It plays on the question of proportions, the original and the copy, and the materiality of things and their value, with some of the bronze heads becoming gold heads in Ai Weiwei's installation. On his blog – subsequently censored – the artist informed the public of the hybrid, Italian–Asian nature of the contested works, defending a concept of culture very far removed from contemporary Chinese nationalism and insisting on the need for a real public debate in China over the history of the country, the 'value that the heads *really* represent', and the extent of the destruction carried out by Europeans in comparison with the damage wrought by China on its own heritage. In short, with this work, it is not a question of proving one side or the other right or wrong, but of recalling that no judgement is possible without precise historical knowledge and collective discussion. As a consequence, it is the very question of the memory of the lootings and their instrumentalization by the Chinese regime that become the object of the work of art. Finally, Ai Weiwei concludes that art is made to circulate – his *Circle of Animals / Zodiac Heads*, exhibited all over the world, attests to this.

## Sharing, giving back, or leaving behind

And on the European side? Ignored or brushed aside for more than a century and a half by Western protagonists, private collectors, and the directors of public museums, the question of justice and restitution (or not) in connection with heritage items has become a burning issue in Asia and in the Asian diasporas around the world, and it has called for reactions in Europe. From at least 2009, public institutions have endeavoured (when not burying their heads in the sand) to invent a discourse likely to gain acceptance for the asymmetry between those who hold the largest share of the world's heritage (the museums of Europe and the United States) and those who have little or next to nothing and are indignant about it (the countries dispossessed in the nineteenth century in conditions of economic, military, or political inferiority). Alongside these public attempts to defuse the situation, some institutional actors in the private sector, particularly in the world of the art market and business, understand the advantages they can draw from the crystallization, in China, of identity-based passions in connection with historical heritage.

Some directors of public museums in the mid-2010s developed a concept that they hoped would be able to calm things down and counter the claims of dispossessed countries: shared heritage. The formula, in a nutshell, suggested that, yes indeed, objects from all over the world are physically to be found in museums in London, Berlin, Paris, or Amsterdam, but that they belong morally and culturally to all humanity – to everyone, so to speak – or to no one. In 2017, for example, the Dutch Ministry of Education, Culture, and Science launched an international training programme for heritage professionals entitled: 'Sharing stories on contested histories.' The focus was on Dutch history – its colonial past, its international relations, the traces of this shared heritage, and the resulting 'contested' histories. The programme explained that archives, museum collections, and also intangible heritage (traditions, social practices, rituals, festivals, crafts, performing arts, etc.) were part of a common heritage of the formerly colonized peoples and the former colonists. In Germany, too – in the very particular context of the former castle of the Prussian kings in the heart of Berlin, demolished in 1949 but rebuilt to house the Museum of Asian Art and the ethnological collections of former Prussia – the concept of 'shared heritage' flourished. It was expressed in the brochures promoting the institution, which in 2016 claimed to be, in its own words, the 'epicentre of shared heritage': 'We are jointly responsible for the cultural heritage of humanity. We must therefore share it with the nations that we once subjected to colonial domination.' Sharing, in the minds of these institutions, did not at that time mean either lend or return, and very quickly the concept turned out to be a dead end. While it is easy for those who own the objects in their museums to affirm that they 'share' the responsibility for them, it is more difficult to conceptualize the idea of 'sharing' on the part of those who do not physically own the objects.

The rhetoric of shared heritage fizzled out. In the private domain, there was an admittedly more sophisticated, but also very political, reaction to China's heritage claims. In 2015, Sotheby's Institute of Art, a private for-profit educational institute dependent on the London auction house, produced and broadcast a short documentary that played on the notion of impossible sharing (or non-consensual sharing). We see in close-up the well-groomed hands and then the face of a relaxed fifty-something in a white shirt – Ian Robertson himself, the then director of the department of studies of the art market and emerging markets at Sotheby's Institute – facing the camera, holding in both hands a small red car.[14] He addresses the viewer directly, asking them to imagine that they are the owner of an ancient statue, and that someone says 'It's mine, not yours.' Then he turns his face, with the camera following him, to address a small boy sitting next to him, and bids the viewer to imagine that this someone is the greatest economic power in the world. The child makes as if to take the toy from the adult's hands, but in vain. He withdraws into himself, sad and frustrated. End of the prologue. The credits announce the subject of the film: Art Repatriation, which, in the form of a cartoon, revisits the history of the Summer Palace and its looting, which it compares with the economic power of twenty-first-century Chinese millionaires. The message: potential Chinese clients, you have the financial power not only to buy back your country's historical heritage on the art market, but also, in a patriotic spirit, to contribute to the 'Chinese Dream' by donating it to your public museums. The double detour through history and the motif of humiliation; the difference between the great who possess and the small who cannot possess anything, the toy that is useless in the hands of the adult but could make sense, or give joy, to the child; the image of a heritage that cannot be shared: in this fable created by Sotheby's, the questions of money, symbolic capital and real capital, collective trauma and individual power, market and heritage are skilfully and inextricably linked. Or, to put it another way: Chinese millionaires, avenge your long-humiliated nation by buying back its honour and its historical heritage from the countries that have been proud possessors of it for centuries and refuse to give it back. Sotheby's subtly invites its potential clients to circumvent the inflexibility of Western institutions and states by investing in it in order to eventually obtain the repatriation and renationalization of lost assets.

This example shows to what extent the art market is linked to the question of translocations and the aesthetic appropriation of art, to the creation of museums, but also to contemporary artistic creation. The worlds of culture, art, economics, and politics are porous. Museums are not just 'places of culture' dissociated from the world of money; and the world of money is not a closed entity, impermeable to other spheres of society. On the contrary: we can clearly see in the case of these bronze heads that money plays a major role in the feeling of cultural and identity appropriation. Because even if several heads have been recovered by China, others have yet to be located and taken back. Like the ruins of Yuan Ming Yuan, the incomplete zodiac recalls the violation of Chinese identity by the Europeans. But, at the same time, it leaves open the prospect of a definitive completion.

## Full circle

Let's return to the Grand Palais in February 2009. The Chinese administration responsible for cultural heritage condemned, as I noted above, the sale of the bronze heads that, through the centuries, had moved from the collection of the emperor of China to that of Yves Saint Laurent and Pierre Bergé. It threatened Christie's, which has been active in China since 1994, with increased customs controls if the sale went ahead.[15] A few days before the event, a group of eighty-one Chinese lawyers also filed a request with the Paris High Court to block the sale, a request that was rejected by a French judge. The plaintiffs were even ordered to pay a fine to the auction house. For the latter, in fact, nothing prevented the bronze heads from being put back into circulation: having changed hands several times over the centuries, they could and must now continue their journey on the global art market. Christie's stated that it had been doing everything possible, for many years, to contribute to the return (repatriation) of Chinese heritage to China, by offering repurchase opportunities to collectors who were then free to take them home. The sale finally took place. The heads were auctioned over the phone, and reached a price of 28 million euros. But the anonymous buyer refused to pay for them. Two days after this sabotage, while the identity of the buyer (a member of the 'Chinese National Treasures Fund', a non-profit association close to the government, responsible since 2005 for recovering looted Chinese treasures) and his moral and patriotic motives were revealed, Pierre Bergé announced that the heads would be reinstated in his collection. The animosity of the Chinese media extended to the whole of France, but also to Christie's, which feared that the highly promising Chinese art market would slip away from it.

Four years later, there was a dramatic turn of events: François-Henri Pinault, chairman and CEO of the Kering group, to which Christie's belongs, took advantage of a visit to China by French President François Hollande to propose to Xi Jinping's new government that he donate the two objects purchased for a secret sum from Pierre Bergé. Officially, the idea was to strengthen Franco-Chinese diplomatic and commercial ties, but also, and above all, it was to repair the severe damage caused by the 2009 controversy – especially since the Pinault group's luxury brands (including Gucci, Yves Saint Laurent, and Balenciaga) – were highly sought after in China. On 28 June 2013, 153 years after they were violently torn from the Summer Palace by French and British troops, François-Henri Pinault, accompanied by his father François, returned the animal heads to China in a highly publicized ceremony at the National Museum in Tiananmen Square. Christie's CEO at the time, Steven P. Murphy, said:

> The generous gift to the people of China of these historic works of art marks a memorable act of philanthropy by the Pinault family. As one of the leading proponents of the importance of cultural heritage, Christie's is delighted to have played an instrumental part in ensuring their return. We welcome the fact that they will now go on display in the National Museum of China where many millions of Chinese and visitors to China will have the wonderful opportunity to appreciate them once again.[16]

In 1861, the republican Victor Hugo had called for a 'France liberated and purified' to return the looted treasures to China. Since the bronze heads had never entered public collections (where they would have been inalienable), it was not the French Republic, but a private actor symbolically replacing it, who carried out the spectacular restitution at the beginning of the twenty-first century. The emperor of China has long since ceased to exist, as has the French emperor under whose auspices the looting took place. Other empires – financial

**1860 to twentieth century**: arrival of animal heads in Europe, where they are put on sale on the art market and moved into various collections before Pierre Bergé and Yves Saint Laurent acquire the rat and rabbit heads.

**2009**: auction of the Pierre Bergé – Yves Saint Laurent collection in **Paris**; a Chinese collector, Cai Ming Chao, acquires the two heads, but refuses to pay for them and demands their return.

**2013**: François-Henri Pinault buys the two heads and returns them to the Chinese government. They have since been exhibited at the National Museum in **Beijing**.

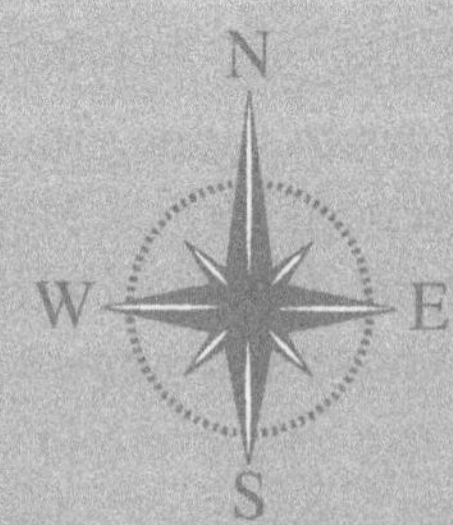

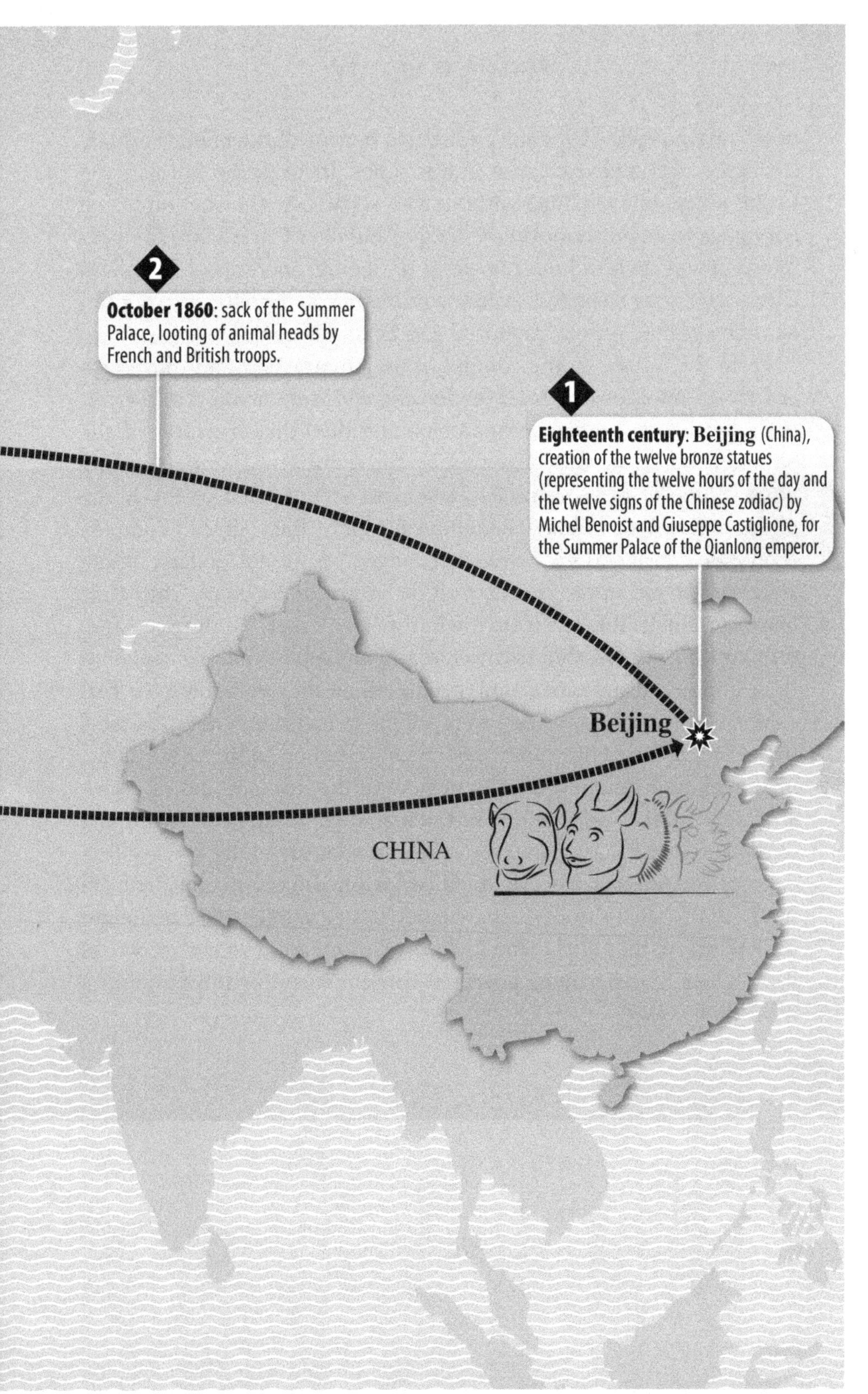
2
October 1860: sack of the Summer Palace, looting of animal heads by French and British troops.
1
Eighteenth century: Beijing (China), creation of the twelve bronze statues (representing the twelve hours of the day and the twelve signs of the Chinese zodiac) by Michel Benoist and Giuseppe Castiglione, for the Summer Palace of the Qianlong emperor.
Beijing
CHINA

ones – have replaced them. A collateral benefit of the affair: in 2013, Christie's obtained exclusive authorization to organize sales in the People's Republic of China without a local partner. The auction house continues to boast about this to the present day: 'Christie's is the only international auction house licensed to operate auctions in Mainland China,' states its website.[17] A fine commercial and political operation has been grafted onto a memorial and historical affair.

From the outset, in the context of the Opium War and the West's economic ambitions in Asia, the looting and translocation of the rat, the rabbit, their bronze companions, and the other treasures of the Summer Palace were determined by the question of money and its flows. Some of the inestimable treasures accumulated at the home of the emperor of China – who himself was at the centre of complex economic constellations – were exchanged on site for dollars; others were monetized upon their arrival in France or England. They thus became monetizable assets on the European market. On the one hand, they concentrated within themselves the immense symbolic capital of their imperial provenance, and, on the other, they embodied the real capital that wealthy collectors were willing to invest in order to possess them. Other forms of capital were also grafted on to them: aesthetic, historical, and military. This is how, over the decades and in retrospect, the market became one of the main beneficiaries of the looting of the Summer Palace. However, in the first decades of the twenty-first century, this market has expanded and opened up to regions that did not have the means to participate before. The customers are no longer only Western; they also come from the regions from which the works were taken. This has huge potential consequences for the geopolitics of world heritage.

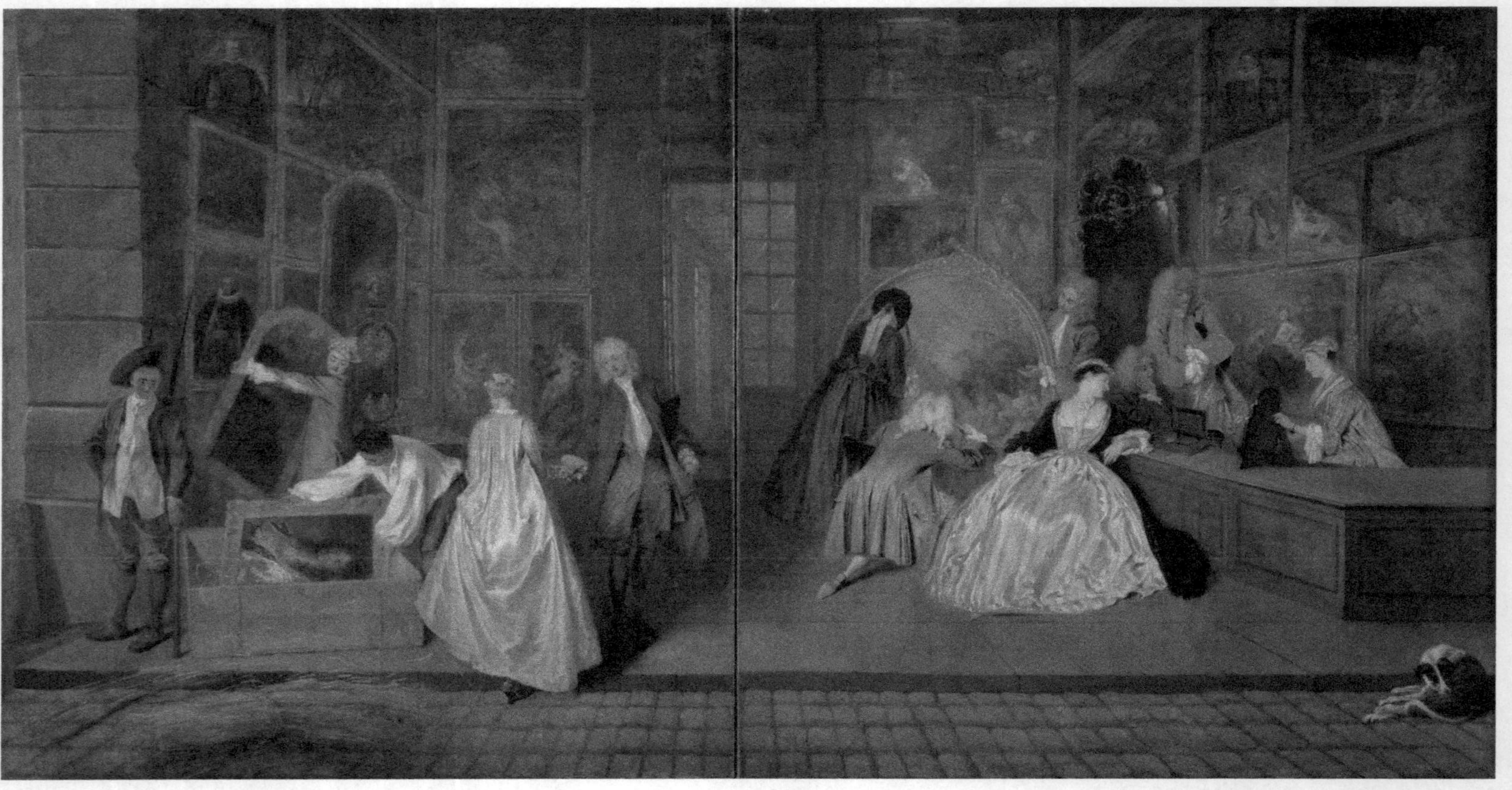

Antoine Watteau, *L'Enseigne de Gersaint*, 1720, oil on canvas, 166 × 306 cm. Charlottenburg Palace, Berlin, Stiftung Preussische Schlösser und Gärten. Photo © Scala, Florence / bpk, Bildagentur für Kunst, Kultur und Geschichte, Berlin.

# 6

# WATTEAU'S *L'ENSEIGNE DE GERSAINT*

In front of this painting, the great art historian Pierre Rosenberg once said: 'It's poignant.' Poignant to know that the painter Antoine Watteau, according to legend, painted it in a few days, at the age of thirty-six, very shortly before his death? Poignant, all those paintings within the painting, this canvas that contains dozens of others? Poignant, the absence of a shopfront, which makes us look at the scene like an eye without an eyelid? Poignant, the harmonies of colours impossible to capture by reproduction or photography? Poignant, the gestures of seduction, the looks, the twisting bodies and faces, the folds of fabrics, wigs, headdresses? Poignant, the concentration of those beautiful people who love art and love themselves (in the mirror on the right)? Or this old couple, the man on his knees, white wig and cane in hand, the woman all in black, who, seen from behind, seem absorbed by the flesh of several young naked women near a spring of water, in the large oval of a rural scene? Poignant, the crating and coffining of a portrait (on the left), when the artist himself feels that his time is running out? Poignant, the little dog scratching its fleas against the century-old cobblestones of Paris, the street that invades the scene, and the bits of straw in such a refined microcosm? Poignant, the melancholy and strangeness of the painting?

*L'Enseigne de Gersaint*, painted at the end of 1720, shows the idealized interior of the gallery of the very young art dealer

Edme-François Gersaint. He had just given free accommodation to his friend Watteau, whose health and business were in very poor shape. In one and the same gesture, the painting says thank you and farewell. It was acquired around 1745 by the king of Prussia, Frederick II, known as Frederick the Great, an ardent lover of French culture, literature, philosophy, and painting. Since the eighteenth century, *L'Enseigne de Gersaint* has been kept in Berlin, to the great regret of various French intellectuals who, in the twentieth century, never stopped calling for its return, because its 'voluptuous blur', to quote Stendhal, is for some the very essence of 'French taste'. But is not a painting that is 'so French' but so far from France, in its very enemy's home, also poignant?

In almost 300 years, between its departure from Paris in the 1740s and our twenty-first century, *L'Enseigne de Gersaint* has been shown in France only four times: at the Palais de Tokyo in Paris in 1937, as part of the International Exhibition of Arts and Technology; at the Petit Palais in 1951, in an exhibition extorted, so to speak, from the museums of Berlin, which will be discussed below; at the Louvre in 1963, the day after the signing of the Élysée Treaty that sealed the reconciliation of France and West Germany, in a very political exhibition on 'eighteenth-century French painting at the court of Frederick II'; and at the Grand Palais in 1984, under the direction of the young Pierre Rosenberg, for the artist's third centenary – the first and 'formidable exhibition'[1] of Watteau's work in France, where *L'Enseigne de Gersaint* rubbed shoulders with other works from West Berlin. 'You have to go straight to the unexpected enclosure where the two Cythères are gathered – the one from the Louvre, cleaned and therefore fresher, and the one from Berlin – *L'Enseigne de Gersaint* and the *Gilles*, outstanding works that have the miraculous power to resurface perpetually unscathed from the daydreams and chatter that we never tire of wrapping them in', as the art historian André Chastel enthused in *Le Monde*.[2]

Why talk of an 'unexpected enclosure'? What was at stake between France and Germany from the eighteenth to the twentieth century with this *L'Enseigne de Gersaint* that aroused such a particular mixture of political and aesthetic emotions? Who owns its blurriness and the grip it exercises?

## The diplomacy of exhibitions

At the end of the Second World War, Berlin's museums were in ruins, like the rest of the largely destroyed city. While the Red Army recovered from their hiding places, tunnels, bunkers, and salt mines in the east of the country the public collections once held by German museums, and shipped them to the Soviet Union, the victorious American army also found in other hiding places, tunnels, bunkers, and salt mines the masterpieces sheltered by the same museums in the west of the country, and grouped them in reserves called 'collecting points'. Then the American authorities selected 200 paintings by old masters and transported them to the United States. For over a year, between the spring of 1948 and the spring of 1949, a spectacular exhibition, 'Berlin Masterpieces', travelled across the country, from Washington to Los Angeles, via New York, Philadelphia, Boston, Chicago, Portland, and San Francisco, to name just a handful of stops. The pictorial jewel of the public collections of former Prussia, which no longer had any legal or political existence and could be considered a dismantled state, was presented to nearly two and a half million American visitors. By Law No. 46 of 25 February 1947, the Allies, victorious over Hitler, proclaimed the dissolution of the Prussian state and expelled the Germans still east of the Oder River so that Polish and Soviet nationals could settle there. The rich collections formed in Berlin by the kings of Prussia, who had become emperors of Germany – their public libraries, archives, and museums: all of these no longer had a master. In 1948–9, the US tour of the paintings from these collections can be understood both as a tribute to European culture, safe and sound after the atrocities of the war, and as an exhibition of trophies snatched by the 'free world' from a finally crushed Germany, as an additional victory over the vanquished. Following the American tour, the military managers of the Prussian collections offered Europe another series of travelling exhibitions, which took place in Amsterdam (1950), Brussels (1950–1), and Paris (1951). It was in this context that *L'Enseigne de Gersaint* was exhibited, between February and May 1951, at the Petit Palais, in the heart of the liberated French capital. The curator André Chamson took care of the museography. He created elegant settings for the works, highlighting them using the most modern lighting techniques: the aim was to serve the message of humanity and peace that the paintings were intended to convey. In a large room hung with velvet, right in the centre of the exhibition, *L'Enseigne de Gersaint* was given pride of place. Mounted in a specially designed frame-base, it was protected from visitors by a heavy twisted cord and a specially appointed guard, and from temperature variations by a hygrometer placed very close. In the opening piece of the catalogue, Chamson emphasized the luxury that such an event represented:

> It was not so long ago that the art lover who dreamed of seeing certain masterpieces could not do so without immediately thinking of long journeys. To see Van Eyck's *Portrait of a Man with a Carnation* or Rembrandt's *The Man with the Golden Helmet*, for example, was to go to Berlin. The work of art could not be separated from the place of its residence, and this geography of masterpieces was one of the elements of our culture. However, no deep necessity linked the *Mona Lisa* to our Louvre, nor the *Woman with a Pearl Necklace* to the Kaiser-Friedrich-Museum. These great works are at home everywhere and solitary everywhere. They had, however, integrated themselves into these large ensembles that chance, pleasure, or science have formed, and that we call Museums. How can we separate the *Mona Lisa* from Paris? Or the *Woman with a Pearl Necklace* from Berlin? So people travelled to see an illustrious painting ... Today, it is the painting that travels.[3]

If the concept of the public museum dates back to the 1750s in Europe, as we have seen, that of the temporary exhibition is much more recent. The art historian Francis Haskell has reconstructed the history of such exhibitions in a work poetically entitled *The Ephemeral Museum*.[4] As products of the nineteenth century, these temporary spectacles flourished in Europe at the same time as the World's Fairs and, according to Haskell, were part of the same logic of national affirmation in an international context. While the World's Fairs mainly allowed nations to present their technological and industrial innovations, even if art was not absent, the monographic retrospectives on artists such as Raphael, Poussin, Dürer, or Michelangelo served as cultural standards to display the greatness of their civilization abroad.

When, for example, Fascist Italy organized travelling exhibitions in Europe on Titian or Tintoretto in the 1930s, the aim was to place the great Renaissance painters at the service of its influence.[5] This was the advent of what is called exhibition diplomacy. Beyond purely aesthetic, historical, didactic, or scientific interests (the 'purely' not existing in these areas), this new diplomacy imposed on the works an extreme mobility that was also a form of mobilization, to flatter certain patriotisms, strengthen alliances, spread ideologies, or arouse phenomena of collective identification. Today, more than ever, many 'national' exhibitions are the subject of clever montages and behind-the-scenes political negotiations. On 2 February 1951, six years after the end of the Second World War, the exhibition 'Masterpieces from the Berlin Museums' was conceived and presented as a moment of reconciliation, while a politically unified Europe was being built. Its inauguration was a major cultural event in Paris. It was accompanied by a programme of art films in the Petit Palais film club; the Office de radiodiffusion-télévision française (ORTF) came to shoot a report for the television news, the press reported extensively on it, and an illustrated catalogue allowed everyone to take home the memory of this exceptional moment. On 24 March 1951, *Le Progrès de Lyon* welcomed the arrival of the Berlin works in Paris. As an effect of style and syntax, in this article the paintings themselves seem to have decided to make the journey, to come and 'stand' before the eyes of Parisians:

> There is something unexpected in the journeys that rich art collections make through space, and people do not sufficiently appreciate the exceptional nature of these journeys that the Museums of Munich, Vienna, and now Berlin have undertaken successively, and of which Paris is always the happy stopover. Seeing the masterpieces that you have dreamed of, works brought together by centuries of taste, finesse, and knowledge, come to you and stand before your gaze in a seductive staging is one of the delights that an era can provide even though it is more likely to disappoint wishes than to grant them.

But, clearly, the arrival of the paintings from the public collections of Prussia, hailed here as an exceptional moment of cultural delight, was also a political act of the first order, whose backstory is mentioned by neither the organizers nor the journalist from *Le Progrès de Lyon*.[6] This act, first of all, was based on a lack of consent: that of the Berlin museums, which were forced to move (at high risk) ancient masterpieces weakened by several years of war. The 20,000 kilometres that 'their' paintings were made to travel in the United States and the European tour in the early 1950s were the result of a unilateral decision taken by the victors of the Second World War, without any agreement, contract, or discussion with the Berlin institutions, the historical guardians of the works for several centuries. In fact, the exhibition seemed to take place *against* Berlin's will.

Placed by the Western Allies and the Parisian art-historical elite under the banner of 'reconciliation', the exhibition was tacitly perceived by Berlin as an additional act of violence against paintings that had just spent ten years of war in precarious conditions of conservation. 'Tacitly', because their position as the vanquished population of an abolished state certainly did not give the heads of the Berlin museums much chance to protest vigorously and in (written) forms that could be found in the archives today. Moreover, the museum curators are not even mentioned in the long list of acknowledgements that opens the exhibition catalogue.[7] 'Additional' because, in addition to the physical stress inflicted on some delicate works, the curators of Berlin museums had to endure being kept completely in the dark about the future of their collections, of which they had had almost no news since the end of the war and whose global circulation was then organized without their say-so. Not only were they ignorant, at the beginning of the 1950s, of the fate of the works transported to the Soviet Union, as we saw in the chapter devoted to Raphael's 'Sistine Madonna', but also they struggled to obtain information on the intentions of the Western military authorities, who, after circulating their paintings in the United States, rather than returning them to Berlin, replaced them in the collecting points administered by them since 1945. At these collecting points, many flagship works, including the bust of Nefertiti, were gathered, far from the former capital of the Reich.

It was from one of these collecting points, in Wiesbaden near Frankfurt, that the paintings left Berlin in 1950 for Amsterdam, Brussels, and Paris. Obviously, the Berlin museums were not involved in the choice of the works, which were different from those that had circulated in the United States. It was the authorities of the three host countries who decided, in dialogue with the American army, which ones they wished to exhibit. They also selected the work to be reproduced on the cover of the various catalogues.

Paradoxically, although the exhibition catalogue was entitled *Masterpieces from the Berlin Museums*, no German painter appeared on the cover. Amsterdam chose a Vermeer (Dutch); Brussels, a portrait by Petrus Christus (Flemish); and Paris, Watteau's *L'Enseigne de Gersaint* – all 'modest' signs of the national intentions and tensions that ran through this moment of pro-European affirmation. At the end of the Paris exhibition, moreover, certain paintings (a Caravaggio, a Velázquez, and engravings by Goya) were sent by the management of the Petit Palais to Milan and Bordeaux, without Berlin being informed.

A polite telegram, dated spring 1951, shows to what extent the Berlin curators were excluded from the game: worried about seeing 'their' works handled, loaned, and moved throughout Europe, they cautiously sounded out the organizers to find out the date on which the Parisian exhibition would end.[8] In other letters, they inquired about the possibility of obtaining a copy of the catalogue[9] and perhaps even (!) of collecting royalties on the postcards sold. This correspondence is more significant than it seems. It testifies to a balance of power and a decision-making geography profoundly transformed by the war, including in the world of arts and beauty, which is also a world of dominant and dominated forces; finally, it testifies to the growing frustration of the Berlin museums, then empty, and to the clearly uncollegial spirit in which the European protagonists – here, the French – operated.

But, naturally, the official discourse of the organizers of the exhibition in Paris overshadowed the 'German question' – namely, the uncertainty that had weighed on the future of the public collections of Prussia ever since this latter state had been abolished. Indeed, at the Petit Palais, the 'Masterpieces of the Berlin Museums' were mobilized to recall, after the trauma of the war years, the existence of a happy, united, and pacified Europe of culture. Coming from Berlin, the Cranachs, Dürers, Rembrandts, Vermeers, Caravaggios, Lancrets, and Watteaus became the representatives, the ambassadors, of friendly nations seeking to rise from their ashes and reconnect with the ideal of a common civilization. When it headlined 'The artistic army of Europe was inaugurated by Mr Maurice Schuman [*sic*]', *Le Provençal* of 21 February 1951 spoke clearly of a mobilization of the arts for post-military purposes. Elsewhere, the press insisted on the wonderful transnational dimension of the project, there was talk of 'United Europe ... at the Petit-Palais'[10] and of 'Masterpieces on a visit'.[11] In the March 1951 edition of *L'Âge Nouveau*, the assistant curator of the Petit Palais, Louis Jondot, deployed the official rhetoric associated with the event:

> Not one of the least curious consequences of the last war is that it raises us towards the peaceful regions of the spirit by proposing for our admiration and our mediation works that have crossed the centuries and their upheavals. It seems that in front of such pieces, judiciously chosen from prestigious ensembles, the visitor escapes for a time the often excessive pace of modern life, by becoming more aware of the grandiose possibilities of the human.

For André Chamson, art historian and curator of the exhibition, it was a particular responsibility of museums to promote, through the benefits of careful museography, the unique human experience of a silent dialogue with beauty. Art was spiritual nourishment. Contemplating beauty and soaking it up, after 1945, was also a way of healing trauma, of 'regenerating' oneself – not from a national or military point of view, but from a cultural, aesthetic, and profoundly human point of view. In one of the eloquent texts he devoted to the exhibition, André Chamson noted:

> It is in the most ornate frames that we should be showing these van Eycks, these van der Weydens, these Petrus Christuses, this Geertgen tot Sint Jans, this Hieronymus Bosch and this Bruegel. There must be silence around the Fouquet and the Georges de la Tour, space around the 'Enseigne de Gersaint', a resting place for twelve Rembrandts and the two Vermeers....
>
> We hope that the visitor can recreate some solitude around these works, the smallest of which are sometimes the most monumental.

> For what gives us the feeling of the precious is perhaps nothing other than the presence of a world in an object that we could hold in our two hands: a world of psychological penetration and knowledge of man, a world open to all the spectacles of nature, from the sea to the mountains, a world of History or of Myths and Legends ... These are all the worlds that these portraits open up to us, these saints meditating in solitude, these young women with their smiles ... To look at such objects is doubtless to contemplate life with the gaze that the gods direct towards men: it is to see everything at a single glance.[12]

And indeed, judging by the photographic traces it has left in the archives, the staging of Berlin's works at the Petit Palais strove to encourage contemplation, introspection, and free aesthetic enjoyment, and even to attenuate noise. The rooms were covered with elegant grey and light pink curtains, with a very airy effect, while innovative neon tubes acted as lighting, and special spaces were dedicated to the main works. Despite a tense economic situation, the French public authorities invested heavily in the rediscovered experience of face-to-face encounters with the paintings. Some were world renowned, such as *The Man with the Golden Helmet*, a flagship piece of the Berlin museums then attributed to Rembrandt, shown in Paris in a kind of isolation booth symbolically enhanced, in the museum's vocabulary, by the presence of a security cordon. Watteau's *L'Enseigne de Gersaint*, for its part, benefitted from a generous spatial layout, and the regulation also provided for 'a guard ... permanently inside the cordon placed in front of [it]. This painting must be the object of special surveillance at all times.'[13] Photos show the guard, in a cap and black uniform, dozing askew on a padded chair, exposed as much as the work of art to the curiosity of men and women in overcoats and hats. The air must have been cold in the winter of 1951.

A 'special surveillance at all times'? But why Watteau? And why this work in particular? In fact, its arrival in Paris in 1951 was the culmination of several decades of aspirations and debates about the 'right place' for the work, about its national belonging. Moreover, the French authorities fought to obtain it. In a letter, written shortly after the opening of the exhibition in Paris, the American officer in charge of the Wiesbaden collections wrote: 'It is impossible to overemphasize the importance, in the eyes of the organizers of the exhibition, of the inclusion of Watteau's *L'Enseigne de Gersaint*.... In brief: the French have given this great painting the special care that its importance demanded.'[14]

In fact, right from the opening of the exhibition, it was this painting, and almost this painting alone, much more than all the other paintings in the Berlin museums, that attracted the attention of the press and the public. All the articles devoted to the exhibition reproduced it in photographs. *Paris-Match* printed it, highly unusually, as a double spread in colour, an expensive process that was generally reserved, at the time, for cover pages and stars. Even before the inauguration of the exhibition, an anonymous journalist exclaimed in *Arts*: 'We will see "L'Enseigne de Gersaint" again in Paris!';[15] elsewhere, insistent plural possessives proliferated: 'This treasure is returning to us at the Petit-Palais after leaving the Pont-Neuf; it has definitely escaped our heritage, but fortunately has been preserved in the heritage of humanity', noted the short-lived magazine *Femmes républicaines* in its February 1951 issue.[16]

Six years after the end of the Second World War, despite the omnipresent European and pacifist rhetoric of the exhibition, the idea that *L'Enseigne de Gersaint* had 'escaped' from France's heritage was deeply rooted in the collective consciousness. Some journalists explicitly claimed ownership of it. In *Paris Presse*, the art critic André Salmon, while welcoming the just return of the Watteau, 'a marvel of French art', suggested that the acquisition of the painting by the king of Prussia had been dubious, and recalled a Franco-German dispute from half a century earlier that had left a bad taste: 'We do not know the circumstances in which the King of Prussia, Frederick II, acquired the twin canvases finally shown to the Parisians. In 1900, Emperor Wilhelm refused to lend them for the (universal) Exhibition. They adorned his private apartments.'[17]

A marvel of French taste in the private apartments of a coarse Kaiser – it would be difficult to suggest more explicitly how much some people at the beginning of the 1950s felt that German ownership of this Watteau was incongruous. This incongruity triggered animated discussions for several decades.

## Potsdam, the 1740s

What do we actually know about the initial move of the Watteau from Paris to Berlin? Contrary to what Salmon suggests, the circumstances of its acquisition by Prussia are well known. Watteau died in 1721 and the painting remained for some time in the hands of his friend Gersaint. But, at the beginning of the eighteenth century, the art trade, of which Gersaint was a major player in Europe – and Paris a hub – did not allow paintings to remain in place for long. Great Parisian collectors, and the sovereigns of Europe from Dresden to Saint Petersburg, via Stockholm, Karlsruhe, Potsdam, and Warsaw, were in search of old masters, mainly Italian and Flemish, to build up the collections in the great public galleries discussed in the previous chapters, or to fill their personal cabinets. At a time when French culture and language were omnipresent in Europe, these representatives of the aristocracy and the upper middle class maintained networks of agents who – in Paris, in particular – acquired for them contemporary pieces considered to be significant, including works by Chardin, Boucher, and Watteau.

After twenty years spent in two Parisian collections, around 1745 *L'Enseigne de Gersaint* was ceded to Count Friedrich Rudolph von Rothenburg, a friend and agent of Frederick II of Prussia. Very early on, while still crown prince, the latter collected French painters of his generation for his own pleasure (and not for the gallery of paintings that he would later form). His extreme aesthetic sensitivity, his taste for men, for music, and for philosophy, clashed with the brutality of his father, nicknamed the 'king-sergeant'. Thus, when as an adult the future Frederick II surrounded himself with French paintings, delightful portraits of children or gallant parties (*fêtes galantes*), this has to be seen as a counter-programme to the education and principles he had endured during adolescence, marked by the execution, practically in front of his eyes, of a young officer with whom he had fallen in love. Like *L'Enseigne de Gersaint* in 1744, one of the three versions of Watteau's famous *The Embarkation for Cythera* known today entered Frederick's collection in the 1740s, by which time he was king. These acquisitions occurred at exactly the same time as the elector of Saxony and king of Poland purchased a hundred paintings from the gallery of the duke of Modena and negotiated in Parma the sale of Raphael's 'Sistine Madonna'. About his Parisian purchases, Frederick wrote to his brother, in French:

> I have received eight paintings from France more beautiful than all those you have seen and of a colouring that puts nature to shame, I am still waiting for fourteen that I picked up by chance for a hunk of bread; they will be used to decorate my Vineyard (Sans Souci) and Charlottenburg; these paintings perhaps give me more pleasure than the king of Poland finds in looking at his gallery in Modena, and certainly there is no comparison between the object and the expense.[18]

Fifteen years later, when Austrian troops invaded Berlin and pillaged Charlottenburg Palace, the Watteaus 'by a singular stroke of fortune' – says a contemporary source – were miraculously spared.[19] In 1806 and 1807, when Napoleonic troops occupied Berlin and Dominique-Vivant Denon, the director of the Louvre, selected from the royal castles and galleries the hundreds of paintings and antiquities 'worthy', according to the vocabulary of the time, of being taken to Paris, he ignored these French paintings, doubtless too contemporary for the Louvre, too well represented in France, and not (yet) corresponding to the taste of the time.

*L'Enseigne de Gersaint* and the other French paintings of Frederick II survived the difficult years of the Napoleonic occupation of Berlin without damage and continued to silently adorn the Hohenzollern castles throughout the nineteenth century. It was only around 1900, in a context of Franco-German enmity exacerbated by the resentment of the war of 1870 and the humiliating proclamation of the German Empire at Versailles in 1871, well after the rediscovery of Watteau and the *fêtes galantes* by the generation of the Goncourt brothers, that French public opinion started to worry about it.

A first drama unfolded during the highly symbolic World's Fair in Paris in 1900 and marked the start of a new century. The German imperial government chose to present there, halfway between what it called a 'tribute to the imperishable glory that the French nation acquired in the eighteenth century in the field of the arts'[20] and a provocation over the ownership of heritage, a vast exhibition of the art collections of Frederick the Great. It was a perilous exercise in cultural and diplomatic balancing. Everything was there: Watteau, the *fêtes galantes*, a famous bust of Voltaire by the sculptor Houdon, furniture imported from France by the philosopher-king. Everything ... except *L'Enseigne de Gersaint* and the 'Berlin' version of *The Embarkation for Cythera*. While Parisian critics noted this without being explicitly bothered by it, this absence gnawed at people's minds as relations between France and Germany became strained in the years preceding the First World War – especially since, on both sides of the Rhine, Watteau and these two works now crystallized an abundant discourse on the singularity of art, taste, and more generally of the French spirit in the eighteenth century. For some in France, these paintings were the pure emanation of a bygone era, for which they fostered a sense of nostalgia. For others, in Germany, they were the space for the projection of an idealized vision of an art of living, whose elegance was opposed not only, in their view, to contemporary Germanic heaviness, but also to the animosity of a neighbour whom they no longer recognized.

In March 1900, the composer Richard Strauss was in Paris and visited the Louvre with Romain Rolland. They were both thirty-five years old. Rolland was then teaching art history at the École Normale Supérieure, and Strauss, who had also studied this discipline, was now conducting the orchestra of the Berlin Opera. They passed in front of the Parisian version of *The Embarkation for Cythera*, and what both noted in their journals allows us to sense with great immediacy the 'Watteau effect' in those years. Romain Rolland writes: '[Strauss] has a real taste in painting, and a taste for fashion.... He recognizes the superiority of the great Watteau; he says that this "Embarkation [for Cythera]" is a kind of *Märchen-Malerei* [a fairy-tale painting]. The happiness and ease of life that emerge from the eighteenth century caress him pleasantly.'[21] For his part, after the visit to the Louvre, Strauss noted in his journal the idea of music for a ballet that he would call *The Island of Cythera* after Antoine Watteau.[22] The work was actually begun, but ultimately remained a fragment. Ten years after its notable absence from Paris, the Berlin version of *L'Enseigne de Gersaint* was exhibited with great pomp at the Berlin Academy of Fine Arts, opposite the French Embassy and a stone's throw from the Brandenburg Gate, where Prussia and the German Empire had become accustomed to celebrating their military victories. In Paris, this 1910 German homage to French painting this time provoked explicit criticism. On the eve of the First World War, Watteau was no longer just a painter. He was the incarnation of an *elsewhere*, a *before*, a dreamed *self* or *other*; he was also and above all a political object.

## Crime, art, and punishment

> They have paintings in Berlin ... many paintings, first-rate, and mainly French paintings! Quite unknowingly and less wittingly than their divine Mozart, our Antoine Watteau never stopped working for the King of Prussia....
>
> At the mere mention of our works of art in exile, we glimpse potential 'repossessions' or 'compensations' that would be part of the formidable indemnity owed to us....
>
> It is not at all a question of stealing, not even from the thieves, but of honestly taking back our property, of retaking without haste and without hatred our dispersed treasures, or of mercilessly demanding compensation. The honour of France demands them.[23]

It was a now forgotten art critic, Raymond Bouyer, who, in January 1919, formulated this demand in the art magazine *Le Cousin Pons*. Directed by a journalist then known for his monarchist ideas and his proximity to the Action Française and Charles Maurras, the magazine gave Bouyer several pages where, under the title 'The question of works of art and the French paintings of the king of Prussia,' he described the destruction of heritage inflicted by the German army on France and the idea of taking back from Germany, as compensation, the Watteaus from the Prussian collections. According to Bouyer, in fact, these collections 'shelter[ed] the distant integrity of an immortal "little France"' exiled in a distant land, works that would need to be repatriated – integrity being the exact opposite of the state of ruin in which post-war France found itself. Applied to *L'Enseigne de Gersaint*, these 1919 demands were part of a more general European movement advocating the payment by Germany and Austria of heavy war indemnities not only in money or territory, but also in works of art – a discourse, as we saw in the chapter devoted to the altarpiece of 'The Mystic Lamb,' which indeed found legal expression in the Treaty of Versailles: it ordered the 'restitution' to Belgium, by the museums of Berlin and Munich, of works that had nevertheless been legally acquired by the latter on the art market in the nineteenth century.

As for Watteau's paintings in the Prussian collections, and despite the pressure exerted by articles such as Bouyer's, they were ultimately not included in the reparations demanded from Germany and they remained in Berlin after 1919. At that time, however, their legal status changed: having been the property of the Hohenzollerns (members of the Prussian royal family who became German emperors) since the mid eighteenth century, they were – after the abdication of Emperor Wilhelm II, the Revolution of 1918, and the advent of the Weimar Republic – declared the property of the German people, as were the imperial castles themselves, most of which were transformed into state museums. But this change in status did not prevent some French intellectuals of the interwar period from continuing to regret their presence on the other side of the Rhine, and imagining their return.

After the Second World War, which they spent partly sheltered from bombing in a mine in the Kassel region in western Germany, Watteau's paintings, including *L'Enseigne de Gersaint,* were found intact by the Allies. Among the Monuments (Wo)men was 'Captain Rose Valland,' a French art historian known for her resistance actions at the Petit Palais museum:

> Very close to Kassel in the Harz, the 1st US Army penetrated the Bernterode mine, reaching a sanctuary dug more than five hundred metres underground where the bronze coffin of the King-Sergeant and that of his son Frederick the Great had been placed.... The crown of Prussia, the globe and the sceptre had been buried next to these mighty dead, with the now symbolic sword of Prince Albrecht of Prussia. The Bernterode mine also offered a safe haven to several hundred paintings from the Potsdam museums. How could we fail to mention with emotion all the masterpieces of our eighteenth century grouped around *L'Enseigne de Gersaint*?[24]

The reunions are not just an opportunity for emoting over artistic heritage. They motivated a second campaign of demands, even more bitter than that of 1919. In a manner typical of the great debates on the restitution of works of art, which systematically escape a binary political reading – where 'right' and 'left' would have well-defined antagonistic positions – it was in the Communist camp, this time, that the demand was voiced. In the spring of 1945, *Les Lettres françaises*, a literary review close to the Communist Party, published two virulent articles by Louis Aragon, 'Les désastres de la guerre' ('The disasters of war') (March 1945) and '*L'Enseigne de Gersaint*' (April 1945), reprinted and expanded a few months later in a book for bibliophiles – printed on numbered vellum, illustrated with a portrait of Watteau as a frontispiece and several details in sepia from *L'Enseigne de Gersaint*, which gave the book its title (1946). With an overwhelming verbal violence and pathos, which can probably only be explained by the immediate, horrifying physical experience of the war, Aragon demanded the painting's return to France. His position could be summed up in these terms:

> French art must return to France. This war would not be over if our prisoners, our deportees, remained in Germany. French art, which is a part of France, cannot remain in Germany when it has to play its part in France, in our renaissance. French art must return to France – from the hands unworthy of holding it, and for a transfusion of this spiritual blood we have shed. Berlin, Munich, Dresden cannot keep this living blood, this warm blood, this red blood of the French spirit while here we remain seated in our ruins, on the open graves of those who would have been the painters, the poets, and the scholars of the future. French art must return from Germany to France. French art, by right, belongs to France.[25]

This is a surprising position, both heavily ideological and rather lacking in nuance in its view of the arts, which here seem to be reduced to fuelling a nationalist phantasmagoria. For Aragon, the Watteau of Prussia intersects with what he calls the 'national question' – that is to say, the idea that artists maintain a visceral link with their nation of belonging. From this perspective, not only are their works of art associated with a people (of flesh and blood) and constitutive of an identity, but there also are peoples unworthy of possessing them. This supposed identity of the work and the country authorizes Aragon to demand not only a restitution, but more generally an atonement by the 'people' who own the work. As an unconditional militant of the Communist Party in the early years of the Cold War, the author here falls in line with the Soviet argument which, in 1945, justified the shipment of the Dresden and Berlin collections to the USSR as trophies, in compensation for lost lives. The juxtaposition of the softness, the blurred lines and the tender colours of Watteau with the experience of Fascist terror is undoubtedly effective. It poses more explicitly than elsewhere the question of the links between art, nation, and nationalism. Who owns beauty? For Aragon, in this text which leaves no room for forgiveness, it belongs to those whose 'spiritual blood' has been shed:

> We will impose on this criminal people a terrible and lasting tax; we will forge and place on the German people one of the heaviest and most crushing yokes that history has ever known. And why not? What can we ask of them in return for what we have lost, something incalculable, something that has no price? In return for the spiritual blood of France …
>
> What will we ask of them? Gold, raw materials, the product of their work as disciplined beasts, the effort of their slavish muscles? Machines? Steel? Coal? For the spiritual blood of France … What a mockery! […]
>
> We must ask for something else, even more: what will cost a little money for the spiritual blood of France. And that is what I want to talk about.
>
> For there are masterpieces of French art in Germany. Stolen or not, that is not the question. The essential fact is that, taken away by their generals or bought by their kings or their financiers, there are paintings, statues, and books from France in Germany. And the German people must be declared deprived of their right of ownership over these books, these statues, these paintings. Because they are relays of French thought, sensitivity, and knowledge and, as such, once returned to France, they will be the only (and still inadequate) remedy to compensate for the harm that the German people have done to the French spirit. For, once set back in the context of their birth, these

> books, these paintings, and these statues can hasten the birth and aid the blossoming of other books, other paintings, other statues in France. In Germany, however strong and happy their influence on Germans may be, this influence will only be exercised for the benefit of Germans and not for ours – not for the benefit of a people in which these works have their source. Ultimately, from a Poussin or a Watteau that are kept elsewhere, nothing will arise that could be born from a Poussin or a Watteau in France. [...]
>
> And when I demand as my due this painting by Antoine Watteau, from Valenciennes, who will dare to say that we are taking advantage of the opportunity to rob the poor Germans who paid a merchant with good German currency for 'L'Enseigne de Gersaint'? I demand the purest and most unequalled product of French genius in return for each sob of a tortured man, a raped woman, a wounded victim finished off in these mountains of our passion. For each tear wrung out by torture. For an unequalled French suffering, the unequalled spiritual greatness of a painter from France on the ever-invaded borders of our Flanders ... 'L'Enseigne de Gersaint' first, and then ... Open the catalogues of the museums of Germany and give us back ... What? Gentlemen? Do you think I'm exaggerating? Ah! Take care lest you do fail to value at its true price the terrible, inconsolable lament of a single little French child who died without having understood why these Germans had come to kill him![26]

Little is known about the immediate reception, in France, of Aragon's extreme demand. But we can consider the display of *L'Enseigne de Gersaint* at the Petit Palais, five years later, as a response to his uncompromising plea, the manifestation of a real effort at European pacification in a context still riddled with hatred and national tensions. This is probably how we should understand the long article by an anonymous author dedicated in March 1951 to the exhibition 'Masterpieces from the Berlin Museums', which seems to draw on Aragon's position in order to denounce what he calls the 'vertiginous abysses of contemporary stupidity':

> Germanic barbarism is encamped on the Champs-Élysées. It is astonishing that, just as three hundred Communists, in the Place de l'Opéra,

> are trying to pass themselves off as a crowd, there are no wheedling voices to denounce this outrage, and no stupid hands to put up posters saying 'No Nazi masterpieces in Paris.' Vienna, Munich, fair enough! But Berlin! ... The Germans are barbarians, the Germans must be barbarians. But if they had the taste to assemble so many masterpieces in their museums, then, then ...[27]

Even today, the presence of Watteau in the rooms of Charlottenburg Palace in Berlin forces some people in France to have to restrain their emotions – as if the fierce discussions of the years 1919 and 1945, covered over by the European rhetoric of the Cold War years, had silently nestled itself into collective consciousness. In 2005, forty-one years after his immense Watteau exhibition at the Grand Palais, Pierre Rosenberg asked Berlin for a renewed loan of *L'Enseigne*, which he wanted to use as a centrepiece of an investigation into French painting in German public museums.[28] But Berlin, once again the capital of a now unified and uninhibited Germany, would not listen and refused to send the painting. In the room reserved for it, at the Grand Palais, Pierre Rosenberg chose to leave empty the place where it would have hung. Perhaps a way of saying that the matter was not – and still is not – closed.

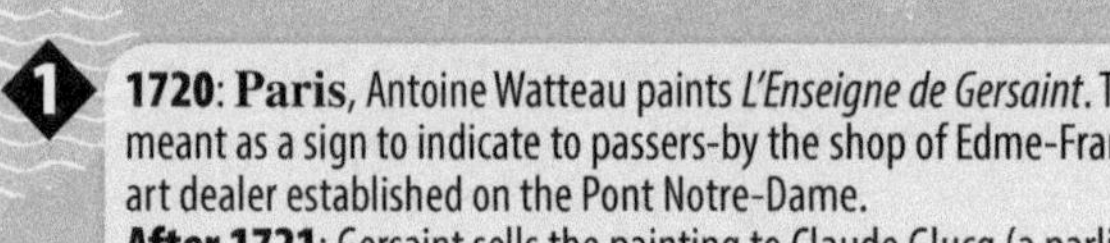

1 **1720**: **Paris**, Antoine Watteau paints *L'Enseigne de Gersaint*. The painting is meant as a sign to indicate to passers-by the shop of Edme-François Gersaint, an art dealer established on the Pont Notre-Dame.
**After 1721**: Gersaint sells the painting to Claude Glucq (a parliamentary adviser and collector in Paris). He gives it to Jean de Julienne (his nephew).

2 **Around 1746**: acquisition of the painting by an intermediary of King Frederick II of Prussia in **Paris** (or Amsterdam), and transfer to **Berlin**, where the *Enseigne* remains until 1937.

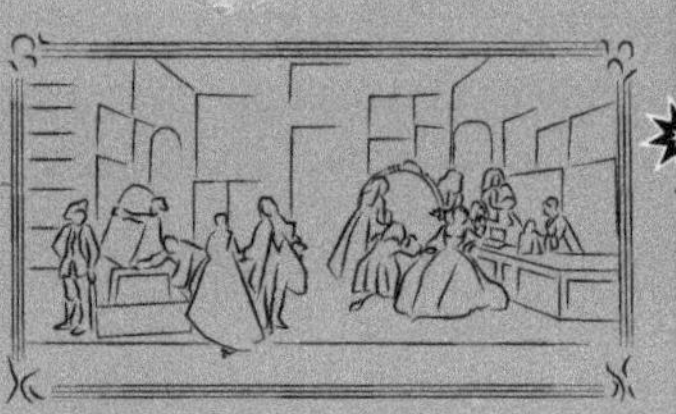

Paris

FRANCE

3 **1937**: temporary return of the *Enseigne* to **Paris** on the occasion of the World's Fair.

5 **February–May 1951**: the *Enseigne* is displayed in **Paris** during the exhibition 'Masterpieces from the Berlin Museums' at the Petit Palais.

8 **1963**: exhibiting of the *Enseigne* at the Louvre, to mark the signing of the treaty between the French Government and the Federal Republic of Germany

9 **1984**: the *Enseigne* is put on temporary display in Paris as part of Pierre Rosenberg's Watteau exhibition at the Petit Palais.

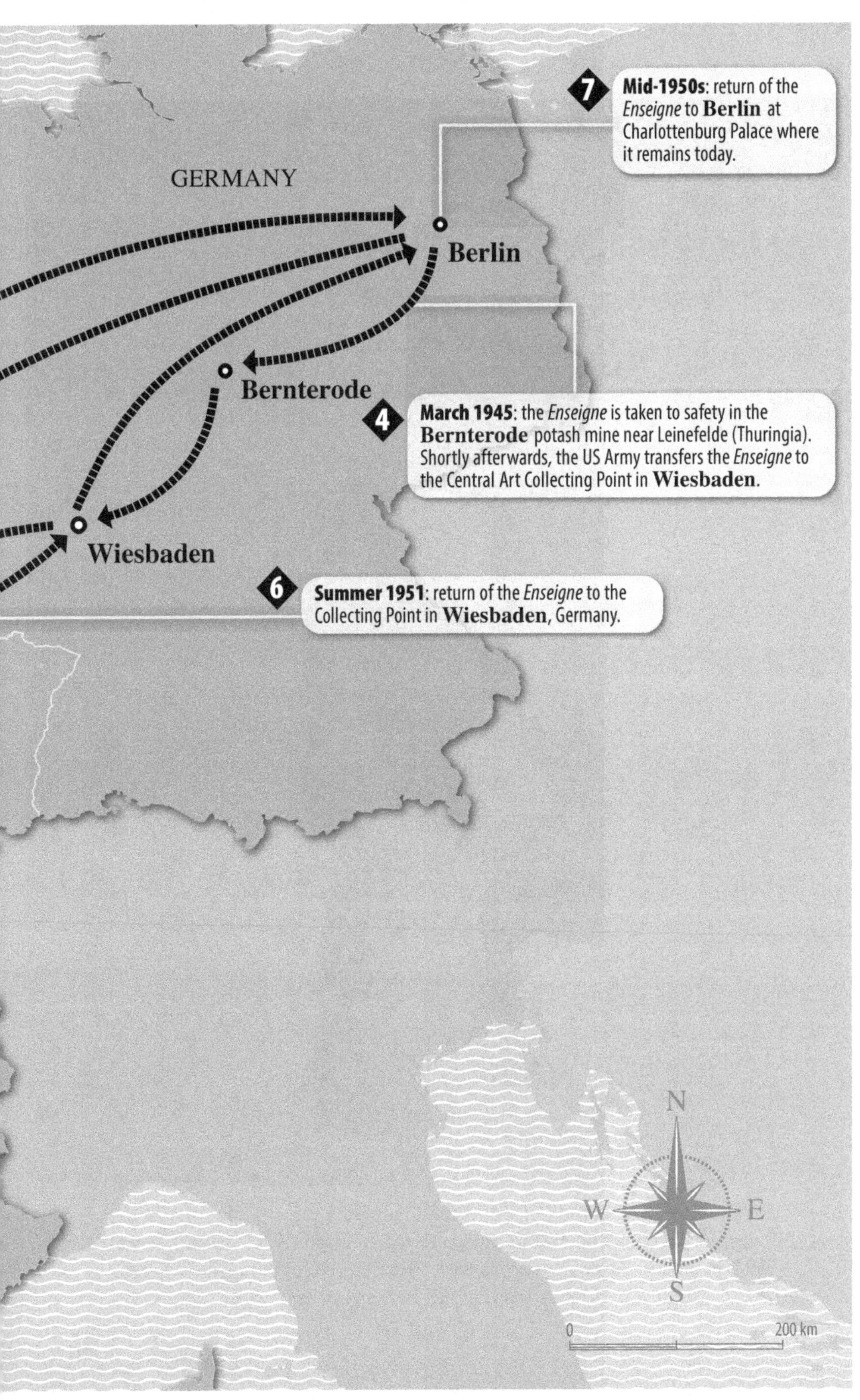
Mid-1950s: return of the Enseigne to Berlin at Charlottenburg Palace where it remains today.
7
GERMANY
Berlin
Bernterode
4
March 1945: the Enseigne is taken to safety in the Bernterode potash mine near Leinefelde (Thuringia). Shortly afterwards, the US Army transfers the Enseigne to the Central Art Collecting Point in Wiesbaden.
Wiesbaden
6
Summer 1951: return of the Enseigne to the Collecting Point in Wiesbaden, Germany.
N
W
E
S
0
200 km

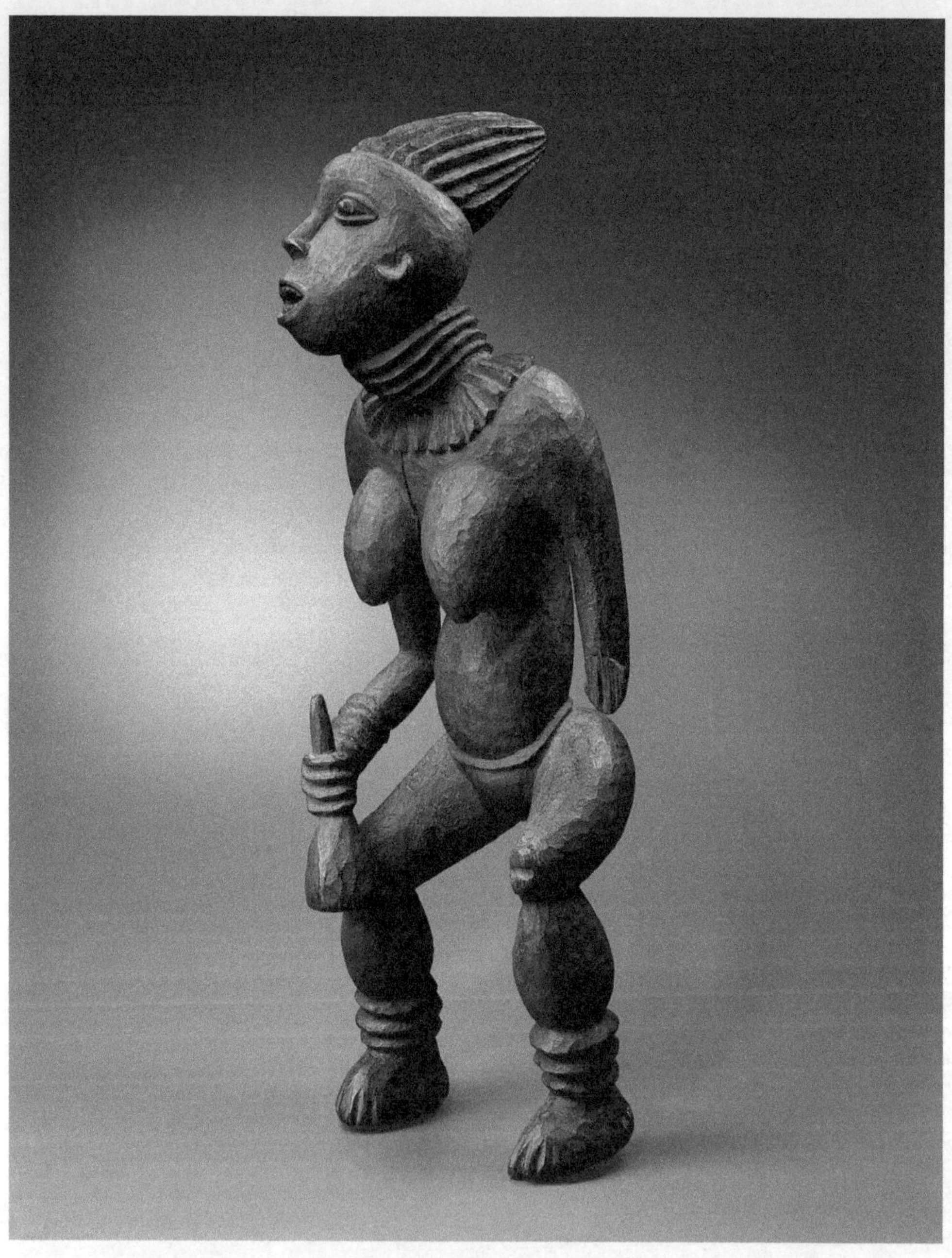

Commemorative statue (*lefem*) in the image of a princess, known as the 'Bangwa Queen', wood and pigments, Fontem region (Cameroon), before 1898, h. 85 cm. Paris, Musée Dapper. Photo © Archives musée Dapper / Hughes Dubois. 

# 7

# THE STATUE OF THE 'BANGWA QUEEN' OF CAMEROON

For over thirty years, it adorned the living rooms of the American millionaire Helena Rubinstein; the photographer Man Ray immortalized it in 1934 in Paris. We have become accustomed to calling it the 'Bangwa Queen' (we will need to discuss this name further); it is one of the most famous works of Cameroonian heritage outside the country. Taken from its community of origin, in the region of present-day Fontem, by a merchant acting for the museums of Berlin when Cameroon was a German colony, the wooden statuette, approximately 80 centimetres high, first spent several decades in the warehouses overflowing with African artworks from the German Ethnological Museum. In the 1920s, at a very fraught time, and probably unaware of its value, the museum sold it to a Berlin art dealer in cahoots with the management, who then transported it to Paris, the hub of the African art market. The famous gallery owner Charles Ratton acquired it and quickly sold it on to Helena Rubinstein, who had recently moved to the capital. Rubinstein, the muse of the global cosmetics industry, was keen on African art, and kept it for the rest of her life. After her death in 1965, the statuette was sold at auction in New York, then it spent a few years with the Franklins, collectors from the American West Coast, who were happy to lend it for temporary exhibitions in the United States. In 1990, the statue crossed the Atlantic Ocean again: it was acquired for the colossal sum of $3.4 million by a private institution, the Dapper Museum, then located in the sixteenth arrondissement of Paris with the vocation of devoting itself to the arts and cultures of Africa, the Caribbean, and their diasporas, until its closure in 2017.

The famous wooden effigy, with red lips and a broken left arm, is a commemorative figure, called a *lefem* in its region of origin – a region located on highlands in western Cameroon, at an altitude of about 1,300 metres, not far from the university city of Dschang. The Bangwa people live there under the aegis of a sacred royalty that today coexists, as in the rest of the region, with the structures of the modern Cameroonian state. If the figure's arm were not broken, we might see her, like other sculptures from the same family, holding a pipe or a musical instrument, shaking a bell with the other hand. Her mouth is open: she is blowing, singing, or speaking. Her knees are bent. This is the image of a woman in motion who really existed and who can be identified by her people. But it is also, as is generally less well known, a striking example of the dispossession of heritage that occurred around 1900 in a colonial context of economic asymmetry and extreme military violence impacting on a royal family from Western Cameroon. At that time, the transfer of the *lefem* effigy to Europe was legitimized by the powerful rhetoric of the 'scientific' museum, which justified massive and systematic cultural extractions from Germany's African colonies in the name of the ethnological knowledge that could be derived from them. In fact, the fate of this figure bears witness to the opposite – the extraordinary inability of Berlin museums, throughout the twentieth century, to study or even exhibit the tens of thousands of works, including statues (sometimes monumental), musical and religious instruments, architectural elements, thrones, weapons, textiles, jewellery, etc., extracted from the *Kolonie Kamerun* on their express instructions.

To whom does the 'Bangwa Queen' belong? To the traditional king, Charles Achaleke Taku – an international lawyer specializing in criminal law, humanitarian law, and human rights; a member of the Executive Council of the Bar Association of the International Criminal Court in The Hague; an initiate of the cult linked to the *lefem*; a descendant of King Asunganyi, abused and despoiled by the Germans from 1899 onwards? To the Berlin museums, which sought and organized the appropriation of several dozen Bangwa sculptures, paying a good price to their local tout, Gustav Conrau? To the international community of all those who love and study the 'arts of Cameroon', as they are usually called, and are delighted to be able to admire them in museums? To the young and old Cameroonians of the European and American diasporas who are demanding a form of 'heritage justice', or at least historical transparency, for the provenance of the works taken out of their country in the colonial era?

The following pages will attempt to untangle the skein. In addition to the 'Bangwa Queen', we will see a male *lefem*, also preserved in Paris, as well as a third, smaller statue, transferred from Cameroon with the two previous ones but stored today on the outskirts of Berlin in the reserves of the Ethnological Museum.

## A massive cultural extraction

One fact must be kept in mind if we are to understand the real and symbolic journey of the (now very American and Parisian) effigy of the Bangwa 'queen' – or, according to some experts, 'princess': her first European stop was Berlin, the capital of the German Empire at the time when Cameroon was one of its colonies. Today, German public museums contain more objects from Cameroon than do all the other countries in the world. This gigantic accumulation, this overabundance of heritage, is a direct product of their past colonial influence. Isolating the biography of a single object such as the statue we are dealing with should not make us forget this fact.

More than 40,000 objects from Cameroon are now preserved in the public museums of the Federal Republic of Germany (FRG). For the purposes of comparison, the entire African collection of one of the most important ethnological museums in the world, the Musée du Quai Branly – Jacques Chirac in Paris, has 69,000 inventory numbers for the entire sub-Saharan region. Unlike in centralized France, where such pieces are mainly gathered in Paris, the German collections are spread across a multitude of institutions throughout the country. In Stuttgart alone, the Cameroonian collection of the Linden-Museum has over 8,000 objects; there are just over 5,000 in Berlin, and just as many in Leipzig. Here again, a comparison is enlightening: in the rich institutions of the British and French capitals, Cameroon is much less present than in Germany – the Quai Branly Museum in Paris records around 8,000 Cameroonian objects, the British Museum in London 'only' 1,468 – while Cameroon was under French or British administration for longer (1920–60) than under German domination (1884–1916/19). How can this be explained?

In 1885, the Berlin Conference – better known on the African continent than in Europe, where it is barely present in the collective consciousness – set the rules for the division of Africa between the European powers:

> Seeking to regulate, in a spirit of mutual understanding, the most favourable conditions for the development of trade and civilization in certain regions of Africa, and to ensure to all peoples the advantages of free navigation on the two main African rivers that flow into the Atlantic Ocean; desirous, on the other hand, of preventing misunderstandings and disputes which might arise in the future from new possessions on the coasts of Africa, and concerned at the same time with the means of increasing the moral and material well-being of the native populations, [the Powers] have resolved, following the invitation addressed to them by the Imperial Government of Germany, in agreement with the Government of the French Republic, to convene a Conference in Berlin for this purpose.[1]

It was with the statement of these principles that the final act of the conference opened; it was signed on 26 February 1885, by the United States, the Ottoman Empire, and fourteen European powers, during the harsh Berlin winter, 10,000 kilometres from the centre of Africa and in the absence of any representative of the African sovereigns. Of the thirty-eight articles in the final act, more than half are devoted to the conditions of navigation on the Congo and the Niger. In this text, Article 6 stipulates that the powers exercising sovereign rights over the African continent undertake to protect and promote 'religious, scientific or charitable institutions and enterprises ... aimed at educating the natives and making them understand and appreciate the advantages of civilization'. The same article specifies that 'Christian missionaries, scholars, explorers, their escorts, assets and collections, will also be the object of special protection.'

The mention of collections and scholars in a document almost exclusively dedicated to territorial and commercial issues is less surprising than it seems: from the very beginning, the collection and export of objects were an integral part of the colonial project, whose ambition was at once political, strategic, and ideological – even psychological. Thus, from the mid-1880s, a mad race began to appropriate not only the natural wealth of the African continent, but also its cultural riches. The archives and inventories of public museums in Europe bear witness to this: while their African collections were modest in size until the mid-1880s – a few thousand pieces at most – they increased at a steady pace after 1885. In Berlin, the Ethnological Museum had only 3,300 African pieces in 1880; there were 11,000 in 1887, 25,000 in 1899, and more than 55,000 in 1919 – of which more than 10 per cent came from Cameroon, including the 'Bangwa Queen'.

But to whom did this statuette belong until then? As its place of extraction suggests, to the community of the Bangwa people, represented by King Asunganyi, born in Fontem around 1865, where he died in 1951. It was a certain Gustav Conrau who took it out of its original context and sent it to Germany. Little is known about him: he was also born in 1865 and shot dead in 1899 near Fontem. Having settled in Cameroon for several years, he lived there, according to his own words, 'from elephant hunting' and missions on behalf of various commercial companies. We also know that he was in contact with the Ethnological Museum in Berlin.

King Asunganyi received Conrau at the end of 1898, in a tense military and colonial context, marked throughout Cameroonian territory by numerous and bloody expeditions – so-called 'punitive' actions – led by the German army against the local sovereigns (a recent survey lists 181 such actions between 1884 and 1914). According to Conrau, this was the first time that a European had entered the sovereign's territory. At that time, the German agent was looking for labour on behalf of the Westafrikanische Pflanzungsgesellschaft (West African Plantation Company), whose main shareholder was the governor of Cameroon himself. He was counting on Asunganyi to provide him with men. At the same time, he was on a quest for precious objects. Several months earlier, in fact, he had set up a lucrative scheme with the director of the Ethnological Museum of Berlin. Their correspondence has been preserved. It provides valuable clues about the mechanisms and costs of heritage translocation that led to the transfer of the 'Bangwa Queen' in 1899.

In line with a process that had been put into practice twice before the discovery of the statuette, Conrau sent objects he deemed interesting to the German museum, which bought them from him and paid him an advance for subsequent deliveries. In 1898, he obtained 410 marks (almost the monthly salary of a German university professor at the time) for the first delivery of a hundred objects from another region of Cameroon. In Bangwa country, where the cultural heritage was still intact, he expected to pick up some excellent finds. So he returned there to settle, some time after his first interview with Asunganyi. Thanks to the growing democratization of photography and the reduction in the size of cameras, which now fitted into the luggage of even the most modest traveller, Conrau took views of the royal palace, which he sent to the Berlin museum: photography had become a means for the institution to make its choices from a distance and to order interesting objects. But, above all, Conrau scoured the region. He chose numerous zoological and botanical specimens ('eighty varieties of plants and seventy-four species of birds'),[2] as well as several dozen 'Bangwa' objects, sent to Berlin in the autumn of 1899, including the 'Queen'.[3] These pieces, according to his correspondence, were obtained through persuasion and gifts – in a colonial context that certainly did not encourage resistance to the desires of the white man. 'The Negroes', wrote Conrau, 'keep the good pieces carefully hidden and one can obtain them only with their trust, *secretly, friend* palabre'.[4] While the correspondence says nothing about the nature of the gifts provided in exchange for the sacred pieces, we do know that Conrau asked the Berlin museum for 1,300 marks for all the Bangwa objects – to be transferred to his father's account in Germany.

A few weeks after this 'excellent operation' (from the museum's point of view), Conrau was found dead: it was not clear whether he had been assassinated or had committed suicide. He was on the run at the time, fearing the anticipated reprisals of King Asunganyi, who had taken him hostage, furious to learn, after long weeks of silence, that the sixty men he had actually provided Conrau with eight months earlier would never return, having died at work in undetermined conditions. The chain of violence that followed this first bloody act has recently been reconstructed: a military expedition against Asunganyi and the Bangwa, with the greatest resources ever assembled by the German army inside the country (according to military sources), the ransacking and burning of his royal palace and the town of Fontem, and fierce resistance by the king and his troops for several months; a price was placed on his head by the German colonial government; he was accused of treason and exiled.[5] Significantly, this episode of violence greatly benefitted German museums. After 1901, not only Berlin, but also Cologne, Brunswick, Stuttgart, and Hanover, saw their Cameroonian collections enriched with prestigious Bangwa pieces – nearly 200 are today listed in the public museums of the FRG alone – as well as human remains taken from the sidelines of the fighting, such as the thirteen skulls sent by a medical officer to the Institute of Anatomy in Strasbourg, a city then in Germany, where they are still preserved today. A letter from 1900, addressed by the director of the Berlin museum to the 'Imperial German Government in Cameroon', clearly shows the (not often very visible) link between museums, colonial apparatus, and 'African art':

> It emerges from photographs sent by Conrau, who has since been assassinated, that the king of the Bangwa has an extremely curious palace with columns ... In the event of a punitive expedition being undertaken, the [Berlin Ethnological] Museum would have a very great interest in ensuring that this house is not burned down. In the scientific interest, it is strongly desired that at least the pillars and sculpted beams should be preserved and transported to Berlin. Furthermore, before the destruction, it would be very desirable for accurate plans and elevations as well as cross-sections of the columned house and the neighbouring dancing house to be made. Likewise, it would be good if the [king's] large signalling and dancing drums, as well as everything in his possession in the way of sculptures, 'fetishes', etc., were not destroyed but rather sent here.[6]

In the German case, on several occasions, the sacking of besieged villages was motivated solely by the greed of the museum, as the military themselves had no interest in transporting entire crates (filled with bulky wooden sculptures, monumental drums that could weigh several hundred kilos, or architectural elements that could be 3 metres high or even more) to difficult regions, with no other means of transport than the strength of local 'porters' (men, women, and children), sometimes during the rainy season. The 'scientific interest' put forward, as we have seen, by the museum director justified considerable logistical and financial efforts, to which the army submitted. The prestige of 'science' in imperial Germany in the 1900s was such that even the military put itself at science's service. At that time, the scientific argument reinforced the already widespread claim that the colonial powers were saving cultures threatened with extinction; it was a matter of 'collecting' the material witnesses to these cultures in order to be able to study them – if not now, at least in the future. At the same time, the idea spread that, in the competition between European nations, the country which possessed the most sumptuous and most complete museums – with the most modern workshops for the conservation, restoration, reproduction, and study of materials, not to mention specialized periodicals, well-assembled exhibitions, and high-level museologists (ideally with academic titles such as *Professor* or *Doktor* in Austria and Germany) – was entitled to be the legitimate guardian of world cultures. Conversely, nations and institutes lowered themselves in the eyes of others if they were not able to maintain their collections in a scientific manner, or at least to pretend to do so. The greatness of nations, the prestige of museums, the demand for scientificity, and the claim to work towards the material and ideal preservation of the world's cultural heritage went hand in hand (and still do today) in the justification of the dismantling of non-European cultures.

## Invisible in Berlin

And yet the arrival of the 'Bangwa Queen' and other statues of the same provenance and quality had no effect in Berlin. The museum added it to the considerable inventory of African works already contained in its stores. It probably already subjected it to the chemical treatment that, in the following decades, would become the norm for all pieces 'from the tropics': disinfection, using powerful insecticides developed in collaboration with the museum and the German chemical industry. The German term used to designate the process was *entwesen*, which literally means 'remove the *wesen*, the being, the substance'. Having been taken from their cultural and historical context, the works were chemically neutralized. Then ... nothing. The information available today seems to suggest that the 'Bangwa Queen' was never exhibited in the halls of the Ethnological Museum in the German capital, or at least not in an 'individualized' manner. No photograph bears witness to it. No press or specialist journal article reproduces the image or mentions it in the two decades immediately following its arrival.

At that time, the African art that aroused the 'scientific' interest of museums and public opinion was that of the court of Benin: the famous bronze heads and bas-reliefs looted by the British army during the sack of Benin City (in present-day Nigeria) in 1897 and brought back in immense quantities to London. These bronzes were so intriguing because it was, as people commented at the time, impossible that they had been created by primitive peoples – they were compared to the finest works of the Italian Renaissance. In Berlin in 1900 and in the years that followed, the Benin bronzes mobilized all the scientific and political energy of the museum's managers, who obtained substantial credits to buy several hundred of them on the London art market. So what came from Cameroon interested no one, with the exception of a gigantic pearl throne from the Foumban region, obtained 'as a gift' from the local sovereign after years of harassment. In total, up to and including 1919, fewer than 25 Cameroonian objects – out of the 6,044 that the museum had at the time of the colony's loss in that year – were scientifically documented or reproduced in the Berlin museum's specialist journals. Even such an avant-garde critic as Carl Einstein, the first to highlight the aesthetic power of African art in his famous book *Negerplastik* (*Negro Sculpture*, 1915), did not mention the statue. He was probably unaware of its very existence. It is not until 1923, and the general work on *Die Kunst der Naturvölker und der Vorzeit* (*The Art of Primitive Peoples and Prehistory*) by the art historian Eckart von Sydow, who was a frequent visitor to the museum, that we find the 'Bangwa Queen' reproduced in a photograph, but without any individual commentary.[7]

In fact, the 'Bangwa Queen' and the other *lefem* spent the three decades following their translocation to Germany completely unnoticed in Berlin. This is all the more surprising given that, all over the world, at the same time, the artistic avant-garde, collectors, and dealers were enthusiastic about the diversity, originality, and expressive power of African sculpture. While a New York exhibition of African art in 1914 became legendary, the guides at the Berlin museum literally ignored the objects presented in the rooms. Displayed – when they *were* displayed – in large collective display cases, it was not their beauty or individuality that was highlighted, but their character as a crude witness illustrating the ingenuity of this or that people, in a racial constellation of which the last edition of the museum guide, published in 1929, gives a chilling overview. The African continent was divided into two large regions, one 'inhabited by the white race', the other 'populated by dark-skinned men, who are usually called Negroes'.[8] The description of their supposed morphology, in particular their 'noses', a few years before the Nazis came to power, gives one goosebumps. The arts of Cameroon, according to this booklet, are gathered in three rooms and a dozen cabinets, to which the guide devotes a total of three short pages.

## International career

But, at that date, the 'Bangwa Queen' was no longer in Berlin. Like nearly 5,540 (!) other Oceanian or African pieces in the German Ethnological Museum, it was sold in 1929 to a very influential ethnographic art dealer active in Switzerland, Germany, and Paris: Arthur Speyer, who had taken over his father's business. Speyer acquired a quantity of objects by scouring the overabundant reserves of German and Swiss museums, then sold them to European dealers who in turn placed them with international collectors looking for exceptional pieces. So, in 1929, the 'Bangwa Queen' was removed from the inventory of the German Ethnological Museum in Berlin. In 1934, it was photographed several times by Man Ray. As a commemorative effigy in its original Cameroonian context, and an inventory number treated with pesticide but never exhibited at the Berlin museum, it then began an unprecedented international career.

In a remarkable article devoted to this journey and the multiple transformations (economic, aesthetic, epistemological) of the 'Bangwa Queen', art historian Maureen Murphy describes one of Man Ray's photographs:

> Adrienne, his companion at the time, poses nude. Her genitals are covered with a shiny fabric. She is seated in front of the sculpture that is placed on a plinth. With her arm extended at the foot of the piece, the model holds herself erect. Her bust leans slightly back, her chest thrust forward, her legs crossed in a pose that combines tension and nonchalance, grace and sensuality. Her face is captured in movement, turned towards the sculpture. The woman observes the figure, while the piece stands hieratically, its clearcut shapes projecting onto the back wall. The shadows echo the shapes, reinforcing the seductive relationship, and amplifying the sensuality of the bodies and the contrasts of values: the bright whiteness of the model's body, very brightly lit, is matched by the dark wood of the piece.... The sensual charge of the sculpture highlighted here is based on the artist's personal appreciation of the work, but it also evokes a vision of Africa conceived as the land of eroticism, of 'ebony' bodies, liberated and without taboos.[9]

In 1935, the Parisian gallery owner Charles Ratton sold 'Queen Bwanga' to Helena Rubinstein. She added the wooden effigy to her personal collection. For thirty years, it was displayed to the prestigious visitors, artists, and art lovers who frequented her Parisian salon. It was also lent to the New York public for major exhibitions: 'African Negro Art' at the MoMA in New York in 1935, the first of its kind in a museum of modern art; and 'Masterpieces of African Art' at the Brooklyn Museum in 1954. Breaking with the practice of European ethnographical museums, American museums gave African art a new significance by adopting the same presentation as for Western and contemporary artworks. For example, African works of art were placed on individual pedestals in order to highlight their aesthetic and plastic qualities, and not their original function or the supposed characteristics of the people who created them. They suddenly became individual objects for aesthetic enjoyment.

**1966**: **New York**, auctioned from the Rubinstein collection at Sotheby's / Parke Bernet. Purchased by Harry A. Franklin, in **Los Angeles**.

**1990**: **New York**, auctioned from the Franklin collection by Sotheby's. Purchased by the Dapper Museum in **Paris**.

**1983**: Harry A. Franklin bequeaths the figure to his daughter Valerie Franklin.

UNITED STATES
Hanover
Flint
Chicago
**New York**
Dayton
Kansas City
Berkeley
Palo Alto
San Francisco
Baltimore
Washington
**Los Angeles**
Houston
New Orleans

*In addition, numerous exhibitions (designated on the map by stars):*

*1935. New York, Museum of Modern Art: African Negro Art (Kat. 319).*

*1954. New York, Brooklyn Museum: Masterpieces of African Art (Kat. 43).*

*1964. Berlin, Hochschule für Bildende Künste: Afrika. 100 Stämme – 100 Meisterwerke (Kat. 54).*

*1964. Paris, Musée des arts décoratifs: Afrique. 100 tribus – 100 chefs-d'œuvre (Kat. 54).*

*1967. Berkeley, Robert H. Lowie Museum of Anthropology of the University of California: African Arts: An Exhibition.*

*1970. Washington, National Gallery of Art: African Sculpture (Kat. 61a).*

*1970. Kansas City, Nelson Gallery of Art: African Sculpture (Kat. 61a).*

*1970. New York, Brooklyn Museum: African Sculpture (Kat. 61a).*

*1984. Washington, Smithsonian Institution, National Museum of Natural History: The Art of Cameroon (Kat. 5).*

*1984. New Orleans, Museum of Art: The Art of Cameroon (Kat. 5).*

*1984. Houston, Museum of Fine Arts: The Art of Cameroon (Kat. 5).*

*1984. Chicago, Field Museum of Natural History: The Art of Cameroon (Kat. 5).*

*1984. New York, American Museum of Natural History: The Art of Cameroon (Kat. 5).*

*1986. Los Angeles, Los Angeles County Museum of Natural History: Expressions of Cameroon Art, The Franklin Collection.*

*1987. Baltimore, The Baltimore Museum of Art: Expressions of Cameroon Art, The Franklin Collection.*

*1987/8. Hanover (New Hampshire), Dartmouth College, Hood Museum of Art: Expressions of Cameroon Art, The Franklin Collectio*

*1988. Dayton (Ohio), Dayton Art Institute: Expressions of Cameroon Art, The Franklin Collection.*

*1988/9. Flint (Michigan), Flint Institute of Arts: Expressions of Cameroon Art, The Franklin Collection.*

*1989. Palo Alto (California), Palo Alto Cultural Center: Expressions of Cameroon Art, The Franklin Collection.*

*1989/90. San Francisco (California), California Academy of Sciences: Expressions of Cameroon Art, The Franklin Collection.*

*2008. Paris, Musée Dapper: Femmes dans les Arts d'Afrique.*

*2011. New York, Metropolitan Museum of Art: Heroic Africans: Legendary Leaders, Iconic Sculptures (Abb.113).*

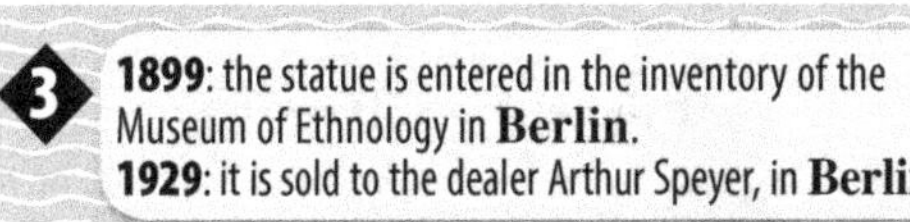

**1899**: the statue is entered in the inventory of the Museum of Ethnology in **Berlin**.
**1929**: it is sold to the dealer Arthur Speyer, in **Berlin**.

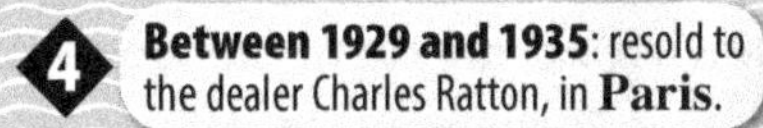

**Between 1929 and 1935**: resold to the dealer Charles Ratton, in **Paris**.

**Around 1935**: resold to Helena Rubinstein, in **Paris / New York**.

**1990–2017**: exhibition at the Dapper Museum in the 16th arrondissement of **Paris** until the building closes to the public in 2017.

**1899**: extraction of the statue from its original context by Gustav Conrau who sends it to the Museum of Ethnology in **Berlin**.



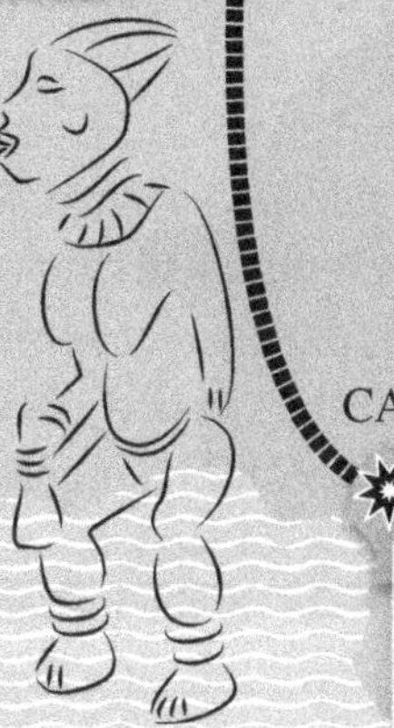

**Before 1899**: creation of the figure in the **Fontem** region (Cameroon), artist's name not documented.

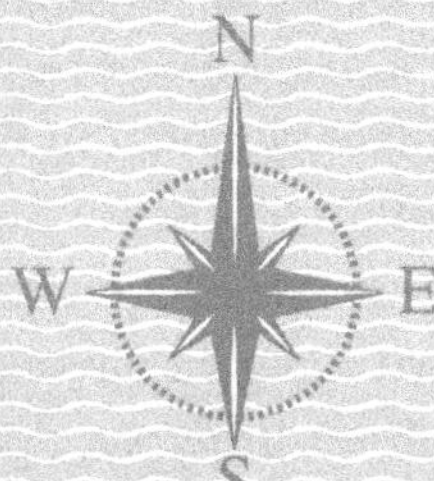

After the death of Helena Rubinstein, the 'Bangwa Queen' was sold at auction in New York in 1966. In California, she joined the extremely rich African collection of Harry A. Franklin, who already owned (or would soon own?) another *lefem* effigy, this time masculine, also originating from the shipment made from Cameroon to Berlin by Conrau in the year of his death. In 1899, the Ethnological Museum had recorded this male figure a few items above the queen in the inventory of its African collections, before also removing it from the same inventory in 1926: it had been sold to Speyer three years before its future consort. According to experts, it was directly through the Speyer family, probably through the son (1922–2007), that Franklin acquired the male Bangwa statue, which would henceforth form a couple with the famous queen. The two were exhibited together on numerous occasions in the United States in the 1970s and 1980s, studied, published, and placed in context in various important American studies of the 'royal arts of Cameroon' – as Western researchers now called them.

One exhibition in particular attracted attention: 'African Sculpture', mounted in 1970 at the National Gallery of Art in Washington and then again in Kansas City and New York, where the 'Bangwa Queen' was presented with her male counterpart. Ten years after the accession to independence of some twenty African countries, the exhibition took place in the context of the rise in power and political self-assertion of the Black American community in the United States. The two statues together acquired, in addition to the layers of meaning and values superimposed since their departure from Cameroon, a major political dimension: that of a collective empowerment, a concept combining self-acceptance and self-esteem, confidence, autonomy, and ambition. In a letter cited by Murphy, addressed to the director of the Brooklyn Museum, which hosted the exhibition in New York and adapted it to meet the presumed expectations of the Black American population in its neighbourhood, we read: 'The large black population that you serve will have, for the first time, the opportunity to see the finest evidence of their cultural heritage ... This exhibition is a unique opportunity.'[10]

The American life together of the two Bangwa effigies ended with the auction of the Franklin collection in 1990. They were photographed one last time for the cover of the Sotheby's catalogue in New York, where the female figure was acquired by the Dapper Museum in Paris for $3.4 million – the highest sum ever spent on a piece of African art. The male figure went to a collector in Japan. In 2009, it was bought by the French entrepreneur and patron Marc Ladreit de Lacharrière, who donated it in 2017 to the Quai Branly Museum in Paris, allowing the works removed from the Fontem region more than a century earlier to be reunited in the French capital, transformed by their successive travels and exhibitions throughout the Western world into icons of African and world art, fashion, luxury, and money. But what about the other statues? And the Cameroonians themselves?

On the outskirts of Berlin, in a glass cabinet in the reserves of the Ethnological Museum, a small wooden figure tells another story. This statue also came from the Bangwa culture, and had been sent from Cameroon to Berlin in the same box as the two prestigious *lefem* figures mentioned above, along with several dozen other pieces. This statue was never displayed to the public, nor published by the Berlin museums before the 2000s. It was not sold in the 1920s, unlike the 'Bangwa Queen' and her future counterpart, and spent its life in the shadows until the start of the Second World War. Evacuated from Berlin with a large part of the African collections in 1942 or 1943, it spent the war in a crate at Bobolice Castle, north-east of Ząbkowice Śląskie, in present-day Poland, before being taken by the Red Army to Leningrad, where it remained with all the other African objects until the mid-1970s. At that time, the USSR returned around 23,000 African works to its sister republic, the GDR. The latter stored the crates unopened at the Ethnological Museum in Leipzig. It was only after the fall of the Wall and the reunification of Germany in the early 1990s that these pieces returned to Berlin, where they are still not exhibited. This is a double loss for Cameroon and the Bangwa people who not only have been deprived of a significant part of their heritage since the German colonial period, but also cannot access it either through publications accessible to the general French-speaking or English-speaking public, or through the internet, where the works are not systematically listed, or even – braving visa difficulties and transport costs – by coming to Germany to visit the museums, which display only a tiny part of them. To add insult to injury, the pure and simple destruction suffered by the African collections of Germany during the

Second World War continues to be ignored, and Russia refuses to say anything about what may have remained there after the 1970s.

In 2023, Germanist researchers from the University of Dschang, in the very region where the Bangwa sculptures were initially created, collaborated with the Technical University of Berlin on a census of the presence of the Cameroonian heritage in Germany – in particular, its absence from Cameroon, and the collateral effects this has had. Their *Atlas de l'absence* (*Atlas of Absence*)[11] depicts a phantom Cameroon (to borrow from the famous title of Michel Leiris):[12] in fact, Cameroon is a phantom twice over, haunting both German museums, which neither exhibit nor publish their collections (despite their value, both in number and in age), and Cameroon itself where, after more than a hundred years, the memory of the works that have left has all too often become blurred or frozen, like that of a missing limb. The only Bangwa works that have been the subject of aesthetic and scientific appreciation in the last hundred years are among those that the Ethnological Museum in Berlin got rid of in the 1920s. It was only after they left Germany that they acquired international fame. Who owns beauty? Certainly not those who do nothing with it.

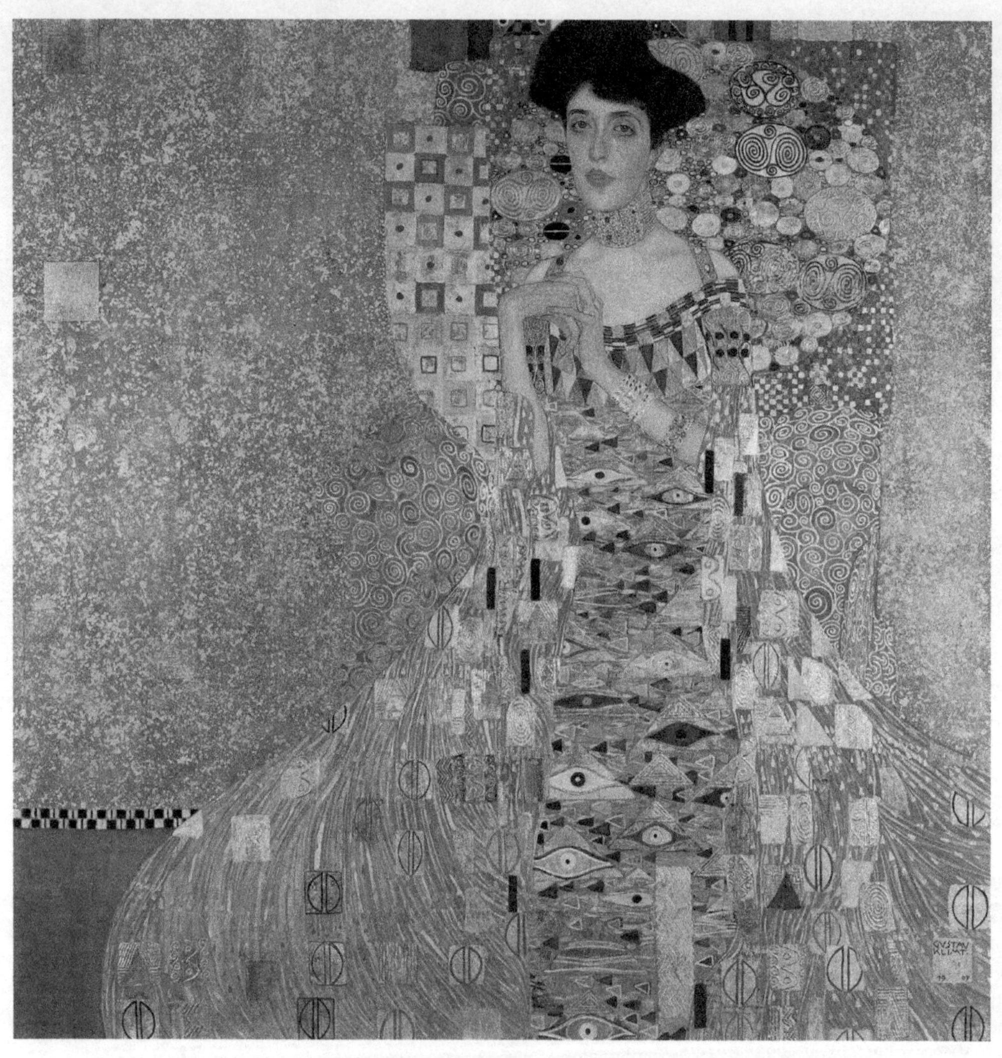

Gustav Klimt, *Portrait of Adele Bloch-Bauer (I)*, 1907, oil and gold and silver leaf on canvas, 140 × 140 cm. New York, Neue Galerie. Photo © IanDagnall Computing / Alamy Stock Photo.

# 8

# THE *PORTRAIT OF ADELE BLOCH-BAUER* BY GUSTAV KLIMT

The painting is a perfect square. It looks like a Byzantine icon, but it is the portrait of a 26-year-old woman, the daughter of a banker and the wife of an entrepreneur. Around her black hair, her diaphanous skin, her neck encircled with diamonds, her parted lips, and her sweet gaze, there unfolds a magnificence of ornaments, small cascading gold and silver tiles, shimmering arabesques, patterns resembling a multitude of eyes or precious stones. The model's dress blends into the background of the painting; we discover the young woman's beautiful face, her neckline and hands at the top, as if by chance.

Since its creation by Gustav Klimt in 1907, the portrait entitled *Adele Bloch-Bauer I* has been on show to a wide audience. Ferdinand and Adele Bloch-Bauer, Viennese collectors and sponsors of the work, circulated it in international exhibitions, with the aim of boosting the influence of Gustav Klimt, whose career they had supported for several years. The original style of the portrait disturbed some, and it is reported that one critic made a daring pun: 'Mehr Blech als Bloch' ('More bling than Bloch'). But at the Venice Biennale in 1910, the international public was captivated: 'L'arte di Klimt è incantatrice' ('Klimt's art is enchanting'), declared the daily *Wiener Allgemeine Zeitung* in Italian on 30 April 1910.

As an emblem of the Vienna Secession – the artistic movement contemporary with Sigmund Freud's discoveries on the unconscious, the mystical compositions of Gustav Mahler and Richard Strauss, the writings of Franz Kafka and Stefan Zweig – the *Portrait of Adele Bloch-Bauer* attracted tourists and art lovers to the Belvedere Gallery in Vienna, where it was the flagship work, until recently. But at the very end of the twentieth century, after several decades spent in this public museum, the painting was claimed by an 84-year-old American citizen: Maria Altmann, a niece of Adele Bloch-Bauer, who believed that her family had been robbed of it. In 2006, Altmann won her case: the painting was taken down from the Belvedere and transferred to the United States. Today, Klimt's extraordinary portrait is on show in the galleries of the Neue Galerie in New York.

Who does the *Portrait of Adele Bloch-Bauer* belong to? To the descendants of the beautiful young woman whose features Klimt captured and transfigured, and, more generally, to the descendants of European Jewish families who were victims of the Holocaust? To the Belvedere Gallery in Vienna, which felt it was its owner, cared for it, and exhibited it for several decades? To the Viennese public, which continues to identify with the work? Asked today, these questions seem quite rhetorical, given that there is now a consensus on the fair restitution of property confiscated from Jewish families persecuted by the Nazi government and its European collaborators. But this was not always the case, and the path that led to this restitution, one of the most publicized and important of the post-war period, was long and difficult.

In the general context of the systematic dispossession of Jewish families in Europe in the 1930s and 1940s, and their post-traumatic treatment by Western democracies after the war, the *Portrait of Adele Bloch-Bauer* is a singular example. As always in matters of restitution, it is important to pay attention to the specific framework of each story. But it must also be kept in mind that these particular cases, added together by the tens of thousands, are part of a larger logic that unites them: the massive and organized looting by states across the whole European continent of private artistic (and other) works of heritage, assembled by Jewish families who were then forced to part with them when they were persecuted, deported, or murdered.

So, in the following pages, I will be discussing the particular fate of the *Portrait of Adele Bloch-Bauer* and its legitimate owners, but also, more generally, the National Socialist policy of heritage looting and the shocking collective resistance of European states when it came to recognizing and repairing, after 1945, the harm inflicted on the citizens of their respective countries. Here, the biography of the people involved is inseparable from the trajectory of the work.

## Collectors, donors, patrons

Before examining in more detail the painting's journey, the perversity of the Nazi system of heritage looting, and the slowness of the post-war authorities to hear the claims of the descendants, it will be useful to take a longer look at a group of actors whom I have touched on in previous chapters, but who have not until now been described as a homogeneous or coherent group. These actors are inseparable from the rise of European museums and the expansion of their collections around 1900. They emerged in all European capitals and in the United States during the last third of the nineteenth century: as patrons, benefactors, and other donors to public museums, they came together in societies such as the 'Friends of the Louvre', or of the Art Institute of Chicago, and of museums in Berlin, London, Odessa, Vienna, and Madrid. Motivated by social considerations and a strong need for gaining distinction through art, they were also motivated by their patriotic involvement in the self-assertion of the national museums of their countries. Around 1900, many of these collectors acquired very valuable pieces on the market, which they then bequeathed or donated to public institutions in their respective cities. Some, through direct funding, enabled the same museums to acquire some prestigious works, the prices of which exceeded public budgets. Many of these collectors came from Jewish families, some of whom had converted to Protestantism or Catholicism during the nineteenth century.

As the historian Véronique Long has shown, the donation of collections was then perceived in these circles as a patriotic act that allowed the respective capitals of the great European states to maintain their place in the international landscape of arts and artists, and for certain American cities to make a mark.[1] For example, in Paris, a few years after the creation of the Société des amis du Louvre in 1898, the

*Journal officiel* encouraged its potential donors with this formula: 'We hold out our hand without blushing, in the name of art and France.'[2] In Berlin, as mentioned in the chapter devoted to the bust of Nefertiti, the great industrialist James Simon not only financed costly archaeological excavation campaigns, but also offered several dozen masterpieces of the Italian Renaissance, including ones by Mantegna and Botticelli, for display on Museum Island. In London, to name just one patron of the arts, Baron Ferdinand de Rothschild, a banker, politician, and passionate collector, bequeathed nearly 300 objects to the British Museum, among which were some very rare princely jewels from the end of the fourteenth and the beginning of the fifteenth century.

In Vienna, the Bloch-Bauers were typical representatives of this generation of industrialists, bankers, and great merchants, of cultivated women and men with sure tastes, developing their own collections and supporting the great national museums. They encouraged contemporary creativity and avant-garde movements by placing generous commissions with living artists. We must bear in mind the commitment of individuals to the common good of nations and of their public museums around 1900, the practice of making artistic legacies and donations that was encouraged by European governments, if we are to understand not only the considerable boom in museums at the threshold of the twentieth century, but also, a generation and a half later, the particular ignominy represented by the looting by European states of the families of those very people who had contributed so much to the influence of their national collections.

## The world of yesterday

Klimt's *Portrait of Adele Bloch-Bauer* was completed in 1907. The commission had been placed several years earlier by the young woman's husband, the industrialist Ferdinand Bloch-Bauer. Originally from a small town near Prague, where he owned an imposing second home from 1909, Ferdinand Bloch-Bauer ran his business from Vienna, then the capital of the Austro-Hungarian Empire, a multi-ethnic and multi-headed monarchy where Prague, Budapest, and Vienna formed brilliant cultural and economic centres. Klimt himself was Viennese by birth. He was around forty years old and at the height of his international reputation when he accepted the commission. He made several dozen sketches of Adele Bloch-Bauer before embarking on the final version. The stages of its creation are well known, as are those of the painting's meteoric rise in the international world of contemporary art, as the Bloch-Bauers did not limit the work's influence to their living room, or its public access to their prestigious friends alone. Between its creation and the end of the First World War, they allowed the work to circulate in various European institutions: first presented in Klimt's own studio in Vienna, it was then loaned to the spectacular exhibition organized for the 300th anniversary of the German city of Mannheim (1907), to the Kunstschau in Vienna (1908), to a solo exhibition of Klimt during the Venice Biennale (1910), and to the Kunsthaus in Zurich as part of the retrospective *A Century of Viennese Painting* (1918). It produced a major impact everywhere. Its image was reproduced in catalogues and art magazines.

In 1912, while the *Portrait of Adele Bloch-Bauer* was circulating in Europe, Klimt produced a second portrait of the young woman, known under the title *Portrait of Adele Bloch-Bauer II*, which also enjoyed great international visibility as one of the painter's last portraits. Klimt died in 1918. His death preceded by a few weeks the dissolution of the Austro-Hungarian Empire by the victorious powers of the First World War. It was the end of a world. As the writer Stefan Zweig wrote retrospectively:

> A remarkable shifting began to prepare itself in our old sleepy Austria. The masses, which had silently and obediently permitted the liberal middle classes to retain the leadership for decades, suddenly became restless, organized themselves and demanded their rights. And it was just in the last decade that politics broke into the calm of easy living with sharp and sudden blasts. The new century wanted a new order, a new era.[3]

This major political change, the transition from a multi-ethnic dual monarchy to an Austrian republic, had a considerable impact on the country's heritage and museum institutions. What belonged to the monarchy was nationalized – in Austria as in Germany, where the empire was abolished at the same time and gave way to the Weimar Republic. In Austria, the new regime was proclaimed on 21 October 1919, with the ratification of the Treaty of Saint-Germain-en-Laye: the Constitution was signed in 1920. This period was marked by violent political conflicts and the rise of extremism, but also by a very strong social commitment on the part of large sections of society who supported the democratic project. This was the case of the Bloch-Bauers, who after the war not only were active members of the association supporting national museums, but also entrusted several paintings from their collection to the Belvedere Gallery of Contemporary Art in Vienna, founded in 1903, reformed in 1912 and renamed the Österreichische Staatsgalerie (the Austrian State Gallery). The *Portrait of Adele Bloch-Bauer* and several other Klimt paintings from the couple's collection were exhibited there on loan from 1918 to 1921, as evidence of a twofold commitment: to the artistic avant-gardes, on the one hand, and to the democratic dissemination of visual culture in a young and fragile state, on the other. However, in 1918, the Bloch-Bauers opted for Czechoslovak nationality. Although they remained active in Vienna, their main residence was now located near Prague.

In 1925, at the age of forty-four, Adele Bloch-Bauer died of meningitis. The couple were childless. The young woman left behind a will requesting her husband, after his death, to donate the brilliant portrait and the other Klimts from his collection to the Belvedere Public Gallery in Vienna. Released belatedly from the archives, this will has been widely circulated since 1998, when the Bloch-Bauers' heirs initiated a claim to their property. It reads:

> My last wishes.
> In full awareness and without being subjected to undue influence, I make the following arrangements in the event of my death:
> I. I appoint my spouse, Ferdinand Bloch Bauer, as universal legatee of all my property....
> III. I bequeath fifty thousand (50,000) Czech crowns each
> 1) to the Viennese workers' association 'Kinderfreunde' ['Children's friends']

> 2) to the Viennese association 'Die Bereitschaft' [an association for social work and the dissemination of social knowledge]
>
> ...
>
> As for my two portraits and the four landscapes by Gustav Klimt, I ask my husband, after his death, to bequeath them to the Österreichische Staatsgalerie in Vienna. And the books from my libraries in Vienna and from our Jungfer-Breschan estate [near Prague], to the Wiener Volks u. Arbeiter Bibliothek [Vienna People's and Workers' Library].[4]

## Discriminations, dislocations

As early as 1936, Ferdinand Bloch-Bauer donated one of Klimt's landscapes to the Österreichische Staatsgalerie in Vienna. Politically, these years were marked in Austria by the rise of the Nazi Party. Although he entered politics in Munich, Adolf Hitler was an Austrian national, and it was in Vienna that he spent the first years of his adult life. The Nazi Party and ideology quickly took root there. Five years after Hitler came to power in Berlin, a large section of Austrian politics and public opinion called for the unification of Austria with Germany. Known as the *Anschluss* and later presented as an 'annexation', this merger took place in 1938. It preceded the annexation by Nazi Germany of part of the Czechoslovak Republic, with its capital Prague; this Republic, like Austria, had emerged from the disappearance of the Austro-Hungarian Empire in 1918. This double territorial extension of the Reich also marked the extension of the systematic German policy of persecution, deportation, and extermination of Jewish nationals from these countries.

Ferdinand Bloch-Bauer's movable property and real estate were confiscated, both in Vienna and in the Prague area, where his residence was successively occupied by the Nazi governor of the 'Protectorate of Bohemia and Moravia', then by one of the main architects of the Holocaust, Reinhard Heydrich, who settled there for several years with his wife and children. Bloch-Bauer was able to take almost nothing with him: he fled to Switzerland in 1938. All of his assets, his business, his collections of ancient and modern art, tapestries, and furniture were now managed by an administrator from the SS, appointed by the Nazi authorities. According to a practice then systematically implemented in Germany and Austria to 'Aryanize' the properties and assets of persecuted Jewish families, this administrator 'relocated' them or sold them. Between 1941 and 1943, in the middle of the war, while the museums were closed, the Österreichische Staatsgalerie was rewarded with four paintings by Klimt from the Bloch-Bauer collection, including the *Portrait of Adele Bloch-Bauer*. Six other paintings, a sculpture, and a tapestry joined the collections of the future Führermuseum, Hitler's megalomaniac museum project in Linz near Vienna. The Bloch-Bauer couple's immense porcelain collection, valued at the time at half a million Reichsmarks, was put up for auction in Vienna in June 1941; before the sale, the director of the city's National Museum of Decorative Arts acquired thirty-four pieces personally for his own home. Ferdinand Bloch-Bauer died in Zurich in 1945. At that time, the works from his collection integrated into the Vienna museums – the *Portrait of Adele Bloch-Bauer*, in particular – were considered the legitimate property of the Austrian state. This was Adele's wish, they claimed. But, clearly, in 1925, she could not have foreseen the war, the Nazi crimes, the Holocaust, or the persecution inflicted on her husband.

The example of the Bloch-Bauers is representative of several thousand other cases of Jewish families being dispossessed of their heritage, in Germany and Austria as well as in Eastern Europe and in the Western European countries occupied by the Nazi army and state apparatus – or actively collaborating with it, as in the Netherlands or in Vichy France. It is also representative of the bad faith, resistance, and obstacles put in the way of victims anxious to recover or, at least, locate their assets in the decades following the end of the war. In many cases, these victims or their beneficiaries emigrated from Europe, to the United States, Australia, or South America, making the process of claiming their property more difficult. In Austria, as in Germany, moreover, it was often former Nazis, members of the SS or other National Socialist organizations, who, until the mid-1970s, continued to hold key positions in the state apparatus, in the ministries concerned with heritage claims, and on the boards of museums of the Federal Republic of Germany (FRG) and the Austrian republic.

These administrative continuities between the Nazi period and the 'reconstruction' of West Germany and Austria, in the context of the establishment of the European Community, have been closely studied. They largely explain why, in these countries, the question of restitution was not debated in the immediate post-war period; it was necessary to wait until the very end of the twentieth century, as in the case of the *Portrait of Adele Bloch-Bauer*, for public opinion to be informed of the provenance of the works offered for viewing in certain public museums, for courts to be formed, and for the beneficiaries of the dispossessed families to win their cases.

In Austria, there was also the widespread idea that the country was itself the victim of an aggression by Nazi Germany and that it had no responsibility to assume with regard to persecuted Jewish citizens. True, reparation and restitution mechanisms were put in place, in Germany as in Austria, after 1945. But the deadline for submitting applications was very tight, and potential applicants, most of whom resided abroad, were not informed of their rights. Furthermore, in many cases, the relocation of assets was difficult to prove with written documents, as the victims in most cases had fled without their personal and professional files. An attempt by Ferdinand Bloch-Bauer, made shortly before his death in 1945, to obtain information from Switzerland on the fate of his collections still in Vienna and Prague failed. In his last will, dated 22 October 1945, he revoked all previous wills and bequeathed all his assets to two nieces (one exiled in Zagreb, the other in Hollywood) and to a nephew (in Toronto). He left nothing to the state or to Austrian museums.

## 'Ciao Adele'

From the 1960s onwards, the Vienna Secession in Austria and the German avant-gardes humiliated by the Nazi regime (for example the expressionist group 'Die Brücke', and the 'Blauer Reiter', denigrated as 'degenerate artists') were given special attention, consciously or unconsciously intended to move away from Nazi aesthetics. By promoting painters such as Gustav Klimt, Egon Schiele, Ernst Ludwig Kirchner, and Karl Schmidt-Rottluff, public institutions, universities, and the media contributed to reinventing positive national identities. This transformation was not self-evident. It was initiated in the United States by galleries and museums sensitive to the presence in their country of many European Jewish immigrants whose world had been lost and who, through art, could connect with it. Gradually, this American interest in the 'Central Europe 1900' aesthetic led to moments of 'rediscovery' and 're-evaluation' on the European continent.

In Vienna, the reconstruction of a positive 'aesthetic identity' was also driven by a more general effort to revitalize international tourism. In this context, the golds, bodies, fluidities, femininities, and musicality of Klimt, completely forgotten since the 1930s, gradually became the emblems not only of an era, but of an entire city, an entire country. The work was suddenly studied, catalogued, and exhibited. The *Portrait of Adele Bloch-Bauer* was reproduced in many kinds of popular media, especially from the 1980s onwards when, seventy years after Klimt's death, the rights to his work passed into the public domain. Mugs, fridge magnets, tea-towels ... the portrait stolen from the Bloch-Bauer family not only occupies a place of honour in the Belvedere Gallery; it is omnipresent in the collective consciousness, in the visual imagination of Austrians and beyond. It does not just *represent* the spirit of the Austrian capital around 1900. It – or rather she – *is* Vienna. A fantasized Vienna, rich, sensual, and mysterious – a city with which the Austrian capital of the twenty-first century readily identifies.

This is evidenced, to cite just one example, by the use of the painting by the French fashion designer Jean-Paul Gaultier and the character of Conchita Wurst, the bearded woman star of the LGBTQ+ community and winner of the Eurovision Prize for Austria in 2014. In a 2015 video clip, Conchita, dressed by Gaultier, brings the painting to life. Transformed into a living portrait of Klimt's Adele Bloch-Bauer, we see her draped in gold, with curled eyelashes, manicured nails, purple eyelids, her neck adorned with diamonds against which her deep and provocative black beard stands out while gold confetti falls from the sky. The video serves as publicity for a major charity gala for AIDS sufferers in Europe. The *Portrait of Adele Bloch-Bauer* seems inseparable from the city where the model and the painter lived. It serves a discourse and an aesthetic of joyful transgression, where tolerance, freedom, and optimism are as if united by the painting – far from the actual history of the work and its owners. And, in any case, by the time the video was filmed, the painting had long since left Vienna.

In August 2000, Marie Altmann, then an American citizen, née Maria Victoria Bloch in Vienna in 1916, filed a lawsuit against the Republic of Austria. She demanded not only the restitution of her aunt's portrait by Klimt, but also that of five of the latter's paintings exhibited in the Belvedere Gallery. At the same time, after half a century of obstruction, the world community agreed in Washington on a series of 'principles' intended to support the efforts of the dispossessed families. Formulated at the International Conference on the Looting of Jewish Cultural Property during the Second World War, in December 1998, these principles were adopted by representatives of forty-four governments. They recommended that states and public institutions in Europe open their archives and simplify the process of research; that cultural property confiscated by the Nazis be reported proactively by the very institutions that possessed it; and that, for works of art which had been verifiably looted, a 'just and equitable solution' be quickly found with the beneficiaries. Despite the existence of these principles, the Austrian state resisted Maria Altmann's request for half a decade; it was finally granted only in 2006. At that time, the restitution to an individual of a work that had been on public display for a long time was far from being a consensus in European public opinion, which seemed to place a painting's or sculpture's accessibility (for example, in a public museum) above the idea of reparation or heritage justice.

When rereading the various statements published by key players in the world of museums and culture in the German-speaking world in the early 2000s, one is retrospectively surprised, or shocked, by the latent anti-Semitism of certain editorials. The weekly *Spiegel* headlined in 2006, 'Morality and millions', suggesting that financial considerations, rather than a concern for justice, were at stake in the claims put forward by Jewish families. In another article, it quoted a German museum director in its headline: 'They are doing business with heritage.' As for the powerful conservative daily the *Frankfurter Allgemeine Zeitung*, it did not hesitate to write in 2007: 'They say Holocaust, but they think money.'

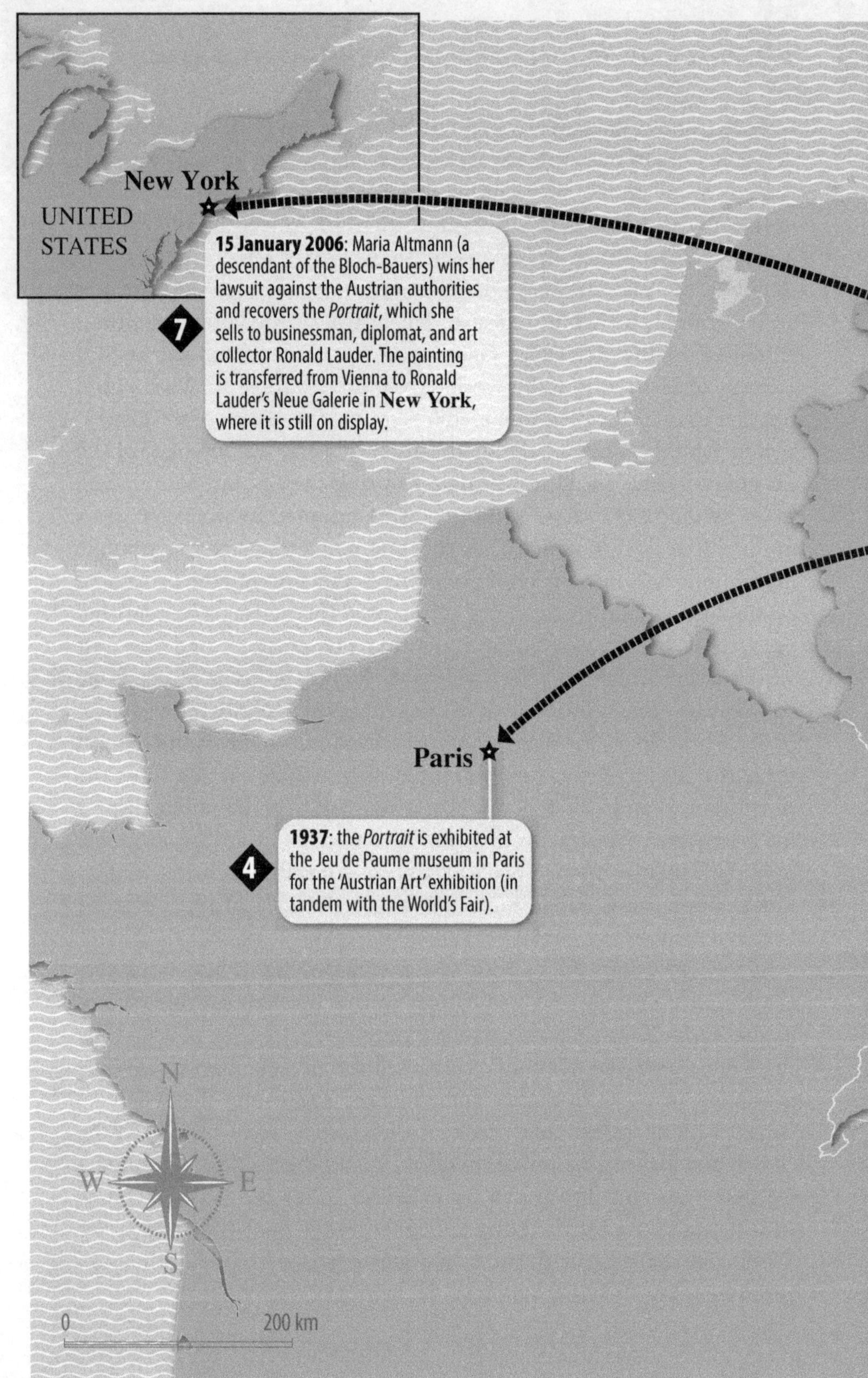
New York
UNITED STATES
15 January 2006: Maria Altmann (a descendant of the Bloch-Bauers) wins her lawsuit against the Austrian authorities and recovers the Portrait, which she sells to businessman, diplomat, and art collector Ronald Lauder. The painting is transferred from Vienna to Ronald Lauder's Neue Galerie in New York, where it is still on display.
7
Paris
1937: the Portrait is exhibited at the Jeu de Paume museum in Paris for the 'Austrian Art' exhibition (in tandem with the World's Fair).
4
N
W
E
S
0
200 km

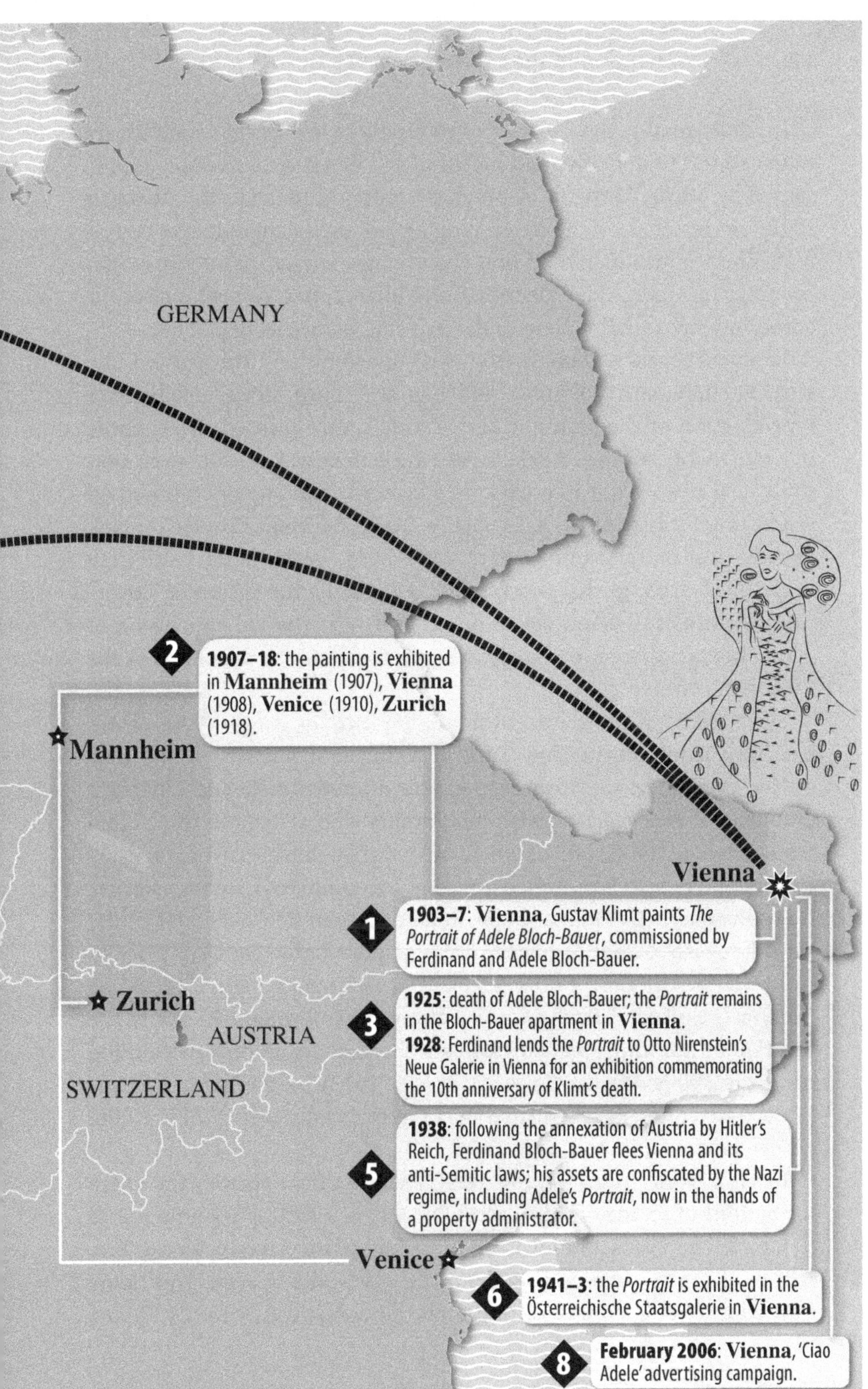
GERMANY
2
1907–18: the painting is exhibited in Mannheim (1907), Vienna (1908), Venice (1910), Zurich (1918).
Mannheim
Vienna
1
1903–7: Vienna, Gustav Klimt paints The Portrait of Adele Bloch-Bauer, commissioned by Ferdinand and Adele Bloch-Bauer.
Zurich
AUSTRIA
SWITZERLAND
3
1925: death of Adele Bloch-Bauer; the Portrait remains in the Bloch-Bauer apartment in Vienna.
1928: Ferdinand lends the Portrait to Otto Nirenstein's Neue Galerie in Vienna for an exhibition commemorating the 10th anniversary of Klimt's death.
5
1938: following the annexation of Austria by Hitler's Reich, Ferdinand Bloch-Bauer flees Vienna and its anti-Semitic laws; his assets are confiscated by the Nazi regime, including Adele's Portrait, now in the hands of a property administrator.
Venice
6
1941–3: the Portrait is exhibited in the Österreichische Staatsgalerie in Vienna.
8
February 2006: Vienna, 'Ciao Adele' advertising campaign.

In 2006, finally, the *Portrait of Adele Bloch-Bauer* was definitively returned to the nephews and nieces of the Bloch-Bauer couple represented by Maria Altmann. A purchase proposal made to the Austrian state was rejected by the latter, judging the sum demanded to be too high. The restitution of the Klimt was then the subject of intense media coverage in Austria; the Viennese were invited, not without pathos, to come and pay a final tribute to the painting before its departure.

In mid-February 2006, in the early morning and throughout the city, 300 billboard columns, and bus and tram stops, displayed a reproduction of the painting, above which were printed these words in white on black: 'Ciao Adele'. A moving collective farewell, one might think ... if it were not in reality yet another marketing operation: two weeks after this campaign, in fact, a thick red band crossed Adele's painted bust on the same posters, with these words: 'What's still here is good advertising that works well! Thanks to the gleaming advertising spaces of the Gewista company.' This was the sad conclusion of a long history shared by the city, its painting, and the exactions of the twentieth century.

Since 2006, Klimt's extraordinary *Portrait of Adele Bloch-Bauer* has been exhibited in New York in a museum founded by its new owner, the American businessman and millionaire Ronald Lauder, a grandson of Hungarian Jewish immigrants who arrived in the United States around 1900, and the son of the great businesswoman Estée Lauder and heir to her immense cosmetics company. Lauder, a former US ambassador to Vienna under Ronald Reagan and president of the World Jewish Congress since 2007, acquired the painting directly from Maria Altmann. In his museum, intentionally named the Neue Galerie (he used German for its name) and founded in 2001, the prestigious painting sits alongside another icon of European painting from the 1900s: the *Berlin Street Scene* (1913) by the painter Ernst-Ludwig Krichner, also returned by a German museum in 2006 to the descendants of a Jewish collector.

In New York, in a way, the Neue Galerie offers visitors the space (or fiction) of an idealized Central Europe, in a setting reminiscent of Vienna in the 1900s and Jewish Europe before the Second World War. It is as if these places, rising from the sidewalks of New York, now formed a more adequate setting than the public museums of Vienna or Berlin that had appropriated the paintings at the expense of their rightful owners. And as if it were possible, thanks to art and beauty, to restore, if not lives, at least a little of that lost, fantasized Europe – the beautiful years of the Vienna Secession with its elegance, its sweetness, its opulence, its cafés, and that immaterial and persistent thing known as beauty. But the paintings are also in New York to recall the path that led them out of Europe, the anti-Semitism of the twentieth century, and the less explicit anti-Semitism which meant that it was only at the beginning of the twenty-first century that many institutions finally agreed to part with property that had been looted, or had entered their collections, during the Nazi era.

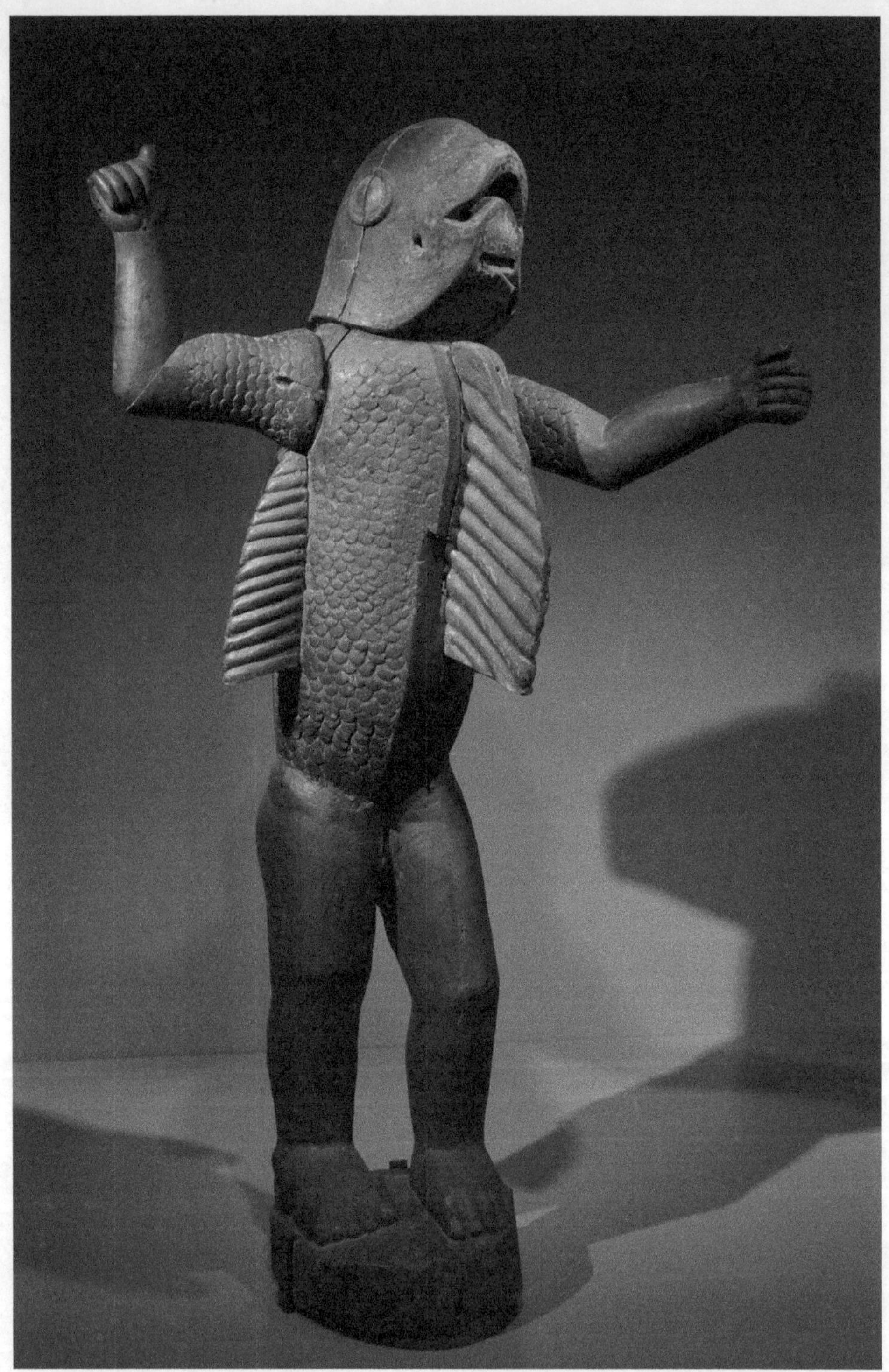

Sossa Dede, anthropo-zoomorphic royal statue (*bochio*) representing Gbehanzin, king of Dahomey, as a shark-man; wood, iron nail, pigments, 168 × 102 × 92 cm, between 1889 and 1892, Abomey region, Benin. Cotonou, National Collections of Benin. Photo: CC BY-SA 3.0 / Myrabella.

# 9

# BENIN'S 'ROYAL TREASURES'

Cotonou, April 2018. At that time, the prospect of a definitive return to Africa of cultural property taken as war trophies by colonial France seemed so improbable that, with an incredulous and melancholy smile, Benin's young interim Minister of Culture, Oswald Homéky, compared it 'to the fall of the Berlin Wall or the reunification of the two Koreas.' Between the unexpected event that the former constituted and the distant hope of the latter, this was a way of tempering his pessimism with the sweetness of a dream: if restitutions were indeed to take place one day, this would have major geopolitical consequences for African art throughout the world.

Three years later, on 9 November 2021, the Wall fell. On that day, the Ministers of Culture of France and Benin, Roselyne Bachelot and Jean-Michel Abimbola, signed in Paris, in the presence of Presidents Emmanuel Macron and Patrice Talon, the act of restitution of twenty-six monumental statues, thrones, architectural elements, textiles, and religious objects from Abomey, the capital of the Kingdom of Danxomè in the territory of the current Republic of Benin. Arriving in France following a bloody military expedition by the French army in 1892 in what was later called the colony of Dahomey, these pieces had immediately been presented to and exhibited at the Musée d'ethnographie du Trocadéro, which became the Musée de l'Homme, then the Quai Branly Museum in Paris. In France, the most familiar of these objects are the three anthropo-zoomorphic statues dedicated to the kings Glele (1814–89) with his wild animal head and raised arms, Gbehanzin (around 1845–89) with his shark scales, and Ghezo (1818–58), a bird man with a raised fist. All three are made of painted wood, human-sized, and powerfully expressive. They had been exhibited once, with great success but only for a few weeks, in Cotonou, in 2006, at the initiative of the Zinsou Foundation for Contemporary Art.

On 10 November 2021, after 129 years of absence, these three statues landed with 23 other monumental pieces (a total of 2.5 tonnes of Beninese cultural heritage), at Cotonou airport, a stone's throw from the Atlantic coast. They were accompanied, in a specially chartered flight from Paris, by Calixte Biah, director of the Ouidah museum. Special broadcasts on all Beninese television channels and the front pages of the daily newspapers described this day as 'historic'. Huge welcome posters decorated the main avenues of the economic capital of Benin, and large crowds gathered along the streets to watch the procession of trucks passing from the airport to the city centre, bringing back the 'treasures of Abomey'. Drones filmed the arrival of the works. The progress of the convoy could be followed by all, live on the internet. The South Korean press and the *New York Times* also covered the event. For the very first time since independence in the 1960s, a sub-Saharan African state had just obtained the physical return to its territory of substantial elements of its culture and history that had been transported to Europe in the colonial era. And France was the first European power to allow this return. It was not only the geopolitics of African cultural heritage that had fundamentally changed, but the very nature of the relationship between former colonized people and colonizers. And, since we are talking about sculptures, creativity, kings, spirituality, and memory, it was also the geopoetics of African heritage that, with this return, entered a new era.

## Heritage moved, heritage replaced

As the trucks arrived in front of the presidential palace, an extraordinary scene took place. In the majesty of their ceremonial outfits, the 'crowned heads' – as traditional kings are called in Benin – together with the notabilities of their respective courts, occupied the front rows of an assembly composed of representatives of the state – male and female – ministers and senior officials of the Republic of Benin, in navy blue costumes and fitted suits. The procession of trucks entered the courtyard; it came to a halt, the back doors of the first vehicle were opened and, for a long while – infinitely long, more than a quarter of an hour but seeming like an hour – in a perfectly regulated ballet but as if in slow motion, with infinite precautions, with millimetric precision and before the eyes of 500 people, 6 men worked gently, very gently, to extract an immense wooden crate: the one that contained the throne of King Ghezo reproduced in photos all over the city, on the truck, and on the crate itself. For the simple removal of a crate from a truck, it took much too long. In fact, time seemed to be suspended. It was not a crate that was being removed. It was more like a metaphorical birth, the arrival or return to the world of a lost heritage, a cultural (re)birth that would leave its mark on the future and on the way people thought. This was followed by a series of speeches that had been carefully composed to welcome the returnees and give them, as we shall see later, a political place in the memorial, constitutional, legislative, and territorial landscape of a modern African democracy.

Who owns beauty? The question, at that time, did not arise in so many words. The virtuosity of the craftsmen and artists who, before 1890, sculpted that throne and those statues, wove those clothes, and decorated those sacred objects, was obviously recognized: the official speeches mentioned in particular one of the creators of those works, the sculptor Sossa Dede; and, in his official capacity, the President of the Republic of Benin, Patrice Talon, insisted on this dimension:

> Statues or sculpted doors, ornate thrones, portable altars or impressive royal staffs – none of them leaves us indifferent. There is no doubt that many of you, in contact with them, will contemplate their beauty, their magnificence and their exceptional splendour, signs of the prodigious skill of their designers. Many will be the voices that, on seeing them, will salute the vision and the greatness of the kings who commissioned them.[1]

But what matters just as much – and, indeed, even more at the time when the works returned to Benin – was the history of the kingdoms linked to these pieces; it was the souls that some people felt were still encapsulated there – the intellectual, religious, and cultural potential that was about to be rediscovered, and perhaps the tourists that they would help to attract. Ultimately, it was the fact that they were returning to the Republic and not to a particular kingdom. For Benin, and more generally for African countries that since their independence had been demanding that former colonial powers return some of the material traces left by their ancient history, the question now arose of the resocialization of sculptures, textiles, and royal insignia – of their reconnection with the realities of the twenty-first century, with the places, old or new, intended to accommodate them, of their reintegration into a cultural fabric to be (re)invented, and of the way they could be given a (fresh) meaning.

How could one come to terms with the European gaze that, for decades, had made these royal or palatial pieces 'museum objects' – classified, studied, and interpreted in accordance with logics that were initially colonial (as trophies), then ethnographic (as witnesses of an ethnic group), and finally aesthetic (as examples of beauty, and of formal originality)? How could they be reset in the systems of meaning and creativity of contemporary African countries, in non-Western forms of the production of knowledge? How could contemporary African societies adopt or readopt pieces that for many, despite their long absence, had not become passive objects but had remained active entities, 'highly charged' pieces, or even active protagonists, ordering the society around them? What was to be made of those statues, textiles, and architectural elements enriched (or impoverished) by years of European exhibition and interpretation (or, when they had remained in storage, by decades of disuse and oblivion)? How were such transformed identities to be negotiated? And what kind of identity could be found in all this, in the twenty-first century, in West Africa, in a world that was obviously no longer what it had been before?

On the African continent, and more generally in states systematically dispossessed of their historical heritage during the colonial era, these questions – due to the lack of large-scale collections on site – had not often been discussed collectively. In Benin, as in neighbouring Nigeria, which was also now preparing to recover a substantial portion of the artistic treasures looted by the British army in 1897 (known as the 'Benin bronzes'), it was necessary to wait for the objects to actually return, for them to be really back home, for heritage discussions to begin. Does a piece taken from a West African kingdom at the end of the nineteenth century belong today to the descendants of the king then in power, to the community of his subjects, to the city where he reigned, or to the modern nation now established on its territories? Should a religious object taken from a particular community be returned to it if the religion in question still exists? Should we spiritually 'recharge' certain pieces, or leave them as material souvenirs? And what about the care to be given to them – ointments, repairs, and transformations that are often incompatible with the Western idea of conservation?

Heritage restitutions are not limited to the physical return of works. They involve important cultural, economic, and social issues. As such, because it was the first African country to have actually physically recovered a considerable part of its heritage, Benin is a privileged observatory for understanding what restitution means: to return and recognize past wounds, certainly, but also – and above all – to open up new horizons and potentialities, to allow forms of reconnection to occur, of which, for the moment, we know nothing.

## Reconnecting through the arts

After a period of 'reacclimatization,' as the authorities responsible called it at the time, the twenty-six historical pieces recovered by Cotonou were – as the first act of their reintegration – the subject of a spectacular exhibition inaugurated in February 2022. Entitled 'Art in Benin yesterday and today. From restitution to revelation,' this exhibition was symbolically held in the former Presidential Palace of the Republic of Benin, over 2,000 square metres directly adjacent to the current presidential residence – a way of signifying without too many words that the works, taken from a kingdom and a king deposed in 1892 (King Gbehanzin), now belonged to the entire republic, which had demanded and obtained restitution from France. Free and open to all, the exhibition welcomed a total of more than 200,000 visitors in a few months, giving the lie to all those in Europe who, for decades, had claimed that Africans were not interested in their heritage; that they had no history, or priorities other than culture; or that they did not know what art is. The international success of the exhibition attracted collectors and art critics from all over the area, well beyond Benin – from its wealthy neighbour Nigeria to Côte d'Ivoire. A West African government thus displayed its capacity not only to obtain and materially organize the return of its precolonial heritage, but also to crystallize public attention around it, bringing together the old and the modern.

For, in this exhibition, it was also works of art that were charged with welcoming the ancient works and reconnecting them with a world that had changed. The objects of the past, the monumental statues of the kings Glele, Gbehanzin, and Ghezo, their thrones and their portable silver altars ('Asen') were presented as remarkable craft achievements, which, thanks to precise historical explanations, maps, and graphs, also brought back to Cotonou the distant and nowadays rarely mentioned history of the precolonial kingdoms. They emphasized the existence, in this region of West Africa, of an ancient culture that was highly developed on linguistic, artistic, and spiritual levels. On the walls, quotations in Fon, one of the five most widely used languages in present-day Benin, allowed the public to make the connection between tangible heritage (the works) and intangible heritage (the language), between past and present. In a separate cabinet, lit like a jewel, was the striped tunic of an Agoodjié from the Amazon Corps, that legendary female unit of the Danxomè army that was reputed to be indestructible. As the last piece in the historical part of the exhibition, the tunic acted as a link to the contemporary part, where 130 works by three generations of Beninese artists welcomed the restored 'treasures', underscoring the continuity of the tradition. Seen all together, they brought the ancient sculptures of Abomey into the twenty-first century. They were a wordless reminder that the sculpted palace doors and the statues of animal-men were also the work of renowned artists long before their arrival in Paris as anonymous war trophies and exotic curiosities at the Trocadéro Museum of Ethnography. They also showed that they could contribute to the affirmation of a decentralized universalism, starting from West Africa. Or, to quote the statement made forty-five years earlier by the

Senegalese intellectual Amadou Mahtar M'Bow, whose words opened the exhibition: 'Returning a work of art or a document to the country that produced it allows a people to recover part of its memory and its identity; it is proof that, in mutual respect between nations, the long dialogue of civilizations that defines the history of the world continues.'[2]

The final effect produced by the return of the treasures of Abomey and their exhibition in Cotonou is worth noting: in the historical section, you could see young children accompanied by their parents discovering ancient statues and asking questions about their origins and their meaning, thus setting in motion a triangular dialogue between different objects and generations. In the contemporary section, traditional chiefs, often very old, in ceremonial dress, were able to view Afrofuturist works such as the sculptures of motorcycle helmets covered in cowrie shells by Emo de Medeiros (born in 1979) from the 'Vodunaut-Hypercyber' series: these works connected mobility, technology, and imagination with the cosmogony of the Vodun religion. Here, the futurist object triggered new discussions, rarely engaged on collectively, between the representatives of tradition and contemporary artistic positions.

Finally, the return of the works and their joint exhibition allowed Cotonou to make of the museum what it is in other countries: a machine with diverse temporalities, which allows us to situate ourselves individually and collectively in time.

In the new geopolitical order of ancient African heritage, a country like Benin has, with the return of artworks and the creation of national collections, put itself in a position to negotiate directly, on its own terms, loans and borrowings of works with other museums in the world, to plan exhibition tours and other forms of circulation – all of which were impossible as long as the country did not have its own collection. On the geopoetic level, we can already see how contemporary creation – and the art market that supports it – is being stimulated by such restitutions.

For the stimulation of artists by artists is at the very heart of the idea of culture and museums. In 1908, in Paris, the young Charles-Édouard Jeanneret-Gris, who had not yet taken the pseudonym of the famous architect he was to become, Le Corbusier, sketched the same royal statues from Abomey, recently brought back to France and exhibited at the Trocadéro Museum of Ethnography. Years later, he noted in his memoirs how much the collections of this museum had marked him – and, indeed, we find traces of the treasures of Abomey among the hundreds of pencil and pen drawings, watercolours, and gouaches that the young man gathered in his sketchbooks. At the Louvre, he drew Egyptian artefacts and Greek vases; at the Cluny Museum, medieval tapestries; at the Guimet Museum, Hindu and Japanese objects; at the Trocadéro Museum of Ethnography, the future architect's interest focused on Peruvian vases with zoomorphic forms as well as on the sculptures of Glele, Ghezo, and Gbehanzin, to which he dedicated at least four sketches known today:

> It's a guilty pleasure that has gripped me since childhood, and I have spent the best moments of my life visiting museums in a large part of the world. You know (you have seen my drawings) that, as early as 1908, being completely foreign to the world of artists, I had already been to make drawings at the Trocadéro Museum of Ethnography, including several pieces that you had exhumed from the jumble where they lay. I was completely unaware that there was a Negro or pre-Columbian question at that time, but I had discovered the ethnographic museum and I was filled with enthusiasm.[3]

In the illustrated press of the time, the large statues of Abomey were considered as the expression of artists who were certainly gifted but 'inferior', as evidenced by this judgement from the colonial administrator and Africanist ethnologist Maurice Delafosse, in *La Nature* in 1894. By pretending to rehabilitate the skills of African artists and craftsmen, he was reinforcing racist stereotypes:

> An opinion, unfortunately quite widespread, tends to represent Negroes in general and Dahomeans in particular, as inferior beings, incapable of any elevated or artistic feeling. The few objects that were able to be saved from the fire of Abomé [*sic*] and which are exhibited at the Trocadéro Museum of Ethnography have come at just the right time to prove the opposite.... I will not go so far as to say that these are models of sculpture. But given the ignorance of the sculptors, their complete

> lack of any kind of instruction, and the inferiority of their tools, one cannot deny that there is in these attempts a beginning of art, capable of improvement.[4]

The message is clear: here the emblems of the Abomey dynasty are reduced to the state of witnesses of a supposed 'development' or 'underdevelopment', of a 'work in progress'. It is interesting, in retrospect, to see that, during their first years in Paris, it was an artist, Le Corbusier, who was among the first to seem to grasp their particular aura. He returned to it in the 1950s: for the World's Fair in Brussels in 1958, he collaborated with his then assistant, the engineer and composer Iannis Xenakis, on the Philips pavilion, intended to house their *Poème électronique*, a multimedia installation. On 3 gigantic screens spread out inside the pavilion, an 8-minute film by Le Corbusier was projected to the sound of a composition by Edgard Varèse broadcast by 450 loudspeakers. The film itself, now lost, was a succession of black-and-white photographs stained with coloured luminous shapes, which through successive flashes created visual associations on the history of humanity and the state of the world. The three statues of the kings of Abomey appeared several times in the film. A black-and-white photograph taken at a performance of *Poème électronique* immortalized the crowd of captivated spectators who, their heads raised towards the screen above them, seemed to be subjected to the threats of the statue dedicated to King Glele with its lion's head, its pointed teeth, and its raised fists. In 1958, in Brussels, the movement for the emancipation of African states colonized by European powers was on everyone's minds.

In the 1960s, the author of one of the first texts devoted to the question of the restitution of works was precisely – and this is certainly more significant than it may seem – a poet and journalist, born in 1931 in what was then still the colony of Dahomey. In 1965, Paulin Joachim published an important editorial in the journal which he then directed in Dakar, *Bingo*. Under the title 'Rendez-nous l'art nègre' ('Give us back Negro art'), he explains the need for young independent nations to reconnect with their intangible heritage (their languages, their philosophies, and their religions), but also their material heritage – namely, the works taken en masse to Europe during the colonial period. In his eyes, this was not a matter of taking revenge or obtaining reparation for the past, but of building the future after a long period of self-denial. He writes: 'There is a battle that must be valiantly fought on all fronts in Europe and America: … the battle to recover African works of art scattered throughout the world.'[5]

When he wrote these words, Joachim had no illusions about the outcome of the fight and he could already imagine the Europeans' response, 'whenever the question gets officially asked': 'But of course, we pillaged to preserve the artistic productions of the black world against worms and termites, against the smoke of the huts. The Africans owe us boundless gratitude for the work we have undertaken.'[6]

Joachim was right. But this kind of response is now a thing of the past. European deafness to the legitimate desire of formerly colonized nations to reconnect with their artistic, cultural, and historical heritage is no more. In 2005, Christiane Taubira, a member of parliament from Guyana, asked the French government to return the spoils of war to Benin. A few years later, in 2013, the Representative Council of Black Associations (CRAN) relayed this call in the French press. These claims remained unheeded. Years later, in August 2016, it was in these terms that the Minister for Foreign Affairs of Benin, Aurélien Agbénonci, requested the return of the Abomey pieces from his French counterpart at the time, Jean-Marc Ayrault:

> I would like to recall that in 1892, following the defeat of the troops of the Kingdom of Danxomè, the French colonial armies, arriving in Abomey, destroyed the palace of King Gbehanzin and took many extremely precious objects that are now in several public and private collections of the French Republic, notably at the Musée du Quai Branly. As you know, these objects have considerable heritage and historical value for all Beninese men and women. But even more, they have considerable spiritual value, insofar as they link us with the souls of our illustrious departed. Cultural property, unique and above all irreplaceable, is the witness of its time and its era. It is for this reason that the international community considers that cultural heritage is a primordial element of national identity and that all peoples have the right to objects that are living witnesses of their civilization. As things stand, and as far as we are concerned in Benin, our cultural heritage,

> a primordial element of our national identity, is found largely outside our homeland. Our parents, our children have never seen these cultural assets, which constitutes a handicap to the harmonious transgenerational transmission of our collective memory. I base my request first on the universal principles and values of UNESCO and the Resolutions of the United Nations, but even more on the natural right of peoples to justice and friendship between our two peoples and our two countries. I am fully aware, M. le Minister, of the time required to conduct such a process.... I can assure you that the Government of my country is at your disposal to discuss the practical conditions and modalities of this restitution, within the framework of an intercultural dialogue that Benin calls for with all its heart.[7]

Formulated in this way, the request put forward a conception of heritage very close to that which the Council of Europe, for example, had drawn up in 2005 with the Faro Convention, which insists on the fact that 'the importance of cultural heritage lies less in the objects and places than in the meanings and uses that people attach to them and the values that they represent'.[8] In a country such as France, where, since the Revolution, heritage has been one of the pillars of the nation, along with republicanism and secularism, Benin's request could not fail to arouse support. However, in his – belated – response in December 2016, the French minister barricaded himself behind complex, almost unpronounceable, legal terms ('inalienability', 'imprescriptibility', 'unseizability') which, like magic formulas, made restitution impossible, but also, given the politeness of the request and the curtness of the response, ruled out any discussion. The French minister acknowledged the importance and value of the concept of national heritage, only in order to better reject Benin's request:

> Yours of the 26th August requesting the restitution of cultural property from Benin's heritage and preserved in France has absorbed my entire attention. France itself attaches great importance to the protection and promotion of cultural heritage, at the national and international levels. It is committed to the universal principles and values of UNESCO and has ratified the 1970 Convention on the Means of Prohibiting and Preventing the Illicit Import, Export and Transfer of Ownership of

> Cultural Property. This convention entered into force in France in 1997 and has no retroactive effect. The property you are referring to has long been part of the movable public domain of the French State, sometimes for more than a century. In accordance with the legislation in force, it is subject to the principles of inalienability, imprescriptibility, and unseizability. Consequently, its restitution is not possible. I am aware of the historical and cultural value of this property for Benin and all Beninese people. I share your wish to make them better known. Large-scale cooperations have already been implemented between the museums of our two countries. I confirm that I am fully at your disposal to develop them even further.[9]

We must bear this exchange of views in mind to understand, beyond the cultural and memorial dimension, the immense political significance of the event represented in 2021 by the signing in Paris of the act of return, under the auspices of Patrice Talon and Emmanuel Macron. This significance was all the greater given that Benin's request in 2016 was part of a long series of heritage claims, forcefully launched by several African countries straight after independence. For France in 2016, the answer was clear and unequivocal: the heritage of a formerly colonized country belonged forever to the person who took it from that country. Five years later in Benin, the return of the works also gave rise to a fascinating effort to transform their status from dynastic, palatial works taken from a king to that of the national heritage of the republic.

Thus, in Cotonou, in February 2022, in his speech inaugurating the exhibition of the twenty-six returned pieces, the president of the Republic of Benin explained to the descendants of King Gbehanzin that the returned objects had indeed been taken from the palace of this king in Abomey, but that it all now belonged to the (multi-ethnic) republic of Benin. He 'republicanized', so to speak, the precolonial heritage and then spent considerable time in the exhibition itself explaining to the 'crowned heads' who came to visit the exhibition, in their different languages, how this 'republicanization' had taken place. The following passages are the literal transcription of a long improvised exchange between the president, traditional dignitaries, and several translators, in Fon, Yom, Yoruba, and French, that took place in front of the ancient works now restored and exhibited to all at the Marina Palace in Cotonou:

> And the peoples of Africa have started to say: 'Send us back what has historical value, what has heritage value – that is to say our common good –, what has value for the memory of the different peoples. Return them to us, these things ... So that your children and your great-grandchildren, so that foreigners, when they come, can see what has marked the history of your country. We too need to see what has marked our history, so that we can know what our country was like five hundred years ago, three hundred years ago, a hundred years ago, and fifty years ago, how the kingdoms evolved, how the peoples of Africa of Benin changed. This is the interest [of restitution]. This is what has made us ask for these goods to be returned to us. So that on our territory there are things that can bear witness to our history. It is important that each people have on their territory things that are part of their heritage and their history, that trace their life for today and for tomorrow.
>
> ...
>
> Today, what is part of the treasures of the kingdom of Nikki, the kingdom of Porto Novo or the kingdom of Kouandé, is the national treasure. This is why these treasures that had left a region of the territory are now the business of all of us; they are our treasure because they bear testimony to what our various kingdoms were. That is why I am delighted that all Beninese men and women can recognize themselves through these works that have arrived already, while waiting for the rest to join them.[10]

This surprising document places its finger on the political, memorial, historical, and museological issues internal to the country linked to the return of heritage objects. If the reappropriation of looted objects will indeed take different forms in each of the nations concerned – depending in particular on the nature of the works, the degree of involvement of local elites, and the will of their current leaders – three features seem to confirm the awareness of heritage raised by the effective restitution of works displaced under conditions of colonial violence: first, the focus of attention on a certain number of objects that crystallize feelings of national cohesion; second, the dynamic process of the centralization of heritage; and third, the importance of issues both aesthetic (the dual exhibition of ancient art and contemporary art) and political (here republican) in the process of recovering the objects.

This dual aesthetic and political dimension comes, finally, with the matter of the return of the works, a moment of recovery that could be described as 'epistemological,' as it consists of reintegrating the works into local systems of knowledge that have either disappeared, or still exist but are far removed from and complementary to the 'Western' systems of knowledge (museographic, ethnographic) into which the works were integrated during the century and a half of their presence in France. The pieces that come back also revive postulates, notions, and constellations of ideas that are embedded in local webs of connection. Or, to be more precise, they seek to be read, seen, and also interpreted in the light of hermeneutic grids specific to the regions from which they come.

## Intellectual reappropriation

When, in the aftermath of independence, one of Nigeria's great intellectuals, the archaeologist Ekpo Eyo, mentioned the possible return of the works looted by the British army in Benin City, he insisted forcefully on the need for these works to be reintegrated into the academic and university discourses of the African continent itself, an essential complement, in his eyes, to the 'Western' readings applied to the works for many decades. In a remarkable text from the mid-1970s, Eyo argued in favour of a renewal of the historiography of Nigerian art that draws on the work of African researchers:

> If Europe has chosen to divorce art from religious or other social contexts, this does not amount to advancement, in fact some would regard it as a retrograde step. For the African, the importance of a sculpture lies outside the realms of aesthetics; it has to do with the reconciliation of his life with his environment – with the problems of birth, survival, well-being, longevity, death and reincarnation: the whole life-cycle. It is only in terms of these social and religious contexts

> – indigenous African ideas, philosophies, religions, economies and politics – that the meaning of a sculpture may be found.[11]

Today, now that a substantial part of Beninese heritage has returned to Benin, the dynamic of intellectual reappropriation described by Eyo seems to be under way – or at least it is on the verge of getting under way. In November 2021, while the returned pieces were still stored in their crates to 'reacclimatize' them, Beninese historians from the University of Abomey–Calavi joined the specialist in African art Didier Houénoudé at a conference to discuss, for example, the question of the language or languages that should be used to speak to the statues. How did their ancestors speak to them? What systems of thought, what words, what melodies, perhaps, were used in the past to address these objects? Do they still exist? So many potential research projects and avenues for the future.

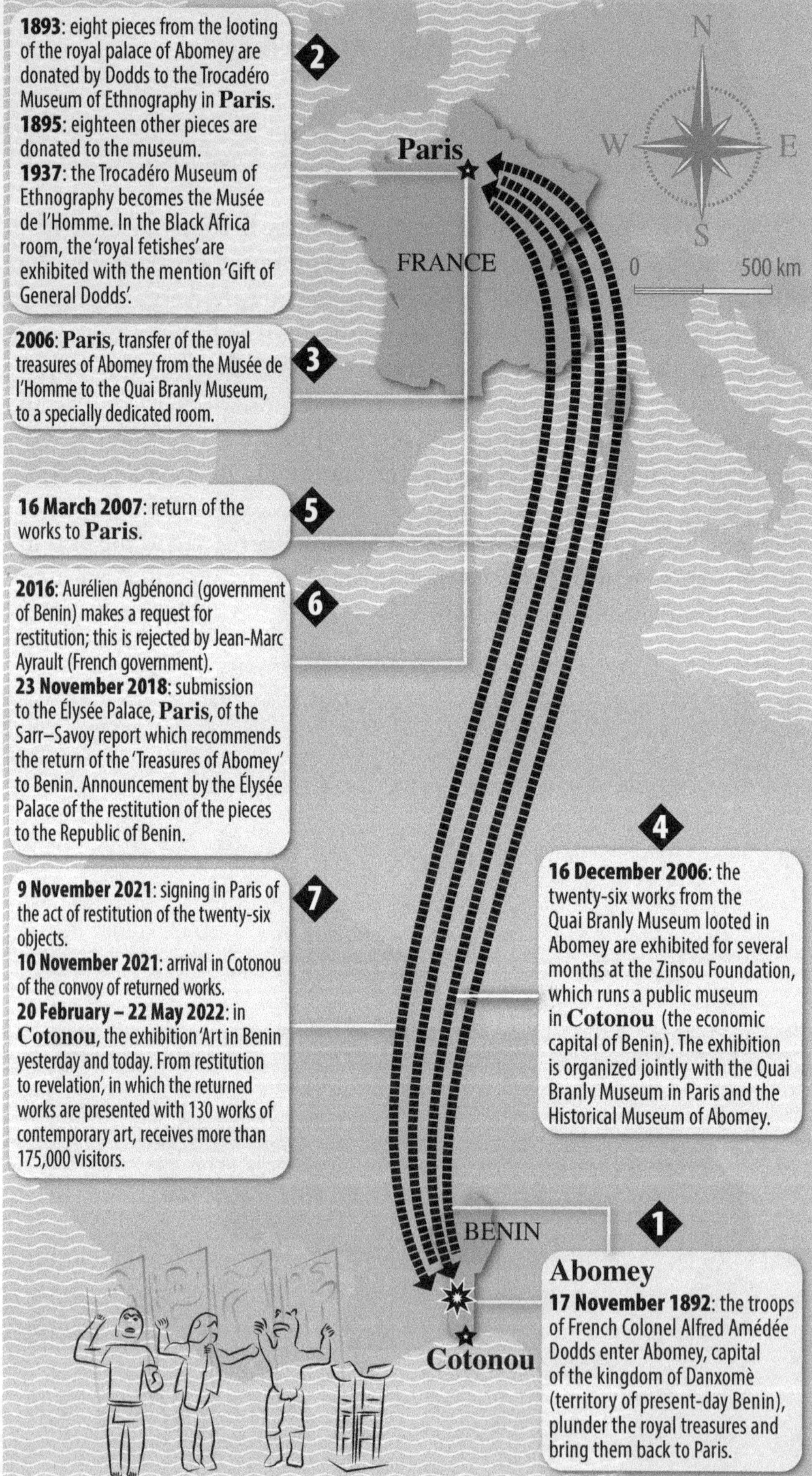

1893: eight pieces from the looting of the royal palace of Abomey are donated by Dodds to the Trocadéro Museum of Ethnography in Paris.
1895: eighteen other pieces are donated to the museum.
1937: the Trocadéro Museum of Ethnography becomes the Musée de l'Homme. In the Black Africa room, the 'royal fetishes' are exhibited with the mention 'Gift of General Dodds'.
2
N
W
E
S
Paris
FRANCE
0
500 km
2006: Paris, transfer of the royal treasures of Abomey from the Musée de l'Homme to the Quai Branly Museum, to a specially dedicated room.
3
16 March 2007: return of the works to Paris.
5
2016: Aurélien Agbénonci (government of Benin) makes a request for restitution; this is rejected by Jean-Marc Ayrault (French government).
23 November 2018: submission to the Élysée Palace, Paris, of the Sarr–Savoy report which recommends the return of the 'Treasures of Abomey' to Benin. Announcement by the Élysée Palace of the restitution of the pieces to the Republic of Benin.
6
4
16 December 2006: the twenty-six works from the Quai Branly Museum looted in Abomey are exhibited for several months at the Zinsou Foundation, which runs a public museum in Cotonou (the economic capital of Benin). The exhibition is organized jointly with the Quai Branly Museum in Paris and the Historical Museum of Abomey.
9 November 2021: signing in Paris of the act of restitution of the twenty-six objects.
10 November 2021: arrival in Cotonou of the convoy of returned works.
20 February – 22 May 2022: in Cotonou, the exhibition 'Art in Benin yesterday and today. From restitution to revelation', in which the returned works are presented with 130 works of contemporary art, receives more than 175,000 visitors.
7
BENIN
1
Abomey
17 November 1892: the troops of French Colonel Alfred Amédée Dodds enter Abomey, capital of the kingdom of Danxomè (territory of present-day Benin), plunder the royal treasures and bring them back to Paris.
Cotonou

# Conclusion

At the end of 2013, a photo of the Ishtar Gate, with its ochre and lapis lazuli enamel bricks and its rows of bulls and dragons, began to circulate on social networks. In Antiquity, this gate had marked the end of the processional route of the city of Babylon, in ancient Mesopotamia. In front of it, kneeling, a London student of Iraqi origin, Zeidoun Alkinani, dressed in a sober and dark outfit, looks into the photographer's lens. He holds in his hands a white sign with handwritten letters: 'This belongs to Iraq.' The photograph must have been taken during the opening hours of the Pergamon Museum in Berlin, where the Ishtar Gate has been preserved since the beginning of the twentieth century. It was first shared on 2 December 2013 by the Facebook account @shakomakodotnet. Since then, it has regularly resurfaced on the networks. While the authorship and date of the photo are not known, the message is unequivocal.

At almost the same time, at the Victoria & Albert Museum in London, a neon installation was set up in the museum's large entrance hall: 'All of this belongs to you.' Here, the museum reminded visitors that they could freely access and interact with the exhibits in its collection during opening hours. However, many of the works in question do not come from the geographical surroundings of the institution. Who is included in the 'you' of the generous welcome?

The historiography of recent decades has established the importance over time of globalized communication and intercultural and transnational exchange. 'Connected history', 'shared history', 'interrelated history', 'entangled history' are among the many labels under which transcultural perspectives are understood. As a general rule, it is the immaterial dynamics (identity constructions, memory conflicts, cultural transfers) that attract the most attention. However, in current museum rhetoric, the vaunted ideal of shared heritage means that museums, as owners of objects from all over the world, take the initiative, not to share the physical power they exercise over these unique and indivisible entities, which remains their prerogative, but simply to 'enter into dialogue' with the countries of origin – to 'set up cooperation' with researchers, artists, and representatives of the 'communities of origin' in order to enrich and enhance 'again' their collections. The world, they say, must be made more readable in this way – through perspectivism and a transcendence of national borders. They thereby avoid the central question of mobility – of the quasi-impossibility, for a large part of humanity, of obtaining the visas that would allow them to come to London, Paris, Amsterdam, or Berlin.

In an astonishing fable written in 2015 and entitled *Des lions comme des danseuses* (*Lions like dancing women*), the French author Arno Bertina depicts the king of Bangoulap in Bamiléké country (Cameroon) and his legal advisers at odds with a Parisian museum.[1] He imagines a cascade of demands at the end of which the king of Bangoulap is graciously granted visas for all Cameroonians, visas valid throughout Europe – provoking the jealousy of the Italian representatives in Brussels, who in turn demand for their nationals unlimited access to all Italian works throughout the world. The European Commission is on the verge of a nervous breakdown when the king of Bangoulap asks the Louvre to lend the masterpieces from its collections to Africa. Upon reading his request, two curators faint.

Who owns the beauty in our museums? The charm of Arno Bertina's fable is that it does not explicitly ask the question and refrains from answering it. With malice and virtuosity, he instead plays with two categories that are barely differentiated in our ordinary ways of using them: possession and property. According to law manuals, possession refers to 'effective power over a thing'. The possessor holds the thing in his power, he or she exercises de facto control over it, independently of a right that would justify it. Or, to follow the etymology of 'to possess' – from the Latin *possidere,* from *potis sum,* 'I can, I am powerful,' and *sedere,* 'to be seated': he is literally 'seated' on the thing. The owner, on the other hand, has legal power over a thing, he or she can do with it 'what they want while excluding others from any interference,' whether or not this thing is actually in their possession. Their property remains attached to them when the thing is taken from them. Etymologically, it has a 'proper' or 'appropriate' character, from the Latin *proprius,* 'personal, particular, special.' A legal educator would say: 'The thief who appropriated your bike is the possessor, you remain the owner.' Applied to our question, this distinction contains a certain liberating potential. If we follow it, museums are the possessors of the objects in their power; the objects are at their disposal, in fact, without necessarily belonging to them in law. The owners, on the other hand, remain those whose object, even if it is lost, remains their 'own.' Yet in the reality of our century, these boundaries exist more than ever and prevent a large part of humanity from approaching Western museums.

For those who possess the works, the formula may appeal. But how much longer will those who no longer possess them and do not have access to them tolerate being kept out of their own history? And how much longer will we in Europe pretend to ignore the fact that the injustice over heritage, an injustice inherited from the nineteenth century, is one of the greatest challenges of the future?

# Notes

## Introduction

1 Antoine Chrysostome Quatremère de Quincy, *Lettres sur le préjudice qu'occasionnerait aux arts et à la science le déplacement des monuments de l'art de l'Italie,* known as *Lettres à Miranda,* ed. Édouard Pommier (Paris: Macula, 1989), letter IV, pp. 109–16 (p. 116).

2 'And snatch'd thy shrinking Gods to northern climes abhorr'd!' in George Gordon Byron, 'Childe Harold's pilgrimage' (1812), canto II, XV: https://knarf.english.upenn.edu/Byron/charold2.html.

3 Victor Hugo, 'L'expédition de Chine – au capitaine Butler,' Hauteville House, 25 November 1861, in Victor Hugo, *Actes et paroles II: Pendant l'exil (1852–1870),* reprinted in Émile Testard (ed.), Édition nationale. Victor Hugo, vol. XL (Paris: Librairie de l'Édition nationale, 1894), pp. 253–6.

4 Paul Valéry, 'La crise de l'esprit' (1919), in Paul Valéry, *Œuvres,* vol. I (Paris: Gallimard, Bibliothèque de la Pléiade, 1957), p. 995.

5 Ibid.

6 Achille Mbembe, *Politiques de l'inimitié* (Paris: La Découverte, 2018), p. 178.

7 James Cuno, *Who Owns Antiquity? Museums and the Battle over Our Ancient Heritage* (Princeton University Press, 2010); Margaret M. Miles, *Art as a Plunder: The Ancient Origins of Debate about Cultural Property* (Cambridge University Press, 2008); Donald Malcolm Reid, *Whose Pharaohs? Archaeology, Museums, and Egyptian National Identity*

*from Napoleon to World War I* (Berkeley: University of California Press, 2003).

8 Cuno, *Who Owns Antiquity?*, p. 146.

9 Ibid., p. xxxii.

10 See Kwame Anthony Appiah, 'Whose Culture Is It?,' *New York Review of Books*, 9 February 2006, www.nybooks.com/articles/2006/02/09/whose-culture-is-it/?srsltid=AfmBOooO0AFCNqSb3nVgIIUED6x3q6Wluw1d811aL9gE1FLBg0JOqltK.

11 1954 Convention for the Protection of Cultural Property in the Event of Armed Conflict, signed on 14 May 1954, entered into force on 7 August 1956 under the auspices of UNESCO: www.unesco.org/en/legal-affairs/convention-protection-cultural-property-event-armed-conflict-regulations-execution-convention?hub=415.

12 Convention on the Means of Prohibiting and Preventing the Illicit Importation, Export and Transfer of Ownership of Cultural Property, signed on 14 November 1970, entered into force on 24 April 1972 under the auspices of UNESCO: www.unesco.org/en/legal-affairs/convention-means-prohibiting-and-preventing-illicit-import-export-and-transfer-ownership-cultural.

13 See Barbara Cassin and Danièle Wozny (eds.), *Les Intraduisibles du patrimoine en Afrique subsaharienne* (Paris: Demopolis, 2014): http://books.openedition.org/égyptien et de la collection de demopolis/515.

14 Marcus Tullius Cicero, *Against Verres*, translated by C. D. Yonge: https://en.wikisource.org/wiki/Against_Verres/Second_pleading/Book_4.

15 Ibid.

16 Cf. Bénédicte Savoy, *Patrimoine annexé. Les biens culturels saisis par la France en Allemagne autour de 1800*, 2 volumes (Paris: Éditions de la Maison des sciences de l'homme, 2003).

17 August Wilhelm Schlegel, 'Die entführten Götter' ('The Stolen Gods'), *Musen-Almanach für das Jahr 1798*, ed. Friedrich Schiller, pp. 199–203.

18 Friedrich Schiller, 'The Antiques at Paris,' in *Poems of the Third Period*: www.gutenberg.org/files/6796/6796-h/6796-h.htm.

19 Jeremy Paxman, in the *Telegraph*, 25 October 2014: www.telegraph.co.uk/culture/museums/11185897/The-Elgin-Marbles-belong-in-Britain-Mrs-Clooney.html.

20 Transcript of *The Train*, https://transcripts.foreverdreaming.org/viewtopic.php?t=107686.

21 Cf. Bénédicte Savoy, 'Musée violé, espaces profanés. À propos de *Fünf Tage – Fünf Nächte* de Lew Arnschtam et Heinz Thiel (1960/61)', in Joséphine Jibokji, Barbara Le Maître, Natacha Pernac, and Jennifer Verraes (eds.), *Muséoscopies. Fictions du musée au cinéma* (Presses universitaires de Paris Nanterre, 2018), pp. 217–33.

22 Daniel Fabre (ed.), *Émotions patrimoniales* (Paris: Éditions de la Maison des sciences de l'homme, 2013).

## 1 The Bust of Nefertiti

1 Ludwig Borchardt, Journal of excavations 1912/1913 [*Grabungstagebuch*], fol. 42, Berlin, archives of the Ägyptisches Museum und Papyrussammlung (Egyptian Museum and Papyrus Collection), quoted in Mariana Jung, '100 Jahre Fund der Nofretete', in *Im Licht von Amarna. 100 Jahre Fund der Nofretete*, exhibition catalogue, Berlin Egyptian Museum, 7 December 2012–13, April 2013 (Petersberg: Imhof, 2012), pp. 421–6 (p. 421).

2 Éric Gady, 'Un impérialisme scientifique? L'exemple de l'égyptologie', in Michèle Battesti and Jacques Frémeaux (eds.), *Sortir de la guerre* (Paris: Presses de l'université Paris-Sorbonne, 2014).

3 Gaston Maspero, *Rapports sur la marche du Service des antiquités de 1899 à 1910* (Cairo, 1912), p. XXX.

4 Ibid., p. XXXI.

5 Account on the division of the finds, quoted by Pierre Lacau in a report to the under-secretary of the Egyptian Ministry for Public Works, 14 July 1925, Archives du Centre Wladimir Golenischeff (EPHE), fonds Pierre Lacau, dossier Néfertiti (henceforth 'Dossier Néfertiti'), no. 5, quoted in Bénédicte Savoy, *Nofretete. Eine Deutsch–französische Affäre 1912–1931* (Cologne: Böhlau, 2011), p. 101.

6 Maria Andreas von Lüttichau, 'Erster deutscher Herbstsalon, Berlin 1913', in *Stationen der Moderne. Die bedeutendsten Kunstausstellungen des 20. Jahrhunderts in Deutschland*, exhibition catalogue (Berlin: Berlinische Galerie, 1998), pp. 130–53.

7 Leaflet for the 'Erster deutscher Herbstsalon' by Herwarth Walden, 1913; Berlin, Staatsbibliothek, PK, Handschriftenabteilung (quoted in Lüttichau, 'Erster deutscher Herbstsalon, Berlin 1913', p. 139).

8 'Kunstausstellungen', *Vossische Zeitung*, 20 December 1913.

9 Lisbeth Stern, 'Ägyptische Funde', *Sozialistische Monatshefte*, 26, 23 December 1913, pp. 1720–1, quoted in Bénédicte Savoy, '"Futuristes,

inclinez-vous!" Fièvre amarnienne à Berlin en 1913–1914', translated by Daniel Barric, *Revue germanique internationale*, 16, 2012, http://rgi.revues.org/1353.

10 Letter from Lou Andreas-Salomé to Rilke, 16 February 1914, quoted in Alfred Grimm, *Rilke und Ägypten* (Munich: Fink, 1997), p. 324.

11 Thomas Mann, *Joseph and His Brothers*, translated by John E. Woods (New York, London, and Toronto: Alfred A. Knopf, Everyman's Library, 2005), pp. 1151–2. (Nefer-Kheperu-Râ-Amenhotep is the name that Thomas Mann gives Akhenaton in this novel.)

12 Adolf Behne, 'Thutmes', *Dresdner Neueste Nachrichten*, 30 November 1913.

13 Maximilian Rapsilber, 'Tell el-Amarna', *Der Roland von Berlin*, 13 November 1913, pp. 1519–23.

14 Letter from Lefebvre to Lacau, 11 October 1915, Paris, Bibliothèque de l'Institut de France, Mss. 6311, fols. 111–12.

15 Letter from Lacau to Lange, 29 April 1919, Paris, Bibliothèque de l'Institut de France, Mss. 6339, fols. 43–5.

16 Letter from Borchardt to Lacau, Cairo, 10 April 1925, 'Dossier Néfertiti', no. 1, quoted in Savoy, *Nofretete*, p. 90.

17 Pierre Lacau, report to the under-secretary of the Egyptian Ministry for Public Works, 14 July 1925, 'Dossier Néfertiti', no. 5, quoted in Savoy, *Nofretete*, pp. 100–2.

18 Ibid.

19 *La Bourse égyptienne*, 31 March 1934, 'Dossier Néfertiti'.

20 Ḥasan Tawfīq al-ʻAdl, *Riḥla Ḥasan Afandī Tawfīq al-ʻAdl, 1887–1892* (Cairo, 2008); for the Berlin museums in particular, see pp. 279–88.

## 2 The Pergamon Altar

1 Revelation 2:12–13 (King James Version).

2 Decree of 24 January 1881, signed by Emperor Wilhelm of Germany and Otto von Bismarck, quoted in 'Amtliche Berichte aus den Königlichen Kunstsammlungen', *Jahrbuch der Königlich Preussischen Kunstsammlungen*, 1 July 1882, cols. XXXXIX–LII.

3 Salomon Reinach, 'Chronique d'Orient', *Revue archéologique*, 2, 1883, passim. Salomon Reinach's views on the East were published in the *Revue archéologique* from 1883 onwards, and then collected in two volumes (vol. I, 1883–90, published in 1891; vol. II, 1891–5, published in 1896).

4 'Regulations on Antiquities (23 [Rebiülahir] 1301 – 21 February 1884)', quoted in Luca Frepoli, *Translocations. Législation. Une anthologie de lois sur la protection des biens culturels mobiles du XVIIe au début du XXe siècle*: https://transllegisl.hypotheses. org/uebersicht/ osmanischesreich-21-02-1884.

5 Salomon Reinach, 'Chronique d'Orient', *Revue archéologique*, 1, 1884, pp. 335–6 (the article mentioned by Reinach is 'Le Vandalisme moderne en Orient', *Revue des Deux Mondes*, 56, 239, 1 March 1883).

6 See, for example, Zainab Bahrani, Zeynep Çelik, and Edhem Eldem (eds.), *Scramble for the Past: A Story of Archaeology in the Ottoman Empire. 1753–1914* (Istanbul: SALT, 2011).

7 Ralf Grüssinger, Volker Kästner, and Andreas Scholl (eds.), *Pergamon – Panorama der antiken Metropole*, exhibition catalogue, Pergamon Museum, Berlin, 30 September 2011 – 30 September 2012 (Petersberg: Imhof, 2012).

8 'Regulations on Antiquities (20 Sefer 1291 – 24 March 1874)', quoted in Frepoli, *Translocations. Législation*, https://transllegisl. hypotheses.org /uebersicht/osmanisches-reich-24-03-1874.

9 Jacob Burckhardt, *Briefe*, 10 volumes (Basle/Stuttgart: Schwabe, 1949–86), vol. VIII (1974), pp. 62–74.

10 Ivan Turgenev, 'Les fouilles de Pergame. Lettre à la rédaction du *Messager de l'Europe*', *Cahiers Ivan Tourguéniev, Pauline Viardot, Maria Malibran*, 19, 1995, pp. 17–20 (translated from the Russian by Alexandre Zviguilsky).

11 Ibid.

12 Guillaume Apollinaire, 'Le Pergamon à Berlin', *La Revue blanche*, 28, 15 May 1902, pp. 146–7.

13 Louis Gillet, *L'Illustration*, 4522, 2 November 1929, p. 510.

14 These were large gastronomic complexes of Berlin that had extravagant decors depicting the Niagara Falls, for example.

15 Albert Flament, 'Tableaux de Berlin', *La Revue de Paris*, 15 May 1932, pp. 445–52 (pp. 451f.).

16 'Pergame et son paysage culturel à multiples strates', Dossier d'inscription au Patrimoine mondial de l'Unesco, January 2013, https://whc.unesco.org /uploads/nominations/1457.pdf.

17 Ibid., pp. 229ff.

18 Ibid., p. 255.

## 3 The Altarpiece of 'The Mystic Lamb' by the Van Eyck Brothers

1 François-Antoine Boissy d'Anglas, 'Courtes observations sur le projet de décret présenté au nom du Comité d'instruction publique sur le dernier degré d'instruction, adressées à la Convention nationale', Paris, 28 germinal an II (17 April 1794), quoted in Édouard Pommier, *L'Art de la liberté. Doctrines et débats de la Révolution française* (Paris: Gallimard, 1991), p. 161.

2 Friedrich von Schlegel, *Descriptions de tableaux*, edited and translated by Bénédicte Savoy (Paris: École nationale supérieure des beaux-arts, 2003 [1803]), p. 92.

3 Ibid., p. 91.

4 Ibid., p. 92.

5 Quoted in Vincent Pomarède, 'Napoléon Ier sur le trône impérial', in Vincent Pomarède, Stéphane Guégan, Louis-Antoine Prat, and Éric Bertin, *Ingres 1780–1867*, exhibition catalogue, Musée du Louvre, 24 February – 15 May 2006, cat. no. 34 (Paris: Gallimard, 2006), pp. 142–5.

6 Letter from Henri Beyle (Stendhal) to Dominique-Vivant Denon, 27 October 1810, quoted in Marianne Hamiaux and Jean-Luc Martinez, 'De l'inventaire N à l'inventaire MR: le département des Antiques', in Daniela Gallo (ed.), *Les Vies de Dominique-Vivant Denon*, conference proceedings, 2 volumes (Paris: Musée du Louvre, 2001), vol. II, pp. 434–5 and illustration p. 441. See also Bénédicte Savoy, 'Unschätzbare Meisterwerke: der Preis der Kunst im Musée Napoléon', in Gudrun Swoboda (ed.), *Die kaiserliche Gemäldegalerie in Wien und die Anfänge des öffentlichen Kunstmuseums*, 2 volumes (Vienna: Böhlau, 2013), vol. II, pp. 407–19.

7 Marie-Anne Dupuy-Vachey, Isabelle Le Masne de Chermont, and Elaine Williamson, *Vivant Denon, directeur des musées sous le Consulat et l'Empire* (Paris: Réunion des musées nationaux, 1999), letter no. 2967, pp. 1018–19.

8 Auguste Marguillier, 'Musées et collections', *Mercure de France*, 414, 1 June 1915, pp. 355–62 (p. 358).

9 Official translation: https://net.lib.byu.edu/~rdh7/wwi/versa/versa7.html.

10 Letter from Franz Graf Wolff-Metternich to the military commander of Belgium, Alexander von Falkenhausen, 4 June 1940, quoted in Birgit Schwarz, 'Alle retten den Genter Altar. Der Weg durch Europa 1940–1945', in Stephan Kemperdick, Johannes Rössler, and Joris Corin Heyder (eds.),

*Der Genter Altar. Reproduktionen, Deutungen, Forschungskontroversen* (Petersberg: Imhof, 2017), pp. 12–25 (p. 13).

11 Schwarz, 'Alle retten den Genter Altar', pp. 16, 13.

## 4 Raphael's 'Sistine Madonna'

1 *Grand Dictionnaire universel du XIXe siècle* (Paris: Pierre Larousse, 1866–77).

2 Pierre-Jacques-Onésyme Bergeret de Grancourt, *Bergeret et Fragonard: journal inédit d'un voyage en Italie, 1773–1774* (Paris: May et Motteroz, 1895), p. 410.

3 Johann Anton Riedel and Christian Friedrich Wenzel, *Catalogue des tableaux de la Galerie électorale à Dresde* (Dresden: Chrétien Henri Hagenmüller, 1765).

4 See the reconstitution of the correspondence by Claudia Brink and Andreas Henning, 'Platz für den großen Raffael!', in Andreas Henning (ed.), *Die Sixtinische Madonna. Raffaels Kultbild wird 500*, exhibition catalogue, Dresden, Gemäldegalerie Alte Meister, 26 May – 26 August 2012 (Munich: Prestel Verlag, 2012), cat. nos. 39–49, pp. 209–22.

5 Letter from Pier Luigi della Torre to Benedetto Vittorio Caracciolo [?], 22 December 1752, quoted in Henning and Brink, 'Platz für den großen Raffael!', cat. no. 41, p. 212.

6 Letter from Roberto Rice, minister of the duke of Parma, to Giovanni Battista Bianconi, 26 June 1753, quoted in Henning and Brink, 'Platz für den großen Raffael!', cat. no. 46, p. 218.

7 Letter from Heinrich von Kleist to Wilhelmine von Zenge, 21 May 1801, http://kleistdaten.de/index.php?title=Brief_1801-05-21.

8 Wilhelm Heinrich Wackenroder, *Outpourings of an Art-Loving Friar*, translated by Edward Morin (New York: Frederick Ungar Publishing, 1975), p. 70.

9 Quoted in Bénédicte Savoy, '"Une ample moisson de superbes choses": Les missions de Vivant Denon en Allemagne et en Autriche, 1806–1809', in the exhibition catalogue of 'Vivant Denon' in the Musée du Louvre, Paris, 1999, pp. 170–81.

10 Letter from Dominique-Vivant Denon to Napoleon, 3 December 1806, quoted in Dupuy-Vachey et al., *Vivant Denon*, letter no. 61, pp. 1319–20.

11 Charles Maurice de Talleyrand-Périgord, *Mémoires du prince de Talleyrand*, 5 volumes (Paris: Calmann Lévy, 1891–1912), vol. I, p. 310.

12 Johann David Passavant, *Raphaël d'Urbin et son père Giovanni Santi*, French edition, revised and enlarged by the author based on the translation by M. Jules Lunteschütz, revised and annotated by M. Paul Lacroix, 2 volumes (Paris: Vve J. Renouard, 1860 [1839]).

13 Lev Nikolayevich Tolstoy, Что такое искусство? [*What is Art?*], in Полное собрание сочинений [*Complete Works*], 90 volumes (Moscow State Publishing House, 1928–58), vol. XXX (1951), pp. 303–426 (p. 380). [Translator's note: This quotation is not in the English translations I have consulted.]

14 Fyodor Mikhailovich Dostoevsky, *Crime and Punishment*, translated by Constance Garnett: www.gutenberg.org/cache/epub/2554/pg2554-images.html.

15 Fyodor Mikhailovich Dostoevsky, *The Possessed, or, The Devils*, translated by Constance Garnett: www.gutenberg.org/files/8117/8117-h/8117-h.htm.

16 Friedrich Nietzsche, 'The Wanderer and His Shadow', in *Human All-Too-Human: A Book for Free Spirits*, Part II, translated by Paul V. Cohn (New York: The MacMillan Company, 1913), §73, p. 218: www.gutenberg.org/files/37841/37841-pdf.

17 Vassily Grossman, 'The Sistine Madonna', in *The Road: Short Fiction and Articles*, translated by Robert and Elizabeth Chandler (London: MacLehose Press, 2010), pp. 181–92 (pp. 182–6).

### 5 The Bronze Heads of the Summer Palace in Beijing

1 See www.lefigaro.fr/culture/2009/02/23/03004-20090223ARTFIG00537-ysl-berge-la-justice-autorise-la-vente-des-bronzes-chinois-.php.

2 See Mira Herrarte, 'Im Tierkreis der Macht', in Merten Lagatz, Bénédicte Savoy, and Philippa Sissis (eds.), *Beute. Ein Bildatlas zu Kunstraub und Kulturerbe* (Berlin: Matthes und Seitz, 2021), pp. 274–7.

3 Hugo Grotius, *Le Droit de la guerre et de la paix (De jure belli ac pacis)* (Paris: Buon, 1625), vol. III, chs. 5–6; see Mariana Muravyeva, '"Ni pillage ni viol sans ordre préalable." Codifier la guerre dans l'Europe moderne', *Clio: Femmes, genre, histoire*, 39, 2014, pp. 55–81.

4 Robert Swinhoe, *Narrative of the North China Campaign of 1860: Containing Personal Experiences of Chinese character, and of the Moral and Social Condition of the Country; together with a Description of the Interior of Pekin* (London: Smith, Elder & Company, 1861).

5 Armand Lucy, *Lettres intimes sur la campagne de Chine en 1860* (Marseilles: Jules Barile, 1861), pp. 112–13.

6 Ibid., p. 113.

7 'Exposition des présents offerts à Leurs Majestés par l'armée expéditionnaire de Chine', *Le Monde illustré*, 23 February 1861, p. 128.

8 *Catalogue des objets précieux provenant en grande partie du palais d'été de Yuan Ming Yuan et composant le musée japonais et chinois de M. le Colonel Du Pin* (Paris, 1862).

9 Ibid.

10 Paris, Bibliothèque nationale de France, département Estampes et photographie, RESERVE FT 6-B-9.

11 Hugo, 'L'expédition de Chine'.

12 Speech made by Xi Jinping on visiting the exhibition 'The Road to Rejuvenation', 29 November 2012: www.neac.gov.cn/seac/c103372/202201/1156514.shtml.

13 Speech made by Xi Jinping at a ceremony marking the centenary of the Communist Party of China: https://english.www.gov.cn/news/topnews/202107/01/content_WS60dd8d8ac6d0df57f98dc459.html.

14 *Art Repatriation in China*, documentary video (9 minutes, 15 seconds), London, Sotheby's Institute, 2015. [Translator's note: The video no longer seems to exist online: I have paraphrased.]

15 See Andrea Wallace, Anne Laure Bandle, and Marc-André Renold, 'Case: Two Bronze Animal Heads – China and Pierre Bergé', Plateforme ArThemis, Art-Law Centre, University of Geneva, 2013, https://plone.unige.ch/art-adr/cases-affaires/two-bronze-animal-heads-2013-china-and-pierre-berge.

16 See www.christies.com/about-us/press-archive/details?PressReleaseID=6539.

17 See https://press.christies.com/in-a-market-first-christies-historic-shanghai-to-london-sale-series-realises-ps249070155-rmb-2087955108-334003078-eur-297389765a-record-for-any-evening-at-christies-london.

## 6 Watteau's *L'Enseigne de Gersaint*

1 André Chastel, 'Watteau, le génie du charme', *Le Monde*, 25 October 1984.

2 Ibid.

3 André Chamson (ed.), *Chefs-d'œuvre des Musées de Berlin*, exhibition catalogue, Musée du Petit Palais (Paris: Les Presses artistiques, 1951), p. 9.
4 Francis Haskell, *The Ephemeral Museum: Old Master Paintings and the Rise of the Art Exhibition* (New Haven: Yale University Press, 2000).
5 See Matilde Cartolari, *Ambassadors of Beauty: Italian Old Master Exhibitions and Fascist Cultural Diplomacy 1930–1940* (Munich: De Gruyter, 2024).
6 See the documentation of the exhibition stored in two boxes and two folders of photographs in the archives of the Petit Palais, Paris, classification mark PPEX1951(1).
7 Chamson (ed.), *Chefs-d'œuvre des Musées de Berlin*, p. 5.
8 Telegram from the Dahlem Museum (Gemäldegalerie), Berlin, to the Petit Palais, Paris, 16 March [?] 1951, file 'Chefs-d'œuvre des musées de Berlin. 1951', Paris, Archives du Petit Palais, PPEX1951(1), box 1.
9 Ernst Heinrich Zimmermann, director of the Dahlem Museum (Gemäldegalerie) to the secretariat of the exhibition of paintings in Berlin, 12 March 1951.
10 Madeleine Ochse, 'L'Europe unie au Petit Palais', undated press cutting, Paris, Archives du Petit Palais, PPEX1951(1), box 2.
11 Robert Rey, 'Chefs-d'œuvre en visite', *Les Nouvelles littéraires, artistiques et scientifiques*, 1222, 1 February 1951, p. 1 and p. 4.
12 André Chamson, undated press cutting, file 'Chefs-d'œuvre des musées de Berlin. 1951', Paris, Archives du Petit Palais, PPEX1951(1), box 2.
13 Security measures for the exhibition, article 3, 1951, Paris, Archives du Petit Palais, PPEX1951(1), box 1.
14 Letter from Thomas C. Howe to Karl Nothnagel, 16 February 1951, Paris, Archives du Petit Palais, PPEX1951(1), box 1.
15 'Nous reverrons à Paris "L'Enseigne de Gersaint"', *Arts*, 12 January 1951, p. 4.
16 'Les Chefs-d'œuvre du musée de Berlin', *Femmes républicaines*, February 1951, Paris, Archives du Petit Palais, PPEX1951(1), box 2.
17 André Salmon, 'Watteau, es-tu là ?', *Paris Presse*, 11 February 1951.
18 Letter from Frederick II to his brother August Wilhelm, 22 September 1746, quoted in Paul Seidel, 'Die Ausstellung von Kunstwerken aus dem Zeitalter Friedrichs des Grossen. I. Friedrich der Grosse als Sammler von Gemälden und Skulpturen', *Jahrbuch der Königlich Preussischen Kunstsammlungen*, 13, 4, 1892, pp. 183–212 (p. 188).

19 Report of the Marquis d'Argens to Frederick II on the destruction wrought by the Austrian army at Charlottenburg, 19 October 1760, quoted in Seidel, 'Die Ausstellung von Kunstwerken,' p. 184.

20 Catalogue of the exhibition, quoted in a report by Samuel Rocheblave, '*Les Collections d'art de Frédéric le Grand à l'Exposition universelle de Paris de 1900, Catalogue descriptif* par Paul Seidel, traduction française de Paul Vitry et J. Marquet de Vasselot ...', *Revue internationale de l'enseignement*, 40, July–December 1900, pp. 178–9 (p. 179).

21 Richard Strauss and Romain Rolland, *Correspondance, fragments de journal* (Paris: Albin Michel, 1950), pp. 136ff., quoted in Willi Schuh, 'Das Szenarium und die musikalischen Skizzen zum Ballett Kythere,' in Willi Schuh (ed.), *Richard Strauss Jahrbuch 1959/60* (Bonn: Boosey & Hawkes, 1960), pp. 59–98 (pp. 84–5).

22 Richard Strauss, note of 17 May 1900, quoted in Schuh, 'Das Szenarium und die musikalischen Skizzen,' p. 85.

23 Raymond Bouyer, *Le Cousin Pons*, January 1919, pp. 425–8.

24 Rose Valland, *Le Front de l'art. Défense des collections françaises* (Paris: Plon, 1961; republished by the Réunion des musées nationaux, 1997), p. 222.

25 Louis Aragon, *L'Enseigne de Gersaint* (Neuchâtel and Paris: Ides et calendes, 1946), p. 24.

26 Ibid., p. 23, p. 27, pp. 49–50.

27 [B. L.], 'Promenade au musée de Berlin,' *Occident*, March 1951, Paris, Archives du Petit Palais, PPEX1951(1), box 2.

28 Pierre Rosenberg (ed.), *Poussin, Watteau, Chardin, David ... Peintures françaises dans les collections allemandes. XVIIe –XVIIIe siècles*, exhibition catalogue, Galeries nationales du Grand Palais, Paris, 18 April – 31 July 2005 (Paris: Réunion des musées nationaux, 2005).

## 7 The statue of the 'Bangwa Queen' of Cameroon

1 *Acte général de la Conférence africaine signée à Berlin le 26 février 1885, ministère des Affaires étrangères. Afrique, Arrangements, actes et conventions concernant le nord, l'ouest et le centre de l'Afrique (1881–1898)* (Paris: Imprimerie nationale, 1898).

2 Letter from Gustav Conrau to Kurt Hassert, 12 June 1899, quoted in Bettina von Lintig, 'On the Bangwa Collection formed by Gustav Conrau,' *Tribal Art Magazine*, 2017, pp. 94–113 (p. 104): https://mag.tribalartmagazine.com/T86EN/page_96. html.

3 Ibid., pp. 96ff.
4 Letter from Gustav Conrau to Felix von Luschan, 11 June 1899, quoted in Andreas Schlothauer, 'Die Kamerun-Sammlungen von Gustav Conrau im Ethnologischen Museum Berlin', *Kunst & Kontext*, 9, 2015, pp. 20–31 (p. 26).
5 See Richard Tsogang Fossi, 'Asunganyi', in Mikaél Assilkinga et al., *Atlas der Abwesenheit, Kameruns Kulturerbe in Deutschland* (Berlin: Reimer, 2023), pp. 372–3.
6 Letter from Felix von Luschan to the Imperial German Government in Cameroon, 10 February 1900, quoted in Schlothauer, 'Die Kamerun-Sammlungen von Gustav Conrau', p. 27.
7 Eckart von Sydow, *Die Kunst der Naturvölker und der Vorzeit. Propyläen-Kunstgeschichte I* (Berlin: Propyläen-Verlag, 1923), p. 115.
8 *Führer durch das Museum für Völkerkunde I* (Berlin: De Gruyter, 1929), p. 128.
9 Maureen Murphy, 'Voyages d'une reine bangwa dans l'imaginaire occidental', *Afrique. Archéologie & arts*, 4, 2006, pp. 23–34 (pp. 26–7).
10 Letter from Herbert M. Katz to Michael Kan, 17 February 1970, quoted in ibid., p. 32. [Translator's note: I do not have access to the original English.]
11 Assilkinga et al., *Atlas der Abwesenheit.*
12 This is an allusion to the account by Michel Leiris of his participation in the Dakar to Djibouti ethnological exhibition, *Phantom Africa*, translated by Brent Hayes Edwards (University of Chicago Press, 2017).

### 8 The *Portrait of Adele Bloch-Bauer* by Gustav Klimt

1 Véronique Long, *Mécènes des deux mondes. Les collectionneurs donateurs du Louvre et de l'Art Institute de Chicago, 1879–1940* (Presses Universitaires de Rennes, 2007).
2 Léon Bonnat in *Journal officiel*, 29 July 1906, p. 5412.
3 Stefan Zweig, *The World of Yesterday*, 4th edition (London, Toronto, Melbourne, and Sydney: Cassell and Company, 1947), p. 55.
4 Adele Bloch-Bauer, will of 19 January 1923, Vienna, Stadt und Landesarchiv, Hauptarchivs-Akten-Persönlichkeiten, A 1, B 35.1: https://web.archive.org/web/20001006235722/http://www.adsele.at/Klage_von__Dr__Stefan_Gulner_m/Vorgelegte_Urkunden/Testament_vom_19_1_1923/testament_vom_19_1_1923.htm. See also Caroline Renold, Alessandro Chechi, Anne Laure Bandle, and Marc-André Renold, 'Affaire six peintures de Klimt – Maria Altmann et Autriche', Plateforme ArThemis, Centre du droit de l'art, University of Geneva, 2012.

## 9 Benin's 'Royal Treasures'

1 Patrice Talon, 'Introduction', in *Art du Bénin d'hier et d'aujourd'hui*, exhibition catalogue, Cotonou, 2022, 2 volumes (vol. I: *Trésors royaux du Bénin. De la restitution à la révélation*; vol. II: *Art contemporain du Bénin*) (Paris, 2022), vol. I.

2 Amadou Mahtar M'Bow, 'Pour le retour à ceux qui l'ont créé d'un patrimoine culturel irremplaçable: un appel de M. Amadou Mahtar M'Bow, directeur général de l'Unesco', *Le Courrier de l'Unesco*, 31, 7, 1978, pp. 4–5.

3 Letter from Le Corbusier to Paul Rivet dated 7 October 1935, quoted by Guillemette Morel-Journel, '"Une véritable révélation ...": La vocation ethnologique de Le Corbusier', in Jacques Guillerme (ed.), *Les Collections. Fables et programmes* (Seyssel: Champ Vallon, 1993), pp. 313–14.

4 Maurice Delafosse, 'Statues des rois du Dahomé au Musée ethnographique du Trocadéro', *La Nature*, 1086, 24 March 1894, p. 262.

5 Paulin Joachim, 'Rendez-nous l'art nègre', *Bingo*, 144, January 1965, p. 7.

6 Ibid.

7 Letter from the Benin Minister for Foreign Affairs, Aurélien Agbénonci, to his French counterpart, Jean-Marc Ayrault, 26 August 2016.

8 'The Convention on the Value of Cultural Heritage for Society (Faro Convention, 2005) was adopted by the Committee of Ministers of the Council of Europe on 13 October 2005, and opened for signature to member States in Faro (Portugal) on 27 October of the same year. It entered into force on 1 June 2011. To date, 20 member States of the Council of Europe have ratified the Convention and 7 have signed it' (www.coe.int/en/web/culture-and-heritage/faro-convention).

9 Letter from the French Minister for Foreign Affairs, Jean-Marc Ayrault, to Aurélien Agbénonci, 12 December 2016.

10 Patrice Talon, spontaneous speech in the rooms of the exhibition 'Art in Benin yesterday and today. From restitution to revelation', 20 February 2022, amateur recording, transcribed by Dieu Ly Hoang, Berlin, 2022.

11 Ekpo Eyo, *Two Thousand Years of Nigerian Art* (Lagos: Federal Department of Antiquities Nigeria, 1977), p. 8.

## Conclusion

1 Arno Bertina, *Des lions comme des danseuses* (Lille: La Contre Allée, 2015; revised edition, 2019).

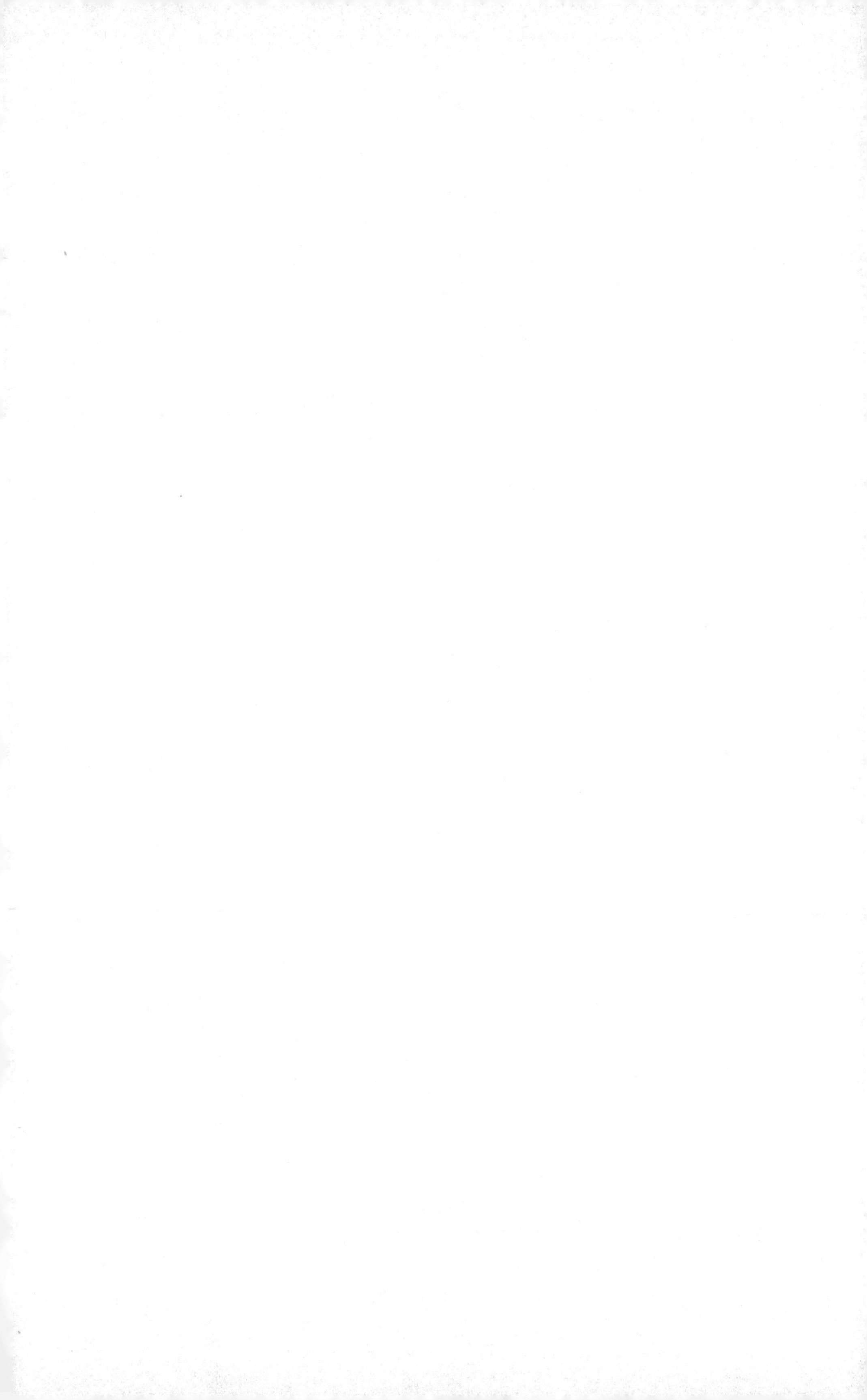